The Swipes of My Life

Kirsten McStay

*They say you've got to kiss a few frogs to get your prince,
weather a few storms to get your rainbow…
But no one said that you had to kiss the whole fucking pond in a
shit-storm!*

1. Love

I've always loved the idea of being in love.

Ever since I was a little girl, watching films and reading books, I always had this fascination with finding 'The One', 'Prince Charming', 'Mr Right', 'Chuck Bass' and later in life... the infamous 'Mr Big'.

I don't know exactly what it was that made me feel that way. I do suspect that from reading fairy tales from a young age, there was something subconsciously drummed into me that happiness always came when the princess found her prince.

For instance, Cinderella wasn't happy until she had that bloody glass slipper on her foot, Sleeping Beauty was about as useful as a chocolate teapot until she was kissed by a prince, and Rapunzel was stuck up a tower somewhere brushing her mane until she was rescued – by a man.

It always seemed that 'Prince Charming' came and 'saved' these helpless princesses and then that was it – happily ever after – how cliche.

Nothing even close to that happened in these days, especially since dating in the modern world is a far cry from a fairy tale and even more so since the majority of dates are set up through various apps.

It's extremely rare that anyone meets in a bar anymore, – and definitely not during a global pandemic.

Growing up with a single mum, I always hated the idea of her being alone and not having anyone to love her the way she deserved to be loved.

I remember being so desperate for her to meet someone that I would come in from school, pick up the local newspaper and circle potential candidates in the lonely hearts column – I would always pick ones that used the good old-fashioned dating terms like 'Good Sense Of Humour' (GSOH) or 'Non Smoker' (NS) because that's what I thought she needed – a man who would make her laugh and didn't stink of fags.

Not that my mum Pamela ever followed up with any of the men handpicked by her eleven-year-old, but I think it made her smile that I wanted her to be happy and loved beyond belief.

Love was something I just knew I wanted in life.

Carrie Bradshaw always banged on about "Ridiculous, inconvenient, consuming, can't-live-without-each-other love" and it's something I just ached to be part of.

I was just always a firm believer of everyone having a 'soul mate' and was totally fascinated with the concept of finding 'The One' and living happily ever after, but it really isn't as simple as that, is it?

After being thrust into the modern dating world back in 2017, I quickly realised that it was more complicated than anything I ever imagined, and it didn't get any better.

Like so many others, I believed the only way to meet 'The One' was with the flick of a finger and a swipe to the right. And my God has it's been a wild ride, so let's start at the beginning.

2. The First Love

I never really planned to settle down at the age of seventeen, but it just kind of happened. I was still so young, entering into my final year of high school when I first properly met Dean.

We had winched down the park a few years back and I wasn't really interested in him at the time, mostly because he had a God fuckin -awful haircut – a mullet to be precise – and also because I was fifteen.

Honestly, the thought of a boyfriend was more of an inconvenience than anything.

After our little kiss in the park, we never saw each other for a couple of years, until he messaged me on Facebook in 2011, *Wits happening stranger?* and that was that.

When we first became boyfriend and girlfriend, it was exciting because I'd never experienced 'love' before.

Because we were so young, we'd sit in his bedroom and watch DVDs and winch all night and then I would go home feeling all giddy and that went on for a few years, that's what 'in love' teenagers did back then, wasn't it?

If I'm being really honest, Dean and I didn't really have anything in common, but he made me laugh and that's what I liked most about him. Admittedly, he also had a cheeky smile, piercing blue eyes, and mousey brown hair.

At eighteen, I was happy. He was all I thought I ever wanted and all I ever really knew, and the more time we spent together, the more I fell in 'love' with him, or what I thought was love at the time.

I was at university and working in a sun bed shop and Dean was a labourer on a construction site, meaning we didn't really have two brown pennies to rub together.

We never went out to fancy places or anything. It was more or less just Nandos and 'Netflix and Chill' – literally.

Dean wasn't allowed to stay at my house for about three years. My stepdad just didn't like the thought of it. My mum on the other hand was a bit more chilled but she respected his wishes and said no too. I was raging at the time but twenty-seven-year-old me gets it now.

I always remember being the one who made all the effort with absolutely everything in the relationship and it really got to me.

When we did go away for an overnight or weekend away, it was always me who booked and paid for it all, and I'm all for equality, but I cannot emphasise enough that I did everything.

Even something as simple as making table reservations – it was muggings here who had to book them. It was like having a man child, and a very fucking lazy one at that.

But now we'd been together for almost six years and at the tender age of twenty-two, it felt like we were an old married couple.

Things hadn't been going so well and it was as if he would do things to deliberately cause an argument with me. Then he would wind me up and make me look like the bad one more often than not and it was clear that our relationship was on the brink of ending.

We had fallen out quite a few times during our time together – like proper fallen 'out, out' over a number of different things.

Despite this, in a bid to make things better, I wanted to start making plans to move in together, but he said he just wasn't ready for that big a commitment, so I decided to do it on my own.

I took it upon myself to rent a two bed, top-floor flat in Motherwell as I just couldn't wait on him any longer, I didn't want to stay with my maw forever and I knew it was what was right for me at that time.

Being independent was always extremely important to me. The minute I got a National Insurance number, I got a job and always worked my arse off to have nice things.

The minute I turned seventeen, I learnt to drive – I've always been determined to do things I set my mind to, but Dean? Not so much. He was happy to just plod along with life, no disrespect to him, but that's just not what I wanted at all.

But now, I was twenty-two and really wanted my own place. It just felt like the time was right. I was ready to be an adult and spread my wings and start a new chapter of my life.

My mum and stepdad were moving out of our family home and into something smaller at the same time as I decided to flee the nest, so they offered me loads of furniture which would save me a fortune, so I totally jumped at the chance.

Dean was just twenty-three at the time, so when I suggested this could be something we do together, he just scoffed and said no.

Yes, we were young, but I thought if we didn't take this jump now, then when? There's no time like the present, surely?

Despite categorically saying no, he practically moved in with me anyway, staying over most nights. He soon had his clothes in the wardrobe, a toothbrush in the pot and I even dedicated an entire drawer to his belongings. He reaped the benefits of living with me but without paying the bills.

One night, I found myself in the kitchen making his pieces for work as he slobbed out on my sofa watching the football.

Is this really what I wanted in life? To make a man's work pieces? Who doesn't even pay his way?

Dean worked really early and still didn't drive at the time, so when he stayed, I would get up when he did at 5 a.m., drive him to where he needed to be or wave him off if he was getting collected by some old guy in a white van.

I bent over backwards for that boy, and seldom got much back from him.

I couldn't stop asking myself, is this what it's going to be like forever?

Don't get me wrong, we'd been away on holiday a few times: Amsterdam, Turkey, and Paris for my twenty-first birthday, which I must admit was one of the most romantic times of my life.

Dean wasn't a totally 'lovey dovey' person at all. He hated most things like that, but he did really make the effort with taking me to Paris.

We drank champagne next to the Eiffel Tower, ate crepes, and did all the other cliche touristy things like putting a lame heart-shaped padlock on the love bridge.

Although I was still so young, this was the only sniff at love I'd ever had. I didn't know anything else.

As we watched the famous Eiffel Tower lights glitter on the hour, he gazed at me and told me he would take me back there one day and propose to me, and I believed him and held on to those words for a few years.

I daydreamed about him getting down on one night in one of the most romantic cities in the world and me crying and uttering the word 'YES' as I slide a shiny rock onto my left finger.

Back in reality, it became apparent that the dream proposal definitely wasn't on the horizon for us, and things gradually deteriorated.

As I said, things had just changed over the last few months. We split up for about a month but after that, it wasn't really ever the same again.

There was one night in particular that was breaking point for us, and it was the moment I knew I deserved better.

I'd planned a night out with my friend Bryony at our local bar.

As I patted thick bronzer on my cheeks before we left, Dean was sitting on my couch, pissed.

Drunk pissed, not pissed off. He had been out the night before and hadn't been to sleep, so when I left at 10 p.m., I could tell he would soon be out for the count.

I loved going out with Bryony, but this night something just didn't feel right.

We downed throat-burning shots and danced until our heels pinched at our toes, but something was niggling at me. I just felt like I didn't want to be there.

I had the strongest urge to go home after only being out about three hours, which wasn't like me at all.

As the music rang in my ears, I was smiling, but deep inside, I was a lost soul. I wasn't happy in the slightest and it hurt my heart putting on this constant front.

Feeling pretty drunk and pouring yet another sour tequila down my neck, I told Bryony that it was time for me to go home.

I knew she could see the sadness in my eyes.

She looked at me and said, 'It's him, isn't it?' I just nodded silently.

Bryony knew as well as I did that it was always going to end in tears.

Dean wasn't treating me the way I wanted or deserved to be treated, but I tried to make it work time and time again.

I tried to please him endlessly, but while I was busy trying to make him happy, I was making myself more and more unhappy.

Bryony and I smoked a menthol cigarette outside the Soul Suite then staggered over to the pavement to flag down a taxi, when I finally told her things just weren't right at home and she just simply hugged me and said, 'What's meant to be will be, Kirst'.

And I knew she was right.

I staggered in the close door, hitting every single brick wall on the way up.

The distinct taste of tequila nipped my mouth as the bricks in the close spun around me.

I looked down to rummage through my electric blue Alexander McQueen bag Dean had surprisingly bought me for my birthday last year, frantically searching for my keys but to no avail.

When they finally came into reach, I put the key through the lock, opened the door, and staggered into the room to find Dean out cold, sprawled across my bed on top of the covers with his phone lying beside him.

The phone just sitting there called out to me. My instinct told me to pick it up immediately.

Looking back, I didn't trust him. I pretended to myself I did, but really, I don't know who I was trying to kid.

I stared at him in his deep, drunken sleep. He was literally dead to the world. And without even giving myself a second to toy with the idea that it was wrong, I picked it up.

Deep down, I knew it was wrong. I would go mad if he picked up my phone and looked through it without permission, but I didn't have anything to hide – and my gut-feeling told me that he did.

My heart was beating out of my chest when the screen flashed as I clicked the lock button.

And the first notification I saw pop up was Snapchat.

Snapchat is every cheater's best friend, it's a picture messaging app where 'snaps' disappear into thin air after they're opened, no evidence and no paper-trail.

Absolutely ideal for anyone looking to conceal any information from their partner.

But when I read the words on the screen, I felt physically sick.

Melissa is typing…

Snapchat from Melissa

Katie is typing…

Snapchat from Katie

Laura is typing…

Snapchat from Laura…

That fucking bastard!

My palms were sweating, and I felt like my heart was beating so fast that it was going to fall out of my arse.

I wasn't going to look at the messages... fuck who was I kidding of course I was, I couldn't trust Dean as far as I could throw him, so I keyed in his very predictable password '0000' and off I went down a dark rabbit hole of lies and betrayal.

To be fair, I did expect to find more than what I did, but Dean was the type of guy who deleted every message on his phone ever, not like me who hoards texts from everybody.

I opened the Snapchat app to find these *'such-and-such is typing'* messages.

I didn't know any of these girls, but surely, they knew he had a girlfriend? God, it's not like I was just new on the scene. I'd been around for almost six years!

One of them was just a reply of 'kissy' emojis. What was he saying to her? The fucker!

I looked over at him snoring his stupid head off and a part of me wanted to smother him with a pillow, but I refrained and continued reading...

Haha OK then, see you soon, babe. Also with a kissing emoji.

I had that horrible feeling in my stomach. That rise in your chest that knocks the wind right out of you.

Hot tears burnt my cheeks.

I was angry, raging in fact, so raging that I could feel sweat seeping out my pores.

You know that way you just feel heat rising in your head? That was me.

Had he invited her to my house? The house that I was paying for or was it something less than that? I didn't know, but what I did know was that I was absolutely ill about it.

He should not have been messaging other girls in the first place, but to have the audacity to do it while in my house when I wasn't even there was just damn right disrespectful.

Part of me was ready to come crashing down on him like a tonne of bricks and start World War III, but another part forced me to lie down beside him and throw the phone back over to his side.

As I lay my head down on the pillow beside him, tears blinded me as I silently sobbed. What did I do to deserve this?

At 5 a.m., I was startled when I was woken up by shouting.

'Kirst, Kirst, wake up!'

Wiping the crust from my eyes in a sleepy daze, I looked over at him as he mumbled that he was going to be sick and asked if I could get him a basin.

Fuck's sake.

Do I bring this mess up now or is he going to spew over my bedsheets?

Reluctantly, I got him a basin from under the sink and didn't say a word as he started throwing up his guts.

Repulsed by the spewing and his actions, I just looked at him in pure disgust and the words 'I'm sorry' escaped his mouth.

Sorry? For what, spewing? Or being a fucking prick?

But I didn't say those words out loud. I stayed silent.

These days, I'm usually quite a hot head when it comes to arguments. I wasn't so much then as I always just wanted things to be fine and rosy with us. If I found myself in that situation now, I would go in all guns blazing and he wouldn't have a leg to stand on.

The following day, we were meant to go to the football together, but of course he woke up with the 'worst hang-over' and said he really couldn't face it.

I was disappointed because we never really did much together that wasn't sitting in the house, but I didn't argue about it as to be honest, I couldn't really think of anything worse than pretending I was OK with him for a full ninety minutes and more.

Over the next few days, I stewed with my thoughts. I didn't confront him right away. I confided in my friends first and they couldn't believe what I was telling them.

'What? I hope you went to town on him!' one of them said in the group chat.

I took the days to decide what I really wanted here.

I was twenty-two, about to turn twenty-three, I had a great job as a journalist for a local newspaper, I had my own flat (well rented) but I'd missed out on so much with my friends such as girls' holidays and wild nights out because I was with him, 'loved up'.

I hate to admit that I was that pal that ditched her friends because she had a boyfriend.

That's another thing, he never socialised with any of my friends. Some of them hadn't ever met him, which after being with each other for so long was bloody ridiculous.

My own brother even says to me now, 'I can't believe you went out with him for six years and I didn't even have his phone number.'

It was strange. My family liked him. They said he was a nice boy, and he was, but we were at totally different stages in life.

He would rather spend his money going out with his pals all weekend and I wanted to go on holidays and weekends away and ultimately buy my own house, but he didn't have much ambition to do the same.

And somewhere in the back of my mind, I always knew it just was never going to work.

After the whole Snapchat fiasco, I knew for a fact that I was never going to be able to trust him again. I worried that every time he picked up his phone, he would be messaging other girls and I just didn't want that anymore.

In my head, I made a decision, and I was surprised that it matched up with the one in my heart.

I was going to end things.

Of course, I was gutted to have to put an end to our six-year relationship. I did love him, and we did have so many fantastic years together, but now they were not so fantastic.

I sat him down and told him about my Snapchat findings and that I didn't want to be with him anymore.

Upon hearing my words, he panicked, said he was sorry, and he didn't remember the messages.

I might have been extremely pissed that night, but those messages certainly sobered me up.

Not wanting to argue about it, I told him my decision was final and that I wanted the keys to my flat back – and my car, and all my belongings from his house and that was it – done.

It was really strange going from all to nothing, being loved-up for six years to being totally and utterly single, but it was something I was just going to have to get used to.

I tried to keep busy to take my mind off it and although it was my decision ultimately, it was still hard.

One week went by in a bit of a blur. I was just pottering around my flat one day when the buzzer went.

'Delivery!' the voice called down the phone.

Without thinking about it too much, I pressed the enter button, expecting it to be my ASOS parcel or something else that I'd unnecessarily ordered online.

I heard a faint knock and my jaw just about hit the floor when I pulled back the door to find a lady standing in front of me clutching a large bouquet of red roses.

I recognised her and it took a minute before it clicked.

The week before Dean and I parted ways, I'd been in this woman's florist shop ordering both our mums flowers for Mother's Day.

'Kirsten, whatever he's done he's sorry.' She sighed, looking embarrassed.

Oh my God.

Equally mortified, if not more, I snatched the glittery red roses from her hands and shut the door.

I was fucking humiliated that even the local florist knew my boyfriend was a virtual cheating twat. He may have not actually been with a girl physically (as far as I know) but in my eyes it was just as bad.

I read the card over and over and over again.

Kirsten, Sorry for my antics, actions speak louder than words. Love Dean xx

Sorry for your antics? Antics? Fucking hell, what a dick-head!

Full of rage, I text him.

Yeah, they do!

Attached to my message was a picture of said flowers in the bin.

He had never bought me flowers before in the six years we were together so I certainly didn't want his tacky, glittery apology roses now.

I was really close to his family. In fact, it's strange to say that I still am. His mum was like a second mum to me for six years so it was hard to cut her off when I really didn't want to but I still speak to her and some of the rest of the family once in a while and they occasionally drop a comment on my latest Facebook post.

About two days after the apology roses, Dean said he would get dropped off at mine after work to gather his things.

When I arrived home after a busy day at the office, there he was sitting on my living room chair looking so helplessly upset and I felt a wave of guilt wash over me.

His eyes were red, obviously from crying, and he asked if this was really it and I nodded.

'It's just not going to work. We've been at this for six years, and it's not getting better, so I think it's time to call it a day,' I said calmly as he wiped a tear from his eye.

On hearing my words, he got up from the chair, gathered his things, and cleared the contents of his bedside drawer into a plastic bag.

The atmosphere was so intense and I couldn't wait to be free from this situation.

Since he didn't drive, I told him I would run him home as I needed to get my car key back from his house.

As fully expected, the journey to his was awkward. I could hear him try to conceal his sniffles with a cough and I honestly felt awful.

Luckily, his house was literally just five minutes up the road, so it wasn't as uncomfortable as it could have been had it taken any longer.

I pulled up outside and he got out without uttering a single word.

I felt like a lifetime had passed as I sat waiting on him, bringing out my stuff. I didn't really have that much, so I didn't understand what was taking so long.

Fiddling with my keys in the ignition, thoughts exploded around my head. This was really it. Things were going to be so different.

Another five minutes passed and he finally returned to my side of the car and handed me my stuff, including my keys, other bits and bobs that were in my drawer at his and then he handed me two random envelopes.

Confused at what they were, I was just about to ask him when I looked up and saw that he was already walking away when it dawned on me.

It was my birthday the following week.

Oh fuck.

I opened the bigger card, which I knew was from him.

To my lovely girlfriend.

'Well, not anymore,' I muttered to myself as I opened it.

And just as I did, a bundle of £20 notes fell on to my lap.

This is not good.

I then opened the second envelope and another bundle of notes fell out, £50 from his mum, dad, and brother.

I suddenly felt nervous that maybe he hadn't told her.

I paused for a minute. I knew I couldn't accept this money. There was £250 sitting beneath my steering wheel. It just didn't feel right at all – we had just broken up!

I stuffed the money back in his card along with the cash from his mum but kept a hold of the actual card from her. I felt it was a bit disrespectful sending that back, too.

Stepping out of the car, I walked up to the door and posted it back through the letter box.

I let out a sigh of relief and walked away.

I knew that was it. That chapter of my life was coming to an end for good.

His mum later sent me a text saying she was disappointed that I didn't take her money, but I explained how I felt to her and thanked her for the card. She was always so lovely to me. I really did feel terrible.

That day I felt like I'd lost a lot, a relationship and the family that came with it, but strangely, I also felt like I could breathe again, and could continue on the path to discovering myself again, finding the girl that had been lost and forgotten about for the last six years.

A few months passed and naturally I would get bored and text him, telling him I missed him, but I didn't miss him. I just missed having someone.

He did the same a few times, and we went back and forth for a few months.

At one point, he was seeing some raging blonde bird but messaged me to say he missed me and that caused a bit of drama with her. She wasn't a happy bunny, but her attitude absolutely stank, so I took great joy in winding her up – she was asking for it to be fair.

Two years ago, we ended up back at mine after a mutual friends' engagement party, but it was what it was and we both knew it.

We met again at the same friends' wedding last year.

We had a nice conversation, asked about each other's families, and it was fine. We had grown up; we were different people, and that was OK.

There was no hate or animosity. He was my first proper love after all; we grew up together and grew apart and that's totally fine.

I still wish the best for him, unlike others who are included in this book.

AMONG THE CHAOS, one thing I did learn from Dean was that I knew what I wanted in a future relationship.

I wanted someone who worshipped the ground I walked on. I wanted a gentleman who would look after me and a person that was genuinely interested in my thoughts and feelings, someone on the same level.

The relationship also taught me to recognise what I didn't want, but there was no way I was even thinking about shacking up with anyone else right now. I was ready to look forward to something totally new – the single life!

Quite a lot of my friends were single at the time, and despite practically ghosting them for almost six years, they picked me up, dusted me off and told me to get ready for going 'out out' because I would be doing a lot of that because that's what single people do apparently.

I was so grateful to be back in their lives again.

I must admit that I wasn't entirely excited for this new chapter of 'being single' because at the start it was a huge change, going from spending most days with the one person, texting the one person, Christ, even having sex with the one person to absolutely no contact at all and no sex whatsoever, was very lonely.

It was weird looking at my phone with no new messages. Usually, I would have a text or two from him saying that he was on his break from work or something else equally as boring, but not anymore. This was something I was just going to have to get used to.

One other thing that worried me though, was that I was so comfy with Dean. I didn't give a flying fuck if I was a mess around him, if I hadn't shaved my legs (or anywhere else) or that I wore scabby non-matching pyjamas. FUCK, I was going to actually have to make an effort again, for someone new – but mostly for myself.

I was a shadow of my former bubbly, outgoing self and I was determined that she'd be back soon.

But there's something I still need to tell you.

About a year before Dean and I split up, I was in Glasgow for a friend's birthday night out – a rare night out at that, but things between me and him weren't the best, so I really needed it.

At this time, I was in my third year of university where I was studying journalism.

I absolutely loved it. Ever since I was a little girl, I used to tell my mum that I wanted to 'read and write' the news and so proud of myself for making my dream a reality.

I slicked on my mascara and coated some shiny gloss over my lips and smiled as I thought about the night ahead.

I planned on getting extremely drunk with my girls because I missed them. I missed the old me, so for one night, I really planned to let my hair down.

I downed my glass of prosecco as one of the girls announced that the taxi had arrived outside.

We clambered into the black Hackney, giggling as we sneaked in bottles of Echo Falls under our coats.

'Where to girls?' the driver asked.

'Bunker in Glasgow, please!'

There was a real buzz about the place. The bar was packing and everyone was having a great time. The music blared, and I was thankful for a night off from Dean and our boring relationship.

I was sipping a long vodka and chatting away to lots of different people in our large group when one of my best friends ran up to me.

'Kirsten, Kirsten! I just met these two guys who are journalists! I told them our friend was studying journalism at uni – come and meet them!'

Great. Typical Shanice, always ends up talking to someone with a story – that girl would literally talk to anyone.

Being polite, I toddled along in my leather pencil skirt and introduced myself to these random two guys, who, by the way, were very easy on the eye.

'Hi, I'm Kirsten!'

Smiling back, they both shook my hand and told me their names and I remember thinking one of them was very handsome, older than me, but a very good-looking guy.

But what did it matter, anyway? I had a boyfriend, plus they're probably thinking, who the fuck are these two steamers?

I got chatting to one of them about work related things and it turns out I'd actually contacted him over email for a uni project – how weird!

We had one drink with them; they bought us a few shots, then we said our goodbyes and continued on with our night.

The whole night was fuelled by tequila and we had a brilliant time, although we actually ended the night in The Glasgow Royal Infirmary – but that's a story for another day.

The hang-over was in full swing the next day and I was slobbing out on the couch when I noticed that Dave (the handsome one), had followed me on Twitter – probably out of courtesy, so I followed him back and nothing else was said, plus it was good to have these contacts for when I actually cracked into the industry.

At the back of my mind, I always thought it was really weird how I'd spoken to him over email before and then just randomly, by chance, bumped into him in a bar in Glasgow.

I often wondered if it was fate. Probably not. It was probably just a total coincidence.

After that, Dave never crossed my mind again, until…

3. The Fuck Man

It had been three days since I split up with Dean; we had still been texting, kind of, more so on his part.

I was bored and I know that it's horrible to say, but I still kind of buzzed off the fact he wanted me and I didn't want him back.

Anyway, the bottom line was that I was bored and had nothing better to do.

Many of my friends said that I should get on Tinder, but I just wasn't ready for that. Christ, it had only been three days! It was far too soon.

My mum always says, 'One way to get over a man is to get under another', and while she is right, I just needed time to breathe and hopefully take to the heartbreak diet because I was the heaviest I'd ever been.

It was a Wednesday evening. I'd just parked my arse on the couch after a long deadline day in the office, when a Twitter notification flashed on my phone screen – I had a message.

When I opened it was from Dave, the journo from that night in Bunker.

What?!

What did he want?

I tapped on the screen…

Hey, kid, how's things? Did you ever get a job in journalism?

Fuck! Why is he messaging me? Kid? What was that about?

It had been over a year since I first met him and now, after me only splitting up with Dean three days ago, he's messaging me? Was he just being friendly, though?

Was this 'fate' again?

Dave was older than me, a lot older… thirteen years to be exact, but maybe he was just being nice?

Fuck's sake, Kirsten, maybe people do just slide into your DMs to be nice and ask how you're getting on? Maybe not everyone who messages you wants to shag … or do they?

I stared at the message for a few minutes and racked my brains thinking about what to say back.

I decided to keep it cool.

Typing back to him, I kept it brief and told him I was working for my local newspaper now and that I hoped he was well.

And almost instantly after I replied, my phone pinged again.

That's good to hear! What have you been up to then? x

Oh, a kiss!

Am I reading into this too much? Probably.

Don't all girls?

We had some general chit-chat back and forth and I had a wee browse over his profile.

I looked at his main picture and my memory served me correctly – he was still as bloody handsome as that night I met him in Bunker.

Ugh, those brown eyes, that peppered hair… I didn't swoon so much over his choice of outfits (ripped skinny jeans and V-neck T-shirts) but you can't have it all, can you?

I didn't really think anything of these messages, so when he eventually asked for my number, I was totally gobsmacked – does he really want to continue talking to me?

Without much deliberation, I handed over my digits like precious gold and eagerly waited for the first message.

And when it arrived, I had butterflies.

The chat seemed easy and we WhatsApped back and forth.

Dave began to ask me about my relationship status and I told him I was very newly single.

Conveniently for me, he said he had just broken up with his girlfriend as well as she cheated too – what is with people?!

I think they'd been together for quite a few years, but he said he was really gutted that it ended the way it did.

The more we chatted, the more I found out about him, about his career, his family and honestly, he had good chat; it was nice to talk to someone who could actually hold a conversation.

Dave then went on to mention that he liked what I was wearing on the night he met me too… my trusty leather pencil skirt, always a winner! I still have it hanging in my cupboard to this day.

But how can he even remember? It was over a year ago and we were lucky to even spend half an hour together.

From what I gathered from these messages, Dave had an attractive personality and I honestly just fancied him so much.

We messaged back and forth for weeks, and he would send me selfies of himself, tall, dark, and handsome with brown eyes. I'm a total sucker for brown eyes. I've said it for years. He was fucking gorgeous!

But it was when he sent me a picture of him posing in the mirror that I cringed slightly. He was totally posing, and it made me 'ICK' slightly, but I let it slide. He was so bloody good looking.

But why was he talking to me? A girl in her early twenties, thirteen years younger than him?

So it transpires that Dave likes a younger girl… I mean I was into older guys. My mum always said she thought I would end up with an older man, but I don't think she meant thirteen years older. It was a bit much, but what had I got to lose? I wasn't talking to anyone else, but I hadn't really put myself out there. Chatting with Dave was just very out the blue.

It was around May time, I was out with a few girls from work in Glasgow sipping cocktails at every outdoor seating area in the town, it was sunny, I had my sunglasses on, a French martini in hand and I was just happy being me for once in a very long time.

I was loving single life, not that I'd even messaged anyone except Dave but the fact I could just do what I wanted, when I wanted, made me feel very satisfied.

I didn't have to consult with anyone else about weekend plans. If the work girls asked me to go out for last-minute drinks, I could go and not feel bad at all.

Previously, I was always made to feel guilty for having a life outside my relationship which was wrong on so many levels, but I know that now.

Since becoming single, I was determined to live the life I missed out on for six years, don't get me wrong, it's partly my fault, I let it happen but I missed out on so much with my friends at the time and it's one thing I deeply regret until this day. So I made a pact with myself that it would not, under any circumstances, happen again.

I told my workmate Shirley about Dave, and how he was older and had been sending me cheeky, flirty texts.

'Just be careful,' she said. 'He sounds like a bit of a fuckboy.'

''Fuck man' more like, he's bloody thirteen years older than me!'

I shrugged at Shirley's lack of enthusiasm. I didn't care what he was, he wasn't my ex and that was already a positive.

The sun shone over Glasgow and I got drunker and drunker as the day went on.

The Cosmopolitan cocktails gave me the courage to send Dave a couple of drunken texts asking if he was out and about.

In one text, I even suggested that he could come meet me, but a few hours went by, and I heard nothing back.

Shirley, Kate and I staggered to the train station to head back to Motherwell. We'd been drinking all day. It was about 8 or 9 p.m. now – my God, what a shift!

I staggered up the stairs of doom once again and before I knew it, I was plopped in front of the couch with a bottle of Pink Moscato.

I deposited more or less the full bottle into one of those massive Ikea wine glasses and silently cheers'ed my new single gal life.

I was about to take my first sip of wine when my phone pinged – it was Dave.

He said he was out with his mates in Glasgow and asked if I wanted to meet him.

Aw fuck! This is just typical – it'd just got home!

I'm back in the Well now, sadly! I typed.

Almost instantly, he replied.

I could come and meet you?

Jesus, does he know that Motherwell is an absolute shit-hole for a night out? Or does he mean 'come meet me' i.e., can I come and meet you… at your house.

After the flurry of cocktails, I'd drunk throughout the day, I was still pretty well on and feeling confident, so thought *fuck it, why not?* – you're single you can do whatever the hell your heart desires, and right now that was having a silvering fox in my bed.

Maybe it wouldn't be like that, though? Maybe he would be a gentleman?

It wasn't long before my buzzer echoed in the hall and I can actually remember thinking, *I can't fucking believe he's actually here.*

I picked up the intercom and just said 'top floor'.

Five minutes went by and I paced up and down the hall with nerves. The three flights of stairs at my flat were a killer for everyone especially when you're steaming drunk, so I assumed that was the hold-up.

As I continued to wait for his arrival, I couldn't shift the feeling of nerves at all. I had the most horrible feeling at the pit of my belly, like butterflies but worse, as if my heart was going to fall out my arse.

This was the first guy other than Dean that had ever been to my flat.

My palms sweated and I must have checked myself in the mirror at least five times since the buzzer sounded.

When I finally heard the faint chap, I pulled back the heavy fire door and there he was.

He stood for a second and kind of swayed from side to side, catching his breath.

'My God, the stairs were never-ending!' he puffed. 'Nice to meet you finally – again.'

He gave me a cuddle and a kiss on the cheek, which was a bit weird.

The kiss felt a bit awkward, but that's normal for a first meeting, right?

I hadn't had any other man in my company like this for six years. Maybe that's why it was weird? And he really was a man, not a boy in his early twenties.

I was really overthinking things now, but I just took a breath and shut the door behind him.

I couldn't help but stare at him as he fumbled to take his jacket off. He was wearing skinny jeans and a bomber jacket. He was older but dressed like a twenty-year-old.

I screwed my face up slightly at his attire before ushering him into the living room.

He flopped down on to the sofa as I poured us a gin each. As I dropped a bit of ice in the glass, I looked over at him, still puffing away from climbing the stairs.

His hair was ruffled, but every time he spoke, I just got lost in his dark eyes. They were mesmerising.

And like every journalist, Dave could talk.

I sat next to him on the couch and just let him gab.

He was at that drunk stage where he was babbling a lot of rubbish to the point, I didn't know what he was saying half the time.

His Dundee accent made me cringe a bit, but nonetheless he seemed like a decent guy.

The chat then turned to him telling me all about how he caught his girlfriend cheating, how it ended badly and how he could never forgive her for doing that to him.

I don't know about anybody else, but don't you just hate when guys bleat on and on about their exes?

Once he finally let me get a word in, I was in the middle of a story when he just leant in and kissed tenderly on the lips and held on to the back of my head firmly.

Oh God.

I remember thinking he was a weird kisser – after the initial soft kiss, he proceeded to ram his tongue right down my throat – and it wasn't pleasant.

I didn't know if it was just because I'd been so used to kissing Dean for the last six years that anything different was just totally weird and abnormal.

Dave's beard rubbed off my chin as we kissed, and as things got heated, he slightly tugged at my hair and pulled me in closer.

His grip got tighter, making it harder for me to kiss him back, but he pulled away, and stared at me and then dug his fingertips into the nape of my neck and kissed me again.

What is he doing?

Of course, one thing led to another, and we ended up entangled in each other on my couch.

His V-neck top came flying off and so did everything else.

'Are you ready for this?' he whispered as he pulled away from my lips once again.

Ready? Ready for what, exactly? I thought.

'There's something you need to know about me.'

I sat up on the couch, fixing my hair back into place. I just stared back at him.

What could he possibly say next?

'I like it rough.'

I burst out laughing and looked at him in a drunken daze. But his brown eyes gazed at me differently, sternly. He was deadly serious.

'I would rather just show you. But I like my girls to be filthy.'

Before I could answer him, he pounced back on me like a horny teenager and pulled at the zip on my jeans.

'I'm going to spank you and you're going to love it.'

Sorry, what?!

I didn't really think much of it in the moment, but as things progressed and more clothes hit the floor, it felt like he was giving me a running commentary of everything he was doing, going to do, and so much more.

I know some people fantasise about things like that but my fucking God did it made me die inside.

He gripped my throat at points and was biting my shoulder and neck and anywhere else he could get his fangs into.

All I could remember thinking was 'is this really happening right now?'

The tips of his fingers became entangled in my long hair extensions, and the first thing that went through my head was that he better not pull them out because I'd just forked out 300 quid for them!

It was weird at first because it was so different from anything I'd been used to before.

'I'm a dominant, baby.'

His words rang in my ears as they made me cringe every time I played them back to myself.

It was the being called 'baby' for me more than anything.

I started to think that maybe Dave had read a copy of *Fifty Shades of Grey* because this was the vibe he was giving me. Although he wasn't quite living up to Jamie Dornan/Christian Grey, he sure as hell was trying to.

I couldn't decide if I liked it or hated it, but I was definitely leaning more towards hating but I went along with it anyway and cringed every time.

It was just so different to what I'd had with Dean. Christ, when I stayed over at Dean's house, we'd only have sex in the best position to make sure the bed didn't squeak while his mum and dad were downstairs.

The next day, I woke up with the worst hang-over ever and absolutely covered in bruises.

After he left, I got a text from Dave asking me if I could wear leather for him the next time.

What?! For real? What? Like a skirt? Or a dog lead?

I laughed it off, thinking it was maybe just the booze making him a bit more adventurous, but when I sat down to digest the whole situation, I began to think…

What the fuck was I playing at?

I did think that maybe that night with Dave at my house would have been a one-off, but I couldn't have been more wrong.

I did see him a few times after that, mostly after nights out when we had both been drinking – it was the most bizarre situation.

For days he would be so needy and then I wouldn't hear from him for months and it went full circle. It really was weird.

One of the times, after not speaking to him for weeks, I ended up going back to his flat after randomly bumping into him in Glasgow at 3 a.m. outside Subway. He was with his pal and I was with a few of mine. One of my girls ended up getting off with one of his friends, who we later found out had a girlfriend… typical.

During one of his needy periods, he was banging on about all the things he was going to do to me the next time he would see me. He would continue to call me 'baby' even though I hated it and say things like 'good girl' it was so weird but I just went along with it again, because we all have needs, eh?

When I was on holiday in Tenerife with my mum Pam, he called me and said he missed me and promised that when I was home, he would take me shopping and buy as much leather clothing items as possible and he would pay for it. Was he proposing that he would be like 'a sugar daddy'?

Fucking hell, this is just too much.

Dave proceeded to tell me that he also wanted to take me away on a 'secret' holiday just me and him so that he could do everything he ever wanted to me.

It was all so bloody odd, but in true Dave fashion, he was all talk and no action as none of this ever happened – thankfully.

I came home from my holiday and didn't hear from him for a while.

He would go off the radar for weeks, then reappear and that was fine. It totally suited me because his neediness was exhausting.

I knew Dave wasn't 'The One'. The butterflies disappeared after the first time I met him, and we didn't go out on any dates or anything. Really, it was just two newly single people having fun.

Or so I thought.

One day, I was sitting at work on my lunch break scrolling through Instagram when all of a sudden, I see that Dave was in Italy on holiday, WITH HIS GIRLFRIEND.

I nearly choked on my Subway salad when I saw the pictures. I was in total disbelief after the complete sob story he gave me about her cheating the first time he met me.

I couldn't help myself but scroll through the series of scenic pictures and there she was, sat beside the Mr Grey wannabe, was the same girlfriend who apparently cheated on him and 'broke his heart'.

I studied every single one of the photos, and even ended up on her Instagram profile too, where I stumbled across more 'they look so happy it makes you sick' pictures.

They were smiling, eating Italian food, drinking wine and looking loved-up – the pair of bastards that they were.

She was fucking beautiful too, he was definitely punching!

38

Blonde hair, green eyes, a body one could only dream of having.

I looked down at my podgy belly, the heartbreak diet never did come to me by the way, and began to question what he even saw in me if his girlfriend or ex-girlfriend, whatever she was, looked like that.

I was mad at my discovery so I clicked back on to his profile and hit the like button for the 'just so you know, that I know, that you're still with her' effect.

I couldn't believe this was happening to me again!

And I don't want to sound like a crazy gal, as I know we weren't together or anything at all like that, but I'd slept with him a few times and he didn't mention anything about reconciling with his 'cheating' ex.

Maybe he told her about me, and they made up? Who knows, probably not though.

So that was it, I didn't hear from him again.

A few months later, I was at the Barrowlands with a group of my friends at a gig, and after it finished, we headed to the taxi rank at Central Station to grab a cab home.

As soon as I joined the queue, I looked up and couldn't believe it... no word of a lie, there he was.

Dave was standing directly in front of me, wearing the skinniest jeans I've ever seen and a tight – definitely too young for him – All Saints T-shirt.

He was swaying side to side. Obviously, he had been out on the booze too.

I couldn't believe that this was yet another bloody coincidence – meeting randomly in Glasgow again without months of contact.

This is so weird...

'Hi!' he said, surprised. 'Fancy meeting you here...'

He looked at me right in the eyes when he was talking to me and it was like being hypnotised. His eyes were amazing, they're my bloody weakness, alongside the several pints I'd scudded at the gig.

Dave had this bizarre hold over me. I was totally mesmerised by him so of course, I ended up taking him home.

After a very touchy-feely, can't keep our hands off each other taxi ride home, we arrived at my flat.

And before I dropped my drawers, I asked him what was going on with his 'cheating ex' and he told me the truth, sorry his truth.

Dave admitted that he had cheated on her, so she cheated on him, and it kind of went back and forth like that for a while.

It was total bollocks.

He explained that he was still with her, kind of. They were trying to work things out but he knew it wasn't working.

Red flag, red flag, red flag.

I should have opened the Juliette balcony of my flat and tossed him out head first.

But I didn't because I'm a stupid girl.

And while the alcohol is partly to blame, I'll totally hold my hands up here and say that I should not have done it because it was wrong, but... yes, I slept with him and I knew he had a girlfriend.

You don't think about it at all when it's happening, you're caught up in the moment of passion but the minute it's over, the guilt comes flooding in.

And it's not just the guilt of him having a girlfriend, but it actually makes you feel dirty.

I really do still feel terrible about it when I think back to it. I'm not going to sit here and pretend that I was oblivious that he was with her because I wasn't. I knew, I did it and I'm sorry. I was young and stupid. I shouldn't have degraded myself like that but I did.

I became his bit on the side and it wasn't even worth it.

What was strange about the whole situation was that he buzzed off the fact I knew about her and I'm pretty ashamed to say that in this instance, I was the 'other girl'.

He used to tell me he fantasied about her finding out about us and knowing what he was up to – like what the fuck? This guy loved playing with fire. What a scumbag! But who am I to talk? I should have called it quits there and then without a doubt.

I remember we drank so much that night that after I dropped him back off at his flat in Glasgow; I had to pull over on the M74 to be sick on my lap. I had a hang-over not only from the alcohol but from him too.

So that was it. I truly believed that was the end of the 'fuck man'… but he popped up again a few months later saying it was over this time.

I wasn't overly bothered about him by this point, the novelty of dating a two-timing, older man (whose hair was more grey than peppered now and the lines on his forehead were there even when he wasn't frowning) had well and truly worn off.

Last year, he text me on my birthday wishing me a good day and asked how old I was, even though he already knew.

When I told him I was turning twenty-five, he replied, *So old, baby, I preferred you when you were twenty-one.*

Ugh, what a prick!

A few weeks after that, he text me again asking to meet up with him again, this time at a hotel in Glasgow. Who knows why he was staying in a hotel, I didn't even bother to ask.

Again, I was out with my pals and as we were drifting off to get drunken kebabs and booty calls, I announced to the group that I was getting an Uber to the hotel Dave was staying at.

'Not the older guy? Thought he was a fuck man?' one of them said.

'He is.' I laughed. 'That's why I'm going.'

He was, but it had been a while and well, you'll learn from the next few chapters of this book that I really do make a lot of terrible decisions when I've been drinking.

So off I jumped into an Uber and made my way to this little out the way hotel in Glasgow.

I arrived at the big revolving glass door.

Taking a deep breath, I swanned in pretending I had a room there, hoping that it didn't look like I was a booty call, or better still, a hooker.

I walked past the male receptionist and smiled at him. His mouth curled ever so slightly – he knew what I was up to and I felt dirty.

I scurried into the lift and was just waiting on some sort of security guard to jump in behind me and usher me back out for not being an official guest there, much like that scene in *Pretty Woman* where Vivienne gets ushered back out by Barney.

I let out a sigh of relief when no one did. The doors closed over and I made my way to the fourth floor and straight to room 452.

I sped up through the corridor and when I came up to my desired door; I knocked quietly, hoping to only grab Dave's attention.

I'd hardly taken my fist off the door when Dave's head peered from behind it, being as discreet as possible.

When he saw that it was me (who else would it be at this hour?) He pulled back the door to grant me entry.

When I turned around to see him, I almost let out a gasp.

There he was, a man at thirty-eight years old standing in front of me for a night of passion, wearing a T-shirt and a pair of PYJAMA BOTTOMS!

He looked so much older now, not the fucking gorgeous guy I'd met in the bar that night a few years ago.

43

And now that same man was standing before me, wearing pyjama bottoms with penguins on them. Was I dreaming this!? Or was this real life?

I blinked a few times just to be sure, and it definitely was penguin pyjamas.

Jesus Christ, it was.

I studied him as he poured us drinks. His hair was definitely greyer than ever before and he had little wrinkles around his eyes. It was obvious that he was ageing and not like a fine wine.

I remember seeing on Instagram a few months before that Dave had been cosy with a brunette woman, more of his age, but there was no mention of her recently, so I just assumed she was out of the picture. Anyway, Dave couldn't nail a bird down. He had too much of a wandering eye and a fetish for a younger girl – that's probably the reason I was here right now.

Still taking in the pyjama fiasco, he handed me the drink and chatted away, asking me how my night was and where I'd been, how work was and just about life in general.

I was drunk and so was he – I didn't even really chat to him much, but I knew that the only way to get those penguin pyjamas off was if we were going to sleep together, so I made my move.

Dave had 100% lost his touch. The sex was absolutely abysmal.

It wasn't as good as I'd remembered it ever being. It wasn't even 'vanilla', which wasn't like him. God, he really was losing his touch, in all ways.

What was I doing here? I was feeling like a slag for being here, but now that I was, it wasn't even worth it!

It was maybe about four in the morning now. We were just lying in bed talking again, not about anything important.

'So how's the single life been treating you then?' I asked, sussing for details on what happened to the last one he had on the go.

'Well… I'm still seeing that Lucy, but I'm not sure. You're going to find this hard to believe, but I actually really like her.'

I burst out laughing, like really laughing, until I turned and looked at him and realised that he was deadly serious.

'What? What do you mean you really like her? How can you say that when I'm literally lying in your bed and we had sex about five minutes ago?'

He looked back at me blankly.

'You know we get on great and stuff, like really great, but I'm not sure if there is something missing. Plus, she has kids.'

And that was it. I was dumbfounded.

This guy seriously has some sort of disorder with his brain if he thinks this is OK!

I didn't have anything else to say to him, so I just turned on the bed and pretended to go to sleep.

'Don't be mad, you know what I'm like, you knew I was with her still.'

And that was it. Conversation done.

'I actually really like her.'

'I actually really like her.'

'I actually really like her.'

'And she has kids.'

'And she has kids.'

'And she has kids.' – that makes it even worse!

The words repeated in my head over and over again.

I lay in that bed feeling really low as Dave drifted off to sleep and my mind was doing overtime – why the fuck did I come here!?

I felt like that dirty 'other girl' all over again. I felt angry tears burn in my eyes.

What is it they say? Play with fire and you get burnt?

Well, this time, I was really fucking scolded, with third-degree burns and more.

I couldn't sleep. It was starting to get light outside, and I knew I had to get out of this situation, and fast.

Overlooking the crumpled penguin pyjamas on the floor, I pulled my phone out of my clutch bag and messaged every single one of my friends in my phonebook the standard Sunday morning 'YOU UP YET?' text, with the hopes that one of them would come and rescue me from this horrific scenario that I, by choice, once again, had put myself in.

'Never again,' I vowed in my cloudy head.

'NEVER A-FUCKING-AIN.'

Unlucky for me, it was only 8 a.m., and everyone was probably still in bed nursing their tequila hang-overs. I had one too, and I needed to go home urgently.

So I picked my phone up again and by this point, I only had about 13% battery and booked another Uber, this time a departing one.

I looked around the dinky hotel room as Dave slept soundly beside me.

It was nice, quite dated though, but why was he here?

Had he maybe fallen out with his bird? You know, the one that he really liked?

I waited until the Uber app showed that my driver had almost arrived before I made my move.

But I was torn. Should I wake him and say, 'that's me away?' or should I just run for the fucking hills silently.

The Uber would be here in three minutes. Three minutes may not seem like much but in this instance, it felt like a lifetime.

I decided that waking him would prolong my time here, so I creeped out of bed and started grabbing my belongings as quietly as physically possible.

I scooped up my belt, heels, and pants… shameful I know, and stuffed them all inside my clutch bag.

Dave opened his eyes in a sleepy daze and saw that I was leaving.

FUCK! I was caught.

He just kind of looked at me and I dashed towards the door.

My heart was beating out of my chest for some reason. I honestly just wanted to go home, but there was no amount of clicking my heels together that was going to make that happen right now.

Scooting down the corridor and back into the lift that carried me into this horrific situation, I remember thinking, *God, I hope no one is up having breakfast downstairs at this time because I'm not a sight for sore eyes.*

The metal doors opened like that fucking lift in *Take Me Out*.

All I could think about was Paddy McGuinness saying: 'Single man reveal yourself!' but instead of a hunky singleton guy, it was me;

Kirsten, 25, from Motherwell with her pants stuffed in her clutch bag.

Now really wasn't the time for jokes.

I kept my head down as I scurried past the pristine female receptionist who was all glammed up in her little navy suit who had evidently just started the morning shift.

Utter shame washed over me. I was the ultimate definition of 'The Fear'.

As if timed to absolute perfection, my Uber driver was waiting at the front door like a knight in shining armour to rescue me from the dragon, which in my situation was greying journalist Dave with the penguin pyjamas.

'Good night, hen?' the driver asked me as me and my extreme 'bed head' stepped into his stale-smelling silver Skoda or, as I saw it at that moment, my carriage of saviour.

Fuck's sake, even my Uber man was judging me for my antics.

I just nodded and kept my head down in my phone before it eventually died. It was the longest journey of my life; the roads were quiet, and the sun was splitting the trees.

I was hung-over and feeling pretty grim – about the amount I drank and also about everything that just happened with Dave.

The driver, God love him, kept trying to speak to me and ask me questions like 'where did you end up then?'

'Aw you know, mate, just back to a hotel shagging some girl's boyfriend and now doing the walk of shame.'

Of course, I didn't say that but just fed him with the usual 'just back to my pals', lie that every girl who has been out on the ran-dan tells their taxi driver when they ask.

Obviously, he knew I was lying, and I could see the smug bastard's face in the mirror, that he enjoyed probing me and hear the lies snake out my mouth.

I arrived back at my house, £40 lighter, bumping bastard!

But I was so relieved.

Maybe if the shag had been decent, I wouldn't have minded as much about doing this godawful walk of shame, but it was just so shite.

I've definitely had more fun at a smear test than I did with Dave just there.

And that was it… I never saw 'Fuck Man' again.

Looking back on the text exchanges between us, I can't believe some of the things he would say to me… they were absolutely wild.

Will you look at me with your amazing eyes while you fuck me?

I'm going to hurt you and you're going to enjoy it.

I'm your boss, baby

Dirty texting hasn't ever really been my thing. I won't lie, I find it awkward as hell and I just cringe at everything, and I never know what to say.

Whenever I'm stuck in this rut, I would usually text my pal, Claire. She's a professional in this department, so I would message her and say, *What do you say to this one?*

Her colourful mind would always come up with something to say back, and that's why I loved her. She was the brains behind my dirty texts, and it was hilarious.

I always just told Dave what he wanted to hear and agreed with everything he said, but I just couldn't bring myself to get into it at all, and he would get annoyed with me for it.

Now, as far as I know Dave is still with the girl, he 'really liked', I unfollowed him on social media so I don't really know what he's up to now, but it wouldn't surprise me if he was still chasing twenty-one-year-olds on the side.

So where did that leave me? Ready to put myself back out there again and be 'single as fuck', that's where.

I was ready to start dating again. If Dave taught me anything it was 'don't be the bit on the side again' and I wasn't going to be.

I'm totally ashamed of stooping so low as to do that and can't believe I belittled myself so much.

But as always, we move on.

WORDS OF ADVICE to future me:

1. When a man (who potentially wants into your pants) calls you kid, run for the hills.

2. If he booty calls you in penguin pyjamas, also run for the hills.

3. Just don't fuck a Fuck Man – run for the fucking hills!!!

4. Sunday Swiping

So there I was again, single, on my own with not a soul on the go.

No good morning texts and definitely no dirty texts calling me baby.

There wasn't any part of me that I thought at any point that Dave and I were actually going to go anywhere, but that was him out the picture, for good.

Good riddance to him and those bloody penguins!

I was in a bit of limbo since my hotel shenanigans and because I didn't have much else to do, I started to go out a lot.

That's what single people do, isn't it?

Go out, get smashed and hope to God that they meet someone.

Let's be honest, we've all been standing in a bar looking around to see if there's any talent and wondering if anyone will randomly come up to you and ask for your number like they do in films.

Let me tell you, it's a fucking myth, unless I've just been going to all the wrong bars.

Anyway, most Fridays and Saturdays I was out drinking with my pals, going weekends away, going to gigs and festivals.

I really had one of the best summers ever.

Although, with all these alcohol-fuelled social events, came me spending most of my Sunday mornings with my head down the toilet pan, spewing up the lining of my stomach.

THE ONE THING I really missed about being in a relationship was Sundays. Sundays were always spent being lazy, eating, cuddling, watching shite TV and just spending the day in bed with your other half.

And also having hung-over sex.

I loved Sundays when I had a boyfriend and now I hated them. Partly because:

1. I was always hung-over.
2. That it was almost Monday already.
3. The loneliness.

During the day was fine as I was too rough to even talk to anyone and sometimes didn't even surface from my bed until 3 o'clock, but when it started hitting five or six, that's when I felt alone, depressed even.

People talk about the 'Sunday night fear' – the peak of your roughness and the thought of starting work at 9 a.m. the next day.

Sometimes I wouldn't get a single text from anyone on a Sunday, except from my mum asking if I was alive or if I managed to get a winch over the weekend.

ONE SUNDAY, I was so bored beyond belief that I decided it was finally time to download Tinder.

And what is Tinder, you loved-up darlings may ask?

It's an app – a shallow one at that – where you swipe left for people you don't like the look of, and right for the ones you do.

If in return, these suitors liked the look of you and had swiped right, it will come up 'You've got a match!' and you can begin chatting with them.

Easy enough, right?

What had I got to lose? Potentially my Sunday hang-overs if I met someone and the way I was feeling at that moment in time, I was OK with that.

So I went into the app store and downloaded it.

I tapped away and began to put in the details.

It wanted to know things like my age, gender and what my job title was.

It then asked me to select a few pictures then write a 'bio'.

Oh God, what will I write?

I racked my brains to try to think of something witty, but in the end, I decided to leave it blank until I had the full thing sussed out properly.

I was set, my profile was good to go, and I began swiping away.

I was still a bit unsure of how it all worked, but basically, I just began swiping left.

It did seem pretty straight forward once you got the hang of it, but I couldn't help but think it was pretty shallow judging someone purely on their looks but then what's the point in getting to know someone if you're not attracted to them?

Swings and roundabouts.

So, there I was, flicking left and right and left, and left, and left. Jeez, this is awful.

His hairline is receding.

He has bad teeth.

What a terrible picture! Why would you use that?

I started to notice the kind of stuff guys were putting in their bios, some boring, some cringe, and some totally outrageous.

I couldn't believe just the variety of people on it. I'm not sure what I expected at all but let me talk you through just a few of them.

MR INDEPENDENT

So I feel like guys on Tinder seem to think they need to use the disclaimer 'own house, own car, own teeth' in their bios to give themselves a better chance of succeeding. And I won't lie, it makes me cringe.

Well, I would like to think so if you're in your thirties, no? But my God, is there really any need to include this? Also, you will get the odd one pictured standing outside a house with a sold sign grinning like a Cheshire cat… we get it you bought a house, but no one likes a showoff!

THE MOUNTAIN SCALER

So right off the bat, I know this type of guy isn't for me.

His pictures will include snaps of him trekking up mountains and taking pictures at the summit of God knows where.

This is the type of guy who is extremely active and has more pictures of them skiing, surfing, rock climbing, and other physical activities which require you to be a regular at a gym (which I am not sadly) and quite frankly, I couldn't really think of anything worse.

Other pictures may include them taking part in Tough Mudder (which is great for them, really) but looking sweaty AF and head-to-toe in mud really doesn't cut it for me, unfortunately.

The Mountain Scaler will also include lines in their bio like 'On a Sunday you can find me bagging munros' or 'looking for someone to see the sunrise with at the top of Ben Nevis', no thanks, I would rather you take me to a bar and buy me a wine, but if that's what floats your boat, great!

THE 'ONLY HERE FOR FUN' GUY

I've come across this type quite a lot.

There are two kinds. There are the ones that write in their bio 'Only looking for a shag' or 'just out a long-term relationship so not looking for anything serious' and I admire them for being honest, but then you get the handsome ones with no mention of it on their bio and message you like: *'Hey I'm clearly highly attracted to you, however I'm not here to exactly find the one. I'm looking to have some adult fun.'*

I never give these guys the time of day to be honest. Because what is the point, really?

A lot of people who find out you're on dating apps (usually people in relationships) always say, 'Oh, is that not just for sex?'

According to these guys yes, and good for them for using it for that but the 'only here for fun guys' don't seem to have a personality at all, merely just a sex robot looking to shove their dicks in anyone who will take it.

I'm sure there are plenty of people who just use it for a quick no strings shag and that's OK.

THE PT

There are so many personal trainers on Tinder... total giveaway is every single one of their pictures is either of them in the gym, posing with their muscles, sometimes even videos of themselves bench-pressing some crazy heavy weights.

They usually say things like, 'I enjoy looking after myself and work out 2/3 times a day, the only thing I'll spend more time with than you is in the gym' (yawn) or 'Fitness freak looking for a workout buddy, you can test out your squats over me if you like' or my favourite 'Don't worry I'll shag you into shape!'

I've never actually been out on any dates with PTs, I'm more of a 'gin girl' than a 'gym girl'.

I can't run the length of myself and I also would probably be judged that I'm not having all egg white omelettes for breakfast followed by a protein shake – give me a bacon roll any day of the week!

I'm sure they're all nice guys, but they do tend to be extreme posers and perfectly groomed in their pictures.

They always seem to wear ridiculously short shorts, a vest top, are covered in tattoos and evidently, a sunbed abuser.

I've spoken to a few of them, and from my experience they don't really have much to say. Maybe it's because from my pictures you can tell I enjoy a good scran. Chunky, but hella funky!

THE TRAVELLER

Another Tinder stereotype which always seems to pop up is 'the traveller'.

Pictures include posing with a drugged-up tiger or at a full-moon party with a bucket of cocktail in Thailand, wearing those horrendous patterned trousers that everyone and their granny wears when they travel Asia.

Their bios sometimes include lines like 'Just back from travelling India, need someone to keep me in the one place' or 'looking for someone to travel the world with'.

I love a holiday myself, but it's so cliche and very, very predictable.

I'll admit I have one picture of myself in the sea in Dubai, not to show off that I've been there, but purely for the fact my tits look great in it.

The traveller tends to be a 'free spirit' and a great believer in '420' (smoking joints) which is something I do not have time for, but each to their own!

THE MARRIED MAN

I have never encountered any kind of conversation with this type, but my fellow Tinderella pal Claire came across it a few weeks ago.

She was chatting to a handsome young man in his thirties. Their chat was so good that he asked for her number.

Once the WhatsApp messages began flowing, he told her he had a confession – he wasn't even the guy in the photos. I mean, what married man would have the brass neck to actually post a picture of themselves on a dating app?

Anyway, he asked her, 'have you got a fuck buddy?' to which she joked, 'no, been celibate ages, lol' and he replied, 'I have a wife and still get none.'

Claire actually thought he was joking until he confessed that the pictures weren't of him and sent her a selfie of a balding forty-something man, followed by a picture of him holding his dick in his hand.

It's fair to say Claire swiftly went ghost on his ass. Sometimes though, I've seen a few profiles saying 'married so will provide pictures on request' which is just so bloody awful. If you're not happy – LEAVE! But sometimes, they say things like 'Wife knows I'm on here, looking for purely just sex'. But still, I don't agree which leads me on to...

THE COUPLE LOOKING FOR A PLUS ONE

I've seen quite a lot of these profiles actually, which totally surprised me. It's always quite unusual to see a picture of a guy with a girl unless it's his granny or something, which even at that, is weird.

But when you see a male and a female pictured together and looking quite cosy, you realise that they're looking for someone to sandwich and let me tell you – I ain't no filling! LEFT!

THE 'HAT-FISH'

You've heard of a catfish, right? Well, the hat-fish is a handsome wee bastard with a hat on in every picture, but once you actually delve into further evidence of their existence, it turns out he is a bald as they come.

A cutie, but with not a single hair on his head. I've tried to see past the hair (or lack of) but these guys tend to be as dull as dishwater. Not all baldies are, of course, but just embrace it for God's sake!

THE VEGAN

A guy usually on the slender side, with a little green plant emoji in his bio along with them stating the fact that they don't date meat eaters.

I don't really know exactly what else because the minute I see it it's a swift left for me. Is that bad? I went vegan for a month as part of a bet in my work and I must say it was easily the worst month of my life. Good for them, but it's not for me.

THE 'ONE PIC PONY'

A guy with one shitty pic and no chat. I always suspect they're a fake profile or someone who has gained 60 pounds in the last year and therefore lacks any up-to-date pictures. Not much really more to say about them – Tinder fact – Everyone's first picture is always their best one, so if you only have one on your profile, I'll assume that only one good picture of you exists.

THE BAM POT

A typical ned or as they call it in England, a 'chav'. Can usually be seen posing topless down the River Clyde with a bottle of some kind in one hand and a fag in the other.

These types usually come with a terrible neck tattoo, usually of their initials. I mean, I'm guilty of owning a few terrible tattoos, but neck tattoos for me are an instant swipe left – sorry!

THE ONE WITH THE HOT PAL

Now, another unwritten rule of Tinder is that if you insist on including a group picture, at least don't use it until the fourth picture. But the one with the hot pal doesn't seem to get the memo.

We want to know what one you are, and we don't want to fall in love with your pal and match you only to find out, in fact, that you're the wee grim looking one at the end. Harsh, but true. All group photo profiles tell me unofficially that you're a munter who's using your pal to trick us into matching with you. Stop it! It's not fair.

THE ONE WITH THE CUTE DOG

Now us girls are all fans of cute dogs on Insta, let's be honest. Many of these guys write things in their bios like 'dog dad' or 'if my dog doesn't like you then you've got no chance' and other boring things along those lines.

They use their cute fluffy pals to lure us in. Some extreme 'doggo dads' have single pictures of them on their profile, which I just totally swipe left for. I want to date you, not your dog! I actually did date one of these guys, but we'll come to him later on.

THE FOOTBALL FAN

My favourite stereotype. This is my type. I love football and me and my daft pal Caitlin go away every year to wherever our team draws in Europe for a weekend of pints, laughs and winching boys.

Anyway, the football fan always has a picture with a football top and/or scarf outside his team's ground or usually tanning pints on an away trip with his equally handsome pals. This one is one to watch though. They always seem to have multiples on the go but we'll get to that later too.

THE 'WORKY'

Again, another one of my favourites. The 'worky' is usually a joiner, electrician, gas engineer or another type of tradesman which requires them to wear their sexy trousers with multiple pockets. I don't know what it is, but a guy in a 'worky' uniform really does it for me. He also tends to be a football fan or a pint scudder. This is my downfall, and you will shortly see why.

SO THERE YOU have it, a short round up of just some of the Tinder stereotypes for those that are not familiar with the app.

I honestly couldn't believe the variety of people on there at all and couldn't help but wonder what type I would end up with.

When I eventually delved into the world of online dating, I must admit, first ever Tinder experience wasn't quite what I imagined it would be, although I wasn't entirely sure what to expect.

The guy that broke my online dating virginity by matching with me was called Jamie, and from his initial photos he seemed decent.

He had gorgeous dark hair and piercing green eyes. He only had two photos right enough, but it wasn't long before he slid into my DMs.

We chatted for a while on the app before he asked me if I had WhatsApp.

OMG! That was pretty quick!

A guy has actually asked me for my number!

I felt smug as everyone always told me online dating was good, but you were most likely to come across some weird ones at some point.

Anyway, I sent over my digits and awaited his first message, but when it arrived, I was left scratching my head.

It read: *Hey do you have leggings?* xxx

What? What was he on about?

I replied, confused.

Leggings?

What was he on about? This had nothing to do with the conversation we just had over on Tinder.

After watching him type for a few minutes, my jaw hit the floor at his response.

You may say yes or you may say no. I've got like the biggest fetish ever for leggings and thongs and I wondered if I could see you in them? I would pay you £300 for ten pics and we can do this regular I promise no nudes or I also like being financially dominated. I'd love you to do a video in leggings demeaning cash from me and showing you in them, the cash limit would be up to you. What you reckon don't be offended gorgeous xxx

What the fucking FUCK!?

I began to wonder if this was a joke, but the more I studied the message, the more I realised that this guy was deadly serious.

Leggings of all things? What the hell?

As much as it would probably be the easiest 300 quid I would have ever made, I decided to just block him and continue on with my new Tinder quest.

I should have known that this was only a sign of what was to come…

5. A Bit Potty

It was definitely a love/hate thing with Tinder because it was almost like a game.

Constantly swiping left and right to try to get to the bottom of a never-ending pit of single men.

You felt a small sense of victory when that wee 'You've got a match!' banner flashed across the screen but also a pang of 'rejection' when you finally gave into a right, only to not be matched back because the reality was that they either hadn't seen you yet or had swiped you left.

But when I did have one of these victories, I was mildly pleased with one of them in particular.

Lewis – a dark-haired, brown-eyed handsome guy, quite muscly and with a bit of stubble. Exactly my type.

Within minutes of matching with Lewis, I knew he was going to be a charmer. He messaged me right away with some cheeky chat up line referring to one of my pictures (the Dubai one to be exact) and he had decent patter which is exactly what I was looking for. I'm highly attracted to a cheeky guy with a bit of banter.

Lewis and I went back and forth in messages, bouncing off each other and since the chat lasted longer than three messages –

which is rare for Tinder so I had heard – I had a good feeling about this one. Could Lewis be my Tinder date debut?

Maybe, as long as he didn't ask for pictures of me in leggings in return for 300 quid.

Oh, a journo, eh? I'm not telling you anything, you'll make it front page news!

This sort of line had popped up a few times when guys found out what I did for a living. One guy even went as far as calling me a 'journo c*nt' and that was that… I unmatched him.

Anyway, I told Lewis his life probably wasn't that interesting to make front page news, and he enjoyed my wit. He was really quite sarcastic, which I liked.

It wasn't long before he eventually asked for my number, and we began texting.

As the chat flowed, I found out more about Lewis and the more I heard, the more I liked.

He was twenty-three – younger than me at the time only by a year – it didn't really bother me at all but I'd always went for an older guy in the past (refer to Chapter 3. The Fuck Man) but maybe it was about time that I tried something new?

Maybe that's where I was going wrong before? Maybe younger guys are the way forward?

We would soon find out, I guess.

One thing about Lewis was that he loved to talk about himself.

He told me that he worked in an office – I still to this day don't actually know what it was he did in said office, it could've been anything really but any time I asked it turned into this big, waffled story so I virtually nodded and accepted that he was one of these guys who like to 'fluff' things up.

He reminded me of a bit of a Del Boy, salesman type, who bigged up something so small into something extravagant. Despite this, I liked Lewis, he talked the talk.

He told me that in his spare time he went to the gym and that he also had a flat of his own about twenty minutes away from me; he sounded absolutely perfect – what was the catch?

One thing that did annoy me about him though, was his ability to use the correct spelling. He didn't know how to use things like they're/there/their or your/you're which, as a journalist, is so fucking frustrating – everyone has a spell checker on their phones these days, do they not!?

But what grated on me even more is that he didn't even spell simple things properly, like 'definitely' he wrote 'definitlie'.

I would correct him in a jokey way because it pettily got to me, but he would just respond with comments like 'oh typical journalist'.

Surely I couldn't be put off a guy due to his terrible grammar and awful spelling? Petty, yes, but I let it slide. He could do worse things like take drugs or be a convicted murderer, you know?

Weeks went by and we were speaking day and night.

IT WAS THE lead up to Christmas and with the time of the year meaning everyone's social lives were really busy, we tried to plan a weekend night date with not much luck.

Every time a date was suggested it was like: 'It's my works Christmas night out that night' or 'ah I have something on, on Friday!', so he suggested we meet on my lunch break that week and go for a coffee since we couldn't have a proper 'date night'.

I'll admit, it wasn't my ideal scenario nor how I imagined my first proper first date to be, but I agreed.

A coffee date. It sounded so grown up. I was just going to meet up with a guy for a coffee. As causal as you like.

I thought back to all these American TV shows I'd watched previously.

Guy and girl meet up for a coffee in an old school diner and the waitress comes over with a pot of coffee and they fall madly in love or it goes horribly wrong.

Snapping myself back into reality, I had to remind myself that I, in fact, was in Scotland and not some cute, rustic New York coffee spot.

The big day soon arrived, and I was incredibly nervous trying to get on with my work in the morning.

My stomach was literally flipping. What if he didn't like me and ran for the hills when he saw me?

What if he was weird? Imagine he kidnapped me? That would make a great story, eh?

Am I the only girl who thinks about every bloody worst-case scenario before a date? It's just a coffee, for fuck's sake!

I'd been clock watching the whole day and before I knew it, lunchtime was fast approaching.

I was constantly touching up my lip liner and fluffing up my hair in the compact mirror I kept in the top drawer of my desk. It was nearly time.

I got up a whole hour earlier than I usually would that morning for this fucking coffee date, so it better be good.

I even dragged my straighteners through my frizzy locks and patted on the good 'going out' Estee Lauder foundation for the occasion, not my wee crappy drugstore one I usually wore to work – I had to look my best.

I opted to wear my cute office pencil dress, the one I only really wore when I knew I was going out for an important interview so to look extra smart paired with my black Calvin Klein trench coat I picked up in the TK Max sale.

I felt slick. I couldn't get truly 'dolled up' like I initially planned, so I might as well look like the sleek journo that I am… who was I kidding? Usually, I wore a pair of black trousers and my hair scraped back in a messy bun and still had crust in my eyes half the time.

But today I made a proper effort. God, I think I even sprayed my good Chanel perfume for the occasion, too. Estee Lauder AND Chanel? He better be worth it!

We arranged to meet in a Costa coffee which was near his office and just happened to be upstairs in a Next store. Not really what I would have picked for a first date, but I let him decide, it's fine it's only coffee, right?

When it hit half twelve, I rushed out the office, into my car and headed straight over there.

I only really had an hour but no one really timed the lunch breaks so it would be fine if I was five minutes late coming back.

It was a frosty day, I had a scarf on, and the cold air bit at my nose making it a bit red, I had that nervous first date feeling again, more so because I was sober too.

I think I phoned every one of my available pals on my way over to take my mind off the nerves right up until the minute I managed to get a parking space amid the crazy Christmas shoppers.

'Good luck, girrrrrl!' my pal Caitlin squealed as I hung up the call.

I checked my lipstick and hair in the mirror one last time before stepping out of the car – God it was cold!

I made my way to Next, thinking back on it now it was a really bizarrely organised date but I didn't know any different – it was my first one!

But I made it past the home-ware section – oh nice cushions – and headed up the stairs… and there he was.

Oh…

Lewis was standing in front of me. All 5ft 4 of him. He was shorter in real life than in his pictures, but I didn't mind that so much being 5ft 3 myself but Jesus, fuck, what was he wearing?

Lewis stood before me wearing the palest grey suit I've ever seen, so pale it looked light blue (think Lloyd Christmas in *Dumb and Dumber*) paired with matching grey brogues and a long grey coat.

What the hell? He looked quite handsome, but really, what the fuck did he have on?

I tried to look past it.

'All right, McStay,' he said, as he kissed my cheek. He had started calling me by my second name in his texts in a sort of endearing way which did make me laugh, but at the same time, it was a bit odd.

'Hello!' I smiled back.

We stood together for a minute and gazed over at the overcrowded coffee shop, wondering where exactly we could sit. It was absolutely bursting at the seams. There were kids running about daft, old dears squashed in tiny tables hovering over a teapot and fruit scones, and shoppers with their countless bags crammed into every corner. I could tell already this was going to be a disaster.

'What you wanting to drink?' he asked.

I opted for a latte, then he ordered me to stand watch for a table becoming free.

This was a bit awkward.

So I scooted into a little booth in the corner which too old biddies had just got up from and I pushed their teapot and cups to the side. I glanced over to see him handing his money over to the cashier and quickly had a look at my phone.

Mum: *Let me know how it goes! Xxx*

I know not everyone tells their mum about guys and stuff like that, but me and my mum are more like sisters than mother and daughter. We are so unbelievably close it's ridiculous. I always ask her for advice on most life situations. She is my absolute best friend.

On the back of becoming newly single, I'd told her that I downloaded Tinder and most days she'd say something like 'So how's the swiping going?' or 'You met the swipe of your life yet?' Always the joker, my mum.

After I split up with Dean, she'd always say 'I knew you wouldn't end up with him' which is kinda annoying to hear, but obviously she didn't want to burst her eighteen-year-old daughter's bubble at the time. She always said he was a 'nice boy' but I thought I needed a proper man's man. I was always the provider in that relationship, and I needed someone to look after me, not in a financial way, but more in an emotional way, and Dean certainly did not do that.

Looking around the cramped coffee shop, I noted that my American diner daydream had well and truly been dashed. And bringing me my coffee was a man in head-to-toe pale grey.

Lewis pottered back over with two coffees on a tray and slid into the cramped little booth.

'Thank you,' I said as he pushed a toffee nut latte over towards me – a firm festive favourite at this time of year, while he opted for a hot chocolate.

We chatted about what our mornings so far consisted of. He was a 'nice guy' but I honestly couldn't stop looking at the suit. It was a real eyesore. But he wasn't an eyesore at all.

He made me laugh with his shitty jokes and quick banter. He had a cheeky smile and the dark stubble on his face was just so attractive. From the neck up, I really quite fancied him. I couldn't stop looking at his brown eyes. They were so sparkly I could get lost in them. I'm a huge sucker for brown eyes, as we know.

It was such a quick half an hour, we chatted about our jobs, holidays, what we had done over the summer, our past relationships.

He didn't give too much away other than he had been in a pretty serious relationship and they lived together. The journalist in me wanted to quiz him on it further, but the single 'playing it cool gal' thought 'don't push it'. When I glanced at my watch, I thought I really need to get going in the next twenty minutes latest. We finished our coffees, and he suggested that we 'had a wee look about'.

Great, my first Tinder date was a stoat around Next Home.

We made our way down the stairs and over to all the Christmas decorations. We browsed awkwardly and dodged past all the frantic Christmas shoppers.

It was a bit weird I'll admit, but maybe he just wanted to spend more time with me? Who knew, but it was easy to talk to him and there were no really awful silences.

After looking at Christmas trees and decorations, we headed out to the car park, and he walked me over to my car which I thought was kind of cute. We said our goodbyes and he gave me a peck on the lips. It was quite nice, but I remember just thinking 'oh my God, what if someone I know has just seen me kiss the guy with the awful suit?'

This is the thing, see if he dressed like a tink, I would be like 'he's awful' and despite the choice of colour, he was smartly dressed and I'm still complaining. I really need to stop being so picky.

'Drive safe, text me when you're back,' he said as he walked away.

I had butterflies a bit when he said it. How nice is that? A proper gentlemanly thing to say, I liked that a lot.

Sitting my arse back in the driving seat, I pulled my seat belt on and smiled. I looked at my clock – shit, I had five minutes to get back to work and was about twenty minutes away.

Better get the foot down!

I was just eleven minutes late getting back into the office, not too bad… no one batted an eyelid so it was all good.

On the way back, I called my partner in crime Caitlin back to give her an update on my coffee date. Caitlin is my most mental single pal. She had also come out of like an eight-year relationship just a few months after I did, so we were both on the same boat and it was nice to speak to someone who went through something similar.

I met Caitlin through my cousin Jodie. Jodie had just recently got engaged and had asked me and her pal Rachael to be her bridesmaids. I didn't really know Rachael that well, but since we were now going to be organising a hen party together, we actually became friends too – she's honestly one of the kindest and most hilarious people I've ever met. And with Rachael comes her sister Caitlin... an equally funny, 5 ft 0, feisty gal and an all-round brilliant person.

We shared a bond over shots of tequila about two and a half years ago, and I've never looked back since.

They're known to me as the Spoon sisters, and I love them both dearly.

Anyway, I told Caitlin all about Mr Lloyd Christmas and she laughed. 'Give him a chance you're being so picky.'

She was right. I was being picky and decided to just give Lewis the benefit of the doubt.

When I sat back at my desk and got ready to start my next news story before heading out on a job, I picked up my phone.

Hey. That's me just back, a little late, but no one noticed. Thanks for the coffee x

I hit send and put down my phone when it almost instantly pinged.

No problem, McStay. Was nice to finally meet u. I had a nice time x

For the rest of the afternoon, I didn't get much work done at all. We texted back and forth all day, even up until 11 p.m. when it was time to go to bed. I really liked Lewis. He had good chat which helped me forget about his fashion faux pas.

We chatted for a few more days and I suggested he come over and watch Christmas films with me through the week and he agreed.

Now, knowing what I know now, you should ALWAYS at least go on three 'date dates' before you invite a guy over to your house… It's my rule now, of course, but I'm still new to the whole Tinder thing at this point but it seemed like a good idea at the time.

That day, once I finished work, I rushed home to make sure my flat was tidy and dolled myself up a bit. I did my make-up and wore my wee Calvin Klein lounge suit – causal, comfy and cute. I didn't want to look too done up for sitting in my house, but I didn't want to look like a slob either and wear my favourite pyjamas that have a hole in the right bum cheek.

We had arranged to order in food too and I don't know about anyone else, but I actually hate eating with guys I hardly know. You need to pretend you don't eat much and disguise the fact you want to ram every single bit of pizza (including his) down your throat.

I waited on Lewis arriving… quickly pacing the floor with nerves, lighting candles, touching up my hair and spraying myself with my trusty Chanel perfume… you've got to smell good!

I jumped when the buzzer rang in the hall, not sure why because I was anticipating it.

Don't answer it right away… don't look too keen, I thought… So, I waited a few minutes and then buzzed him in.

I knew from the minutes that passed by that he must be struggling with the stairs. Imagining him puffing up them reminded me of the times I used to wait on Dave arriving and how he was always drunk when he came over.

We never did anything sober together, we never ordered food or watched films together. We just had drunken sex and that was it. Good riddance to him anyway, the pig!

When I heard the loud knock at the door, I stood a few seconds before I went to answer it, sticking with the 'not too keen' vibe that I was going for.

When I pulled back the door there he was holding on to the wall.

'Jeezo… you not got a lift in here?'

I knew it.

Before I could reply… I was too fixated on the fact that the stupid bastard was wearing shorts. Shorts in December. What!?

They were weird shorts. Like baggy basketball shorts, black with some sort of white logo at the bottom. He was wearing a black T-shirt with a zipper.

This was a far cry from the Lloyd Christmas I met for a coffee… Jesus Christ, is this the same person? He was coming over to chill out, not shoot some hoops – no hoops would be shot tonight that's for sure.

I just laughed and remembered Dave also huffing and puffing as he made his way to the 'penthouse'. It really wasn't as bad as they made out.

'No, sadly not. Come in.'

He took his shoes off at the door, which was nice. Dave never bothered his arse before!

My house was like a mini-Santa's grotto. I absolutely loved Christmas, and this was the first year I had my own place at Christmas time, so I had my tree covered in rose gold baubles and lights wrapped round the railings on my Juliet doors.

'Nice place you've got here,' he said as he parked himself on the couch and I sat down next to him.

'What we watching, then?' he said as he put his arm around me as casual as you like.

'Whatever you want,' I smiled.

Before I even got the chance to flick through films on Netflix, Lewis pulled me in closer and turned his head to kiss me.

Jeezo, he had only been in the door five minutes. I was pleasantly surprised although his stubbly beard rubbed against my face, I enjoyed it – he was a good kisser.

I pulled away.

'Right, what we watching?' I said, grabbing the remote.

He laughed and leant in once more.

We ended up kissing again and again and the next thing I knew he pulled me over on top of him on the couch and we were winching like a couple of teenagers with me straddled over him.

He better not try anything funny, I thought. I've got 'grains'. Grains?

Me and Caitlin always joked that on a first date you had to make sure you always had 'grains' to ensure you don't end up sleeping with a guy the first time you meet him.

Let me explain grains… 'grains' is referring to your pubic hair. It does sound a bit grim, but my waxing lady, Lisa, always says your pubes should be the size of grains of rice before you can get waxed again. Caitlin and I have this running joke that if you've got grains, you can't do anything. No guy wants grains!

Plus, if I slept with him just now that would fuck up my waxing cycle and an emergency shave is not ideal. It's sore, grows in horribly, and means you need to rearrange all future waxing appointments. My waxing lady is like my therapist… she always asks what the occasion is at every appointment or more importantly who the occasion is. Lisa isn't judgy and I totally love that.

I was booked in with Lisa for the following week so absolutely nothing would be happening with Lewis tonight, and besides this was only the second time I'd seen him so it shouldn't be happening this early on.

Anyway, back to the couch.

Lewis ran his hands through my hair and down my neck... I've got a thing for guys touching and kissing my neck... it gives me goosebumps, literally.

His hands then slid all over my back and moved them down to my bum... he slipped his hand down my Calvin Klein leggings and I jumped back.

'Behave!'

I sat up, caressing my chin, which now looked like it had been attacked with sandpaper, and fixed my clothes back into place.

We ended up watching *Home Alone* and ordered in Domino's pizza.

As we tucked into the pizza, Lewis gabbed away. Telling me stories about times he was out with his friends and the antics they got up to. A bit boring to listen to, but he would just talk and talk and talk. I liked it because there were no awkward silences, but I don't think he even allowed the opportunity for awkward silences as he talked so much, but it also let me enjoy my pizza and nod away to everything he said.

But he did make me laugh a lot, he just seemed like a happy go lucky guy.

We kissed some more; he once again tried some funny business but obviously failed (thank God for grains or I might have been tempted) and 11 p.m. rolled round and it was time to go.

As I waved him off, again examining the basketball shorts as he pulled his trainers on, he pulled me in for a sloppy kiss at my front door, he pushed me against the wall and rammed his tongue down my throat as he held my neck in his hands. He kissed me one last time and whispered, 'See you later.'

I shut the door, and I asked myself, did I want to see him later? Did I like him? I was unsure… I couldn't put my finger on it. Did I see myself being with him with him? Probably not. Is it normal to be asking this question on the second 'date'? Probably not.

Time to call Caitlin and give her a debrief.

I told her about the shorts, the kissing, the two cheeky attempts at a hand slip and also the fact that I 'didn't know' about him.

'Hen, how can you know if this is only the second time you've seen him?' she asked.

I always believed that when 'you know you know' like everyone always said. I remember hearing people saying, 'I knew the moment I met him that he was the one' and when I met Lloyd Christmas… I certainly didn't even know if I wanted to be seen with him, never mind if he was 'The One'.

I liked him… but I didn't get those butterflies the second time I saw him. I thought that maybe they would come in time, but they definitely weren't there to begin with. I think that was all down to the suit… and you know how I felt about that.

At this time, as well as being a journalist, I had a part-time job in my local Starbucks making coffees. I've always been a grafter and would do anything to fund the many holidays and weekends away that I enjoyed going on with my pals. It enabled me to book a trip to Singapore, Bali, and Dubai in the March the following year, so I kept it on.

It was tough, but I was making a fortune. I would work as a journalist 9-5 then have an hour break, then go and work 6 p.m. until 11.30 p.m. in Starbucks. I did this three times a week, and I was always bloody shattered.

One night, Lewis and his pal appeared at the shop while I was working and tried to blag some free drinks. On this occasion when I saw him, I was wearing my lovely green apron and my hair in a big messy bun… I really wasn't looking my best, but I didn't care, I was so tired.

Clocking him chatting away to his pal, I noticed that for the first time Lewis actually dressed normally in jeans and a T-shirt, I remember thinking that I wish he looked like that when I first met him and maybe I would have got those initial butterflies.

When I got a spare minute, I went over to speak to them as they sat in the café. I felt nervous seeing him while I was working. I was a supervisor and as the store was a large café with a drive thru, we all had to wear headsets to communicate with each other and to the cars coming around to order drinks.

As I went over with two sneaky free coffees and spoke to Lewis and his pal, my colleagues were shouting down the headsets…

'Check Kirsten flirting with the guy with the beard,'

'On yourself, hen, get in there he looks handsome,' another added.

My Starbucks colleagues were more like family. They had been there for me through lots of difficult times and the laughs we had on shift honestly brightened up my day. They always used to laugh and say I was the best supervisor as I was the most laid back out of everyone because truth be told, I let them do whatever the fuck they wanted. I hold my hands up and say that because working there was my second source of income and basically just pocket money, I didn't put my heart and soul into it like I did with being a journalist. I lived and breathed for that job; I really did. I was awarded Young Journalist of the Year in 2018 and honestly, it's something I'm still so beyond proud of.

As I placed the two freebies down on the table, I chatted with Lewis for a bit, he asked how my shift was going and I asked what the pair of them were getting up to and that was about it.

But our conversation was cut short as duty called me and one of the team had told me through the headset that I was needed on drive thru. I said goodbye and pottered off to get some work done.

'Have you shagged him yet then?' My work pal Ethan asked.

'No… not yet.' I joked. Did I want to though? The thought didn't make me weak at the knees or give me flutters, it made me cringe more than anything, particularly the thought of ripping off those godawful basketball shorts.

Lewis and I continued to text for a few more weeks, although we would go a few days without talking to each other – I wasn't that overly bothered. I was so busy working crazy shifts to really give a shit.

On one of our chattier days, he asked if I wanted to go over to his to stay.

Stay over at his house? We all know what that means. But why was he not asking me to go out on another 'date, date'? Did he not like me in that way? To be honest, if he continued to dress the way he did, then maybe it was best that I wasn't seen with him in public for the foreseeable. Kissing him in the Next car park was bad enough but I anyway I agreed.

Thankfully, I'd been to visit Lisa in case things might progress down there, so if anything, I would be getting a shag at least.

I had work the next day but he told me I could just bring my things and leave from there.

So that's exactly what I did. I put his address into Google Maps and headed over.

After ending another pre-date phone call with Caitlin, I arrived at his house. I hadn't ever been to this area before, so I parked up my car behind his and knocked on the door.

He lived in one of those flats where there's a door at the side of the building with stairs – a maisonette I think it's called? It looked nice anyway.

He answered the door wearing the same style basketball shorts but in red, and it crossed my mind to just turn away there and then and go home but I didn't.

His house was a typical guy house. Basic furniture with the odd little Ikea candle here and there, it looked tidy, that was the main thing.

Lewis told me that he had a new couch arriving early the next morning. He had just repainted the living room and his new couch would finish it off. The couch we sat on was tiny. I literally had to put my legs over him to sit on it. I put my 'overnight bag' in his room, which was literally a double bed, two bedside tables and a TV. It was fine. He had some kinda weird flowery bedsheets, I'm assuming his ex picked when she lived here. He told me they had this place together. Well, he had bought it but she stayed there with him.

As I came out the bedroom, I looked around the hall. It must be a two bed as I could see another door unless it was a cupboard. I didn't want to snoop around – maybe I would ask him for a tour later.

I went back into the living room; he passed me a beer, and we cuddled up on the couch.

Even if I didn't want to cuddle him, I didn't really have a choice given the size of the sofa, but it was a good job that I didn't mind and he shoved on some crap film on Netflix. We got cosy once again and kissed just like we did at my flat.

Things got heated and we did some bits.

Let me tell you about bits, you probably get the gist… touchy-feely things not quite full-on sex but almost… you get the idea.

As the end credits started rolling on the screen, we stopped slobbering all over each other and I still couldn't figure out if I liked this guy or not. He was a decent kisser, but I wasn't overly enthused about him even after the 'bits' – he was too hashy bashy.

'Where's your bathroom?' I asked, about to wet my pants.

'Out there and to the left,' he pointed to the door down the hall.

I lifted my legs off him and toddled to the door.

I remember he had one of those string lights that you pull down, I was nervous in case I pulled it off from the ceiling, but I got there in the end and no damage was done.

As the light flooded the room, I could see that the bathroom was heavily dated.

The first thing I spied was a wooden toilet pan, ICK.

Eyeballing it and its grimness, I really didn't want to park my arse on it, but I was so desperate for a pee that I didn't really have any other option.

I pulled down my jeans and my lacy pants – I wore my fanciest ones in the event he might get to see them – and hovered over the pan from the 70s.

While relieving my bladder, I looked round at all the products lined up in his shower like his anti-dandruff shampoo, Lynx Africa shower gel (classic guy) and a random rubber duck.

I finished peeing and reached for the toilet roll when I noticed something bright tucked in the corner of the bathroom.

What the? Is that a… potty?

A pink potty graced the corner of Lewis's bathroom. Why? I kind of laughed to myself. Why is this in his house?

I pulled up my fancies, flushed the toilet, washed my hands, and returned to the living room.

I sat back down, and he put my legs over his once again.

'Whose potty is that in your bathroom?' I laughed, expecting a ridiculous reply about how maybe one of his pals acquired it after their daft nights out, he had told me they always ended up doing stupid shit when they were drunk.

He stared back at me in silence, before finally replying.

'Em… it's my wee girl's.'

Wee girl? WHAT?

'You've got a wee girl?' I croaked. 'Why didn't you say?'

'I thought you knew, from my pictures?' he mumbled.

Admittedly, I'd seen the occasional picture of a wee girl on his Instagram, but I just assumed it was his niece and as he hadn't mentioned it, I had no idea he was a dad.

HE PRODUCED A CHILD!

'No, I didn't know. I thought you would have mentioned it?'

The atmosphere was now very awkward. I wanted to pull my legs back over, but I couldn't really do that, there was no room.

Should I have looked into this? Why did I assume it was his niece? Was I being a bitch for being mad? I wouldn't have had a problem with him having a child, I mean it's no big deal but the fact he failed to mention it for the weeks we had been 'dating' was fucking weird.

'Is that a problem for you?' he paused.

'No, not at all.'

I just let him think it wasn't, I don't know why I didn't bombard him with questions but I think I was just in shock.

'What age is she?' I asked trying to be nice but sound interested. 'Three, her name is Laila.'

'Aw! That's a cute name.'

And that was that. End of discussion.

'Should we go to bed now?' he said, finishing off the last of his beer. To be honest, by this point I didn't really want to stay but I had a few beers so I didn't really have a choice as I couldn't legally drive home.

We headed into his bedroom. I stupidly forgot to pack pyjamas, so he threw the pair of shorts he wore to my house a few weeks ago at me and I put them on, I looked as ridiculous as he did when he wore them.

I pulled my toothbrush from my bag and went back into the bathroom to face the potty and brush my teeth.

As I scrubbed back and forth, I just stared at the pink bowl of plastic which was covered in Peppa Pig stickers.

I really didn't have an issue with him having a child, what I had an issue with is that he failed to tell me about the most important thing in his life. Why would you not want to talk about your biggest life achievement?

I rinsed my mouth and headed back into the room.

Pulling back the flowery bed sheets, that Lewis was already lying under, I reluctantly jumped in beside him.

The minute I pulled the cover back over me, he turned the lights off but turned the TV on.

Celebrity Juice was on and the next thing I knew, he pulled me over on to his chest. I couldn't not kiss him now; he would know something was up.

I pressed my lips against his and he pushed my wrists on to the bed and pulled himself on top of me.

I squirmed a bit. I for sure knew then that I didn't want to sleep with him, the moment had gone, and I just didn't want to but we'd already done 'bits' so I knew he was going to try.

Every time he did, I whispered, 'No, I'm tired,' and I could literally hear him roll his eyes.

I could see he was getting frustrated, but I just wasn't in the mood at all and by judging from our earlier fumble, it wouldn't be up to much anyway.

He eventually took the hint that he was in fact not going to get lucky that night and instead just put his arm around me as I lay on his bare chest. It was about twelve o'clock now, I was wearing a lacy bra and the pair of basketball shorts and feeling awkward as fuck.

We were watching the end of *Celebrity Juice* and I looked up to notice Lewis had fallen asleep, and I couldn't help but feel relieved.

I crept off his chest and rolled over on my side with my back to him and picked up my phone.

I turned the brightness down on my screen in case it woke him and I text Caitlin.

SOS, couldn't make this up, fill you in tomorrow xxx

I put the phone down and shut my eyes, all sorts of things running through my head.

I jumped, as I heard a few loud thuds. Lewis sprung up and pulled a T-shirt on quickly. I was confused as to what was happening, I still had sleepy eyes and I looked at my phone. It was 7 a.m.

'What's that?' I said pulling the flowery covers over to hide my bra.

'It's my couch,' he beamed, looking as excited as a kid at Christmas.

'Oh yeah,' I whispered. I forgot he said that was happening but Jesus, I didn't realise it would be here this early on.

I decided to get up and sort myself for work. He offered to make me a coffee but I declined, I would stop by Starbucks before I started since I was going to be early, I wasn't going to hang about here any longer than I needed to.

I made my way to the bathroom with my packed toothbrush in hand and noticed two guys pushing part of the new sofa up the narrow stairway.

So I rushed in to avoid showing any other men my underwear.

Turning on the tap, I let the cold water run down the plug hole until it was freezing cold and splashed my face.

Wiping off the mascara from last night, I once again clocking the potty that changed everything and I wondered what Lewis was like as a dad.

I wondered about his little girl and what she was like. Then I remembered the other door in the hall, which must be his little girl's room. I really wanted to look. Lewis was in the kitchen making himself a coffee, so I decided, while the toothbrush was still in my mouth, to creep across the hall and peek behind the door.

I tiptoed over and pushed the door open to reveal every little girl's dream.

Every corner of the room was painted pink and covered in toys and Disney princesses.

I smiled as I noticed a lilac dolls' house in the corner, and it reminded me of my room when I was a wee girl.

Closing the door back over, I stopped in my tracks for a minute, with the toothbrush hanging from my gub still, and it really hit me that Lewis was responsible for a three-year-old little girl.

Back in the bathroom, with thoughts whizzing around my head, I spat my toothpaste out and put my hair in a neat bun.

Once I was ready, I went into the kitchen, and was met with the sofa guys who were unwrapping the plastic from Lewis' new couch.

'I'm going to shoot off,' I whispered, not wanting to be heard.

'Oh OK, you sure? You're going to be really early.'

'Yeah, I'm going to nip home quickly. I forgot my laptop,' I lied.

'OK.' He pulled me in and kissed me in full view of the delivery guys who were just about done with their job. How awkward.

92

'See you later!' I lied again.

'I'll give you a text after. Drive safe.'

I got in my car and let out a sigh of relief. What actually just happened? Handsome Lloyd Christmas was in fact a dad and I didn't know about it.

Driving along the motorway, I couldn't help but think about that pink potty and imagined Lewis eagerly clapping as he towered over a cute little girl who eventually took a piss in it.

It was really bizarre.

By the time I'd parked my car up at Starbucks, it was only about 8 a.m. I had one whole hour before I started work, so I decided to grab a coffee and some breakfast and chill for a bit.

None of my actual work besties were on the early shift, so I couldn't even vent to any of them about my baby daddy drama.

So I called Caitlin as I knew she'd be heading to work and told her everything.

'Hen, you're not ready to be a stepmaw, you can hardly keep a plant alive in your flat – or yourself for that matter.' She laughed.

She was right. I was only twenty-four, I really didn't want to date anyone with a child as bad as it sounds, it's just not a situation I'd seen myself being in, but if the right person came along who did, then absolutely but I definitely didn't see myself being with someone who kept their child a secret.

I decided not to text Lewis. I think he got the hint that I wasn't that into him.

He did text me a few times after that, but it was just general chit-chat. He never asked to see me and I never asked to see him and that was that.

Even now, he occasionally sends me a drunken message along the lines of *What's happening, McStay*, but I never respond.

So, back to the drawing board. Lloyd Christmas wasn't the one, clearly, so it was time to get swiping again.

WHAT DID I learn from Lewis Christmas then?

1. Always do a thorough check on Facebook for traces of secret offspring.

2. Never go on a date to Next.

3. Never waste a good waxing appointment on someone who wears basketball shorts.

6. Vegan Vision

'What do you mean you stayed at his house? You've only just met him!' My mum Pamela scolded as I told her about potty-gate.

'But nothing happened, don't worry, and I won't be seeing him again, so chill,' I replied.

Like I said before, Pam is not a 'regular mom, she's a cool mom'. OK, I don't tell her in detail about what happens with guys, but I tell her all about them otherwise. She's always been on hand to give me advice about men when I need it.

Occasionally, if I match with someone on Tinder who looks like you could take him home to meet your mum, I'll send her a picture and say, 'What do you think of him?' usually she'll say, 'Handsome, very your type' or 'Hmm don't like his haircut', 'No he looks like a burglar' or something along those lines. Not quite sure what she meant by a burglar but OK, Pam.

Before I met Dean, my mum bought me a book called *The Rules: How to Capture the Heart of Mr Right* by Ellen Fein and she would always say, 'Have you read *The Rules* yet?'.

Even to this day I've still not read *The Rules* but she always pestered me to.

I flicked through it once and always remember one that stands out: If he asks you to do something at the weekend after a Wednesday, always decline.

Maybe I should practice that, but the rest of them, from what I could see at a glance, were extremely old-fashioned and were most definitely set for dating in the 90s as it talks about e-mailing and leaving voicemails.

I explained to Pam that I hadn't read it because it was dated and she took it upon herself to order me the updated version: *The New Rules: The Dating Dos and Don'ts for the Digital Generation.*

Great, what was my excuse now? It's still to this day sitting in a drawer gathering dust.

By now, it was a cold and dreary February, two months had passed since 'potty-gate' and Caitlin and I had planned to go out with the girls to Angels, a bar in Uddingston on the Friday and I couldn't wait for a proper night out.

The quiet January had passed, and everyone's funds had eventually picked up from the big Christmas spend and we were all ready to go out and get steaming.

The thought of pouring several tequilas down my neck and getting dolled up pleased me greatly and I couldn't wait.

At the end of January, I'd agreed to take part in a bet at work to go vegan for the whole month of February. My work colleagues said that I would categorically not be able to do it and I was determined to prove them all wrong.

So I munched my way through carrots and hummus like they were going out of date, don't get me wrong it was hard but it did wonders for my shape and I was feeling good despite constantly craving a Big Mac, without the pickles, of course.

The Tinder game had been quiet for a while, but I'd recently matched with a guy called Josh out of pure boredom. I sympathy swiped him for sure as he was nothing like my type at all. Josh was short, bald and in his late thirties, although he did have a nice smile in his pictures.

I don't even know what possessed me to match with him if I'm honest, he really wasn't for me.

Josh had messaged me first after we matched. *Wow, you're just absolutely gorgeous, your smile and teeth are unreal.* Normally, guys like this made me cringe, but at the moment I had nothing else on the go, so I entertained him.

Thanks, they're all my own, I typed back.

Josh was the quickest replier I'd ever come across in my life. He was very keen which I wasn't that into. Why is it us girls love the guys that keep us on our toes and don't text us back right away, but we're put off by the eager beavers who send double, triple, and quadruple texts?

Josh was a fitness coach I think, not that you would know. He wasn't ripped or anything, or remotely fitted into the PT stereotype.

His chat was OK. It was slightly irritating to have a conversation with him because he dropped compliments like bombs every two minutes, but I had nothing better to keep me occupied so I allowed it.

When he asked for my number, I hesitantly gave him it although I hated constantly chatting on Tinder, I didn't want to be speaking to someone on there on my lunch break in the office in case anyone walked past and saw me on a dating app.

Not that there was anything wrong with it at all, but some people are judgy – particularly married people – and like I said, anyone who doesn't know much about it just thinks it's for hook-ups.

Josh would text me all the time, and I text him back when I could be arsed.

What really grated me was that he never finished a sentence in one message, he did it in about five.

It was clear he fancied me. He always would tell me I was stunning and shower me in compliments, which got quite annoying after a while, but it was secretly nice to know that someone fancied me, even if the feeling wasn't mutual.

I was sitting in work on the Monday when Josh text me.

What you up to this weekend? xxxxx

Out with the girls Friday, you? xx

Nothing, quiet, babe. I'll pick you up on Friday if you want xxxx'

I'll see xx

I absolutely loathe being called babe, baby, darlin' as you know. I don't know what it is it just makes me die inside, but he continued to do it, which probably added to my case of the ICK, along with his extreme enthusiasm for me.

Work absolutely flew in that week. It was also my third week as a vegan and I was really struggling. All I wanted to tan a McDonald's and bacon rolls, but had to resort to salads, fruit, coconut porridge and veggie chilli. Why did I agree to this again?

It was finally Friday, and I was buzzing for yet another early finish. I usually loved it too because we had 'Fat Fridays' in the office and we'd order in the rolls and square sausage, but obviously being vegan, I had to resort to something shit like granola and soya yoghurt instead.

I watched on as my colleagues Shirley and Stef wafted their bacon rolls in front of me, teasing me in the hopes that I would cave but I didn't give in and pretended that the granola was as equally pleasing as their buttered up, greasy rolls.

When finishing time rolled around and I shut down my computer, I skipped out the office and headed home to plaster myself in fake tan and put my hair in pin curls in prep for my big night out.

I was so looking forward to it. We were having dinner first at Angels. Fuck knows what I would eat being vegan but we'd worry about that later on.

I rested my pin curls down on the pillow for a disco nap, and when I woke up, it was soon time to get ready. My empty stomach rumbled and panged in hunger, so I poured myself a vodka to keep myself full until dinner.

Deciding what to wear was easy, I pulled on my trusty leather skirt – you know the one – and got my glam on with the tunes blaring.

My mum had agreed to drop me off and arrived at my flat to take me over to the Spoon sister's house for pre-drinks.

Instead of waiting on me in the car, she tackled the stairs of doom and came up to my flat as she had some of my ironing to drop off anyway – it was perfect, she could take a picture of me for Instagram before I left too – God bless Pam.

'Oh, you look lovely, Kirsten. I wonder if you'll get a man tonight.' She beamed, snapping away like Regina George's mum in *Mean Girls*.

'Maybe.' I laughed. I hadn't told my mum about Josh. He wasn't anything to shout about and I already knew that nothing would come of it, anyway.

'Are you ready to go?' Pam asked, jingling her car keys and pointing to her watch.

'Another picture first, please!' I smiled, taking a large gulp of my vodka.

She rolled her eyes; she knew the drill. Pam knows how to take a picture; I'd taught her well – hold the camera high with the flash on.

After standing in a few different positions in the hall in front of my door, Pam snapped away some more and it was time to go.

I took my trusty peep toe Steve Maddens off to walk down the stairs of doom. I didn't want to break my neck before leaving the house.

We were heading over the motorway. Caitlin and Rachael lived in Bothwell so it wasn't that far a journey.

'So, how's the swiping going this weather then?' she asked, prying for info.

'It's quiet just now, not much happening at all.'

Even though I was partly lying, it was true, there was nothing interesting going on in my love life, it had been two months since potty-gate and I hadn't slept with anyone since Dave, the bits with Lewis were pretty poor too so that technically didn't count either, in my opinion anyway.

After the short drive, I arrived at my pre-drinking destination.

'Have a good night, be safe!' Pam called as I stepped out the car.

'I will, don't worry, love you!' I shut the door and walked up the driveway ready to start the night.

I always had a great time with Caitlin and Rachael. There were a few of us going out tonight. My cousin Jodie was going and Caitlin's best pal Andrew too, so we were guaranteed to have a great time.

After a few Proseccos, we ordered taxis to take us to our destination; it wasn't far but none of us were willing to walk the short distance in our heels.

By this point I was absolutely starving and was so far feeling merry from the pre-drinks, I could practically taste tomorrow's hang-over already.

We arrived at Angels and sat down to our table, someone Rachael and Caitlin knew sent over a bottle of prosecco on our arrival so that was spanked in no time.

Before we even had menus in our hands, Caitlin ordered in the shots. I admired her enthusiasm for the sesh, I really did, but I needed to eat something or I would be sick!

When the waitress arrived with the menus, I browsed over mine and I began to panic. Fuck what was I going to have?

'Chicken... pork... beef... fish... halloumi... Everything I couldn't have.

'Excuse me, do you have any vegan options?' I asked, embarrassed.

The table erupted in laughter and I had to explain that I wasn't normally a vegan and that it was part of a bet as my cheeks blushed.

'Let me check with the kitchen and I'll get back to you' she said, looking uncertain.

This was well before vegan food became extremely popular and wasn't at all like it is nowadays.

Once everyone except me had ordered, we toasted our shots and downed them, it was sambucca, ugh! I could feel my oesophagus burn as I pulled a face and washed it down with some more prosecco. I could still taste it, it was absolutely fucking grim!

'I'm not doing that again', I said, 'It's tequila or nothing!'

The waitress returned and told me that the kitchen said they could make me fajitas, but without the meat, the cheese and the wraps. It would literally just be vegetables in fajita spice.

'That's fine.' I nodded, instantly dreading it.

In true 'us' fashion, we somehow managed to make our way through two bottles of prosecco before our food even arrived.

I had a buzz; I wasn't quite drunk yet but I would be crossing that line just shortly.

We giggled, and chatted, ordered cocktails and our food eventually arrived.

My plate was put down in front of me and again, everyone erupted in laughter. I think the kitchen took every vegetable they had and threw fajita spice over it, peppers, onions, carrots and broccoli, sweetcorn – that was it.

Who the fuck puts broccoli in fajitas?

'I can't believe you're eating that.' Caitlin sniggered, tucking into steak.

I couldn't believe I was eating it either, it was absolutely minging, I think I ate the peppers and that was it.

I was starving, but would have to just fill up on drink. This was a disaster, I could already see that in the short future I would be absolutely wrecked.

As the night went on, I got drunker and drunker and drunker.

I felt like every time I blinked there was another shot and glass of prosecco plopped down before me.

I could feel my words slur in conversation too – it was still so early!

Disaster waiting to happen.

At night, the restaurant turns into a bar area with a sort of dance floor, Angels Friday was a thing and everyone went, it was absolutely jam-packed and we had a brilliant time dancing and laughing and for me – staggering.

I looked at my phone with one eye shut. I had a message from Josh.

Hey gorgeous, how's your night going? xxxxx

I replied.

Good, I'm pisssedddd xxxx

I put my phone back in my bag and tanned another shot. Probably not a good idea, but I hadn't been 'out out' in ages so, fuck it.

It was almost twelve now. We got there at 7 p.m. and had drunk a ridiculous amount of alcohol – the food, or for me lack of, really didn't help matters.

I felt my phone vibrate in my bag. It was Josh again.

You want picked up? xxxx

Yeah, OK. I'm at Angels xxx

I was so, so drunk, the room was spinning, and I just wanted to go home, Caitlin and the others had spoken about going somewhere else after Angels but there was no way on this earth I was in a fit state to go anywhere other than my bed.

'Are you OK?' My cousin Jodie asked as she put her arm round me for a drunken cuddle.

'Yeah, I'm just steaming. I'm going to head home, though. I'm getting a lift,' I slurred.

'OK, text me when you get home safe.'

I was shutting my eyes at this point. Fuck, I was drunk. I needed a drink of water.

I'm outside, black BMW. See you soon xxxxx

I staggered my way round what was left of the group and said my goodbyes and made my way outside.

The black BMW was parked at the side of the road, and I clambered over to it like Bambi on ice.

I pulled it open, or tried to, but it was locked from the inside.

When I heard the click, I threw the door open and tossed my bag in and then fell in myself.

'Hiiiii, Josh. Nice to meet you. I'm drunk.' I smiled.

'Nice to meet you, drunk, let's get you home, eh?'

I silently scolded at his response in my head. It was such a 'dad' thing to say, wasn't it?

I looked at him, he didn't really look like his pictures one bit; he looked older in person, and he was a petite guy from what I could see but he was sitting down so it was hard to tell, especially with my beer googles on.

I can't even really remember how the conversation went, if I'm completely honest. I think he asked me about my night and I probably chatted some amount of shit.

Before I knew it, we had pulled up into the car park of my flat. I mean we didn't pull up, we were parked, in a space. He must be coming up to make sure I get in OK, I think?

I fumbled about my bag to find my keys before stepping out, and he got out too.

My God, he was so short! I had 5-inch heels on and was really tall next to him, I took them off to be able to climb the stairs of doom and I was about the same height as him, maybe even taller.

Fucking hell what had I done? I stared at him in disbelief. I couldn't get over the height of him.

'You're quite short, eh?' I mumbled as we made our way upstairs.

'Yeah, short and sweet.' He laughed.

Oh, fucking hell, my head hurt and this whole situation was just making it much worse than it needed to be.

After completing the stairs, I turned around to find Josh lagging behind me.

After trying a few times, I struggled to get my key in the door... I was drunk but fully aware of where I was, what I was doing and unfortunately, who I was with.

When we finally got in, Josh took his shoes off, and I studied him for a minute.

He really is not my cup of tea at all. AT ALL!

I threw my bag on the floor and fell on my bed and he followed.

'Are you OK?' he asked.

106

'Yeah, I'm fine.' I was sobering up and holding on to my already aching head.

'Awww, come here.' He pulled me in for a cuddle and planted a kiss on my lips.

It was awkward, so I kissed him back. I was grateful for the lift, but I wasn't sure I wanted to kiss him, but I did it anyway out of politeness.

He kissed me again. He was actually a really good kisser and one thing led to another…

I won't go into details, but it happened, and it was… awful.

I remember cringing like mad like mid-way through our very short-lived encounter. What was I doing?

'Uh, you make me so horny. I've wanted to do this to you for days,' he moaned in my ear.

If you ever looked up the definition of the ICK in the dictionary, Josh's name would be there.

My. Fucking. God.

I wanted to die on the spot.

Why. Is. He. Saying. Things. Like. This!!! I thought.

'You're just so fucking beautiful, my God, uh, honestly, you're amazing.'

My head was thumping, and I physically and emotionally couldn't take any more of his talking.

Thankfully, it did only last a few minutes and when it was done it seriously crossed my mind to roll over and leg it, jump out the window.

'Hey. That was amazing!' he purred in my ear.

I screwed up my eyes and rubbed them vigorously, praying that when I opened them it was simply just a dream but sadly, it didn't, it was a living nightmare.

Trying to subtly ghost this bald man in my bed, I turned my back to him and drifted off to sleep and he did too.

The birds whistled outside, and I tried to open my eyes but my false lashes had really stuck them together. My mouth as dry as the Sahara Desert, and I needed a drink of water badly.

I lifted my head from the pillow and it hurt like mad. I could taste that horrible alcohol taste in my mouth. My teeth felt furry, and they cried out for a good brush.

I peeked through my hands to see if Josh really was still there and he sadly was – dead to the world, snoring away.

I studied his face in the morning light peeking through my blinds.

Jesus, he was even worse looking than I remembered. He looked old. What the fuck was I thinking!?

Had being a vegan blurred my fucking vision? Christ, I'd eaten enough carrots in the last week, so surely not.

Now was not the time to be making jokes…

In the film *Coyote Ugly*, Lil says the meaning behind the phrase 'Coyote Ugly' is the feeling of waking up after a one-night stand and discovering that your arm is caught underneath someone so 'physically repulsive' that you would rather chew your arm off than wake them up.

It was true. Right now, I felt Coyote Ugly… how was I going to get him out? If I was in his house, I would grab my bag and run for the hills like I did when I met Dave in the hotel room, but Josh was in my house. I felt trapped.

The soles of my feet ached from dancing in my heels as my bare toes padded their way to the bathroom.

Blasting the tap until it was freezing cold, I filled my palms with the cold liquid and threw it over my face.

I squeezed toothpaste on to my toothbrush and attempted to banish the absolutely horrendous taste in my mouth and the coated feeling from my teeth.

As I brushed away my sins, I began retching, oh my God I was going to be sick!

I dived straight over to the toilet and stuck my head down the pan, praying that me wrenching my guts up didn't wake the beast that was currently gracing my bed.

Because my stomach was empty, literally nothing was coming up apart from pure yellow bile. That's the worst kind of spew possible. I remember the taste being so awful I had to brush my teeth again afterwards.

This was not good. Not good at all.

I looked in the mirror. My make-up was still on from last night and I had mascara all down my cheeks.

I looked like death warmed up.

I didn't care, I wasn't trying to impress Josh, and if anything, I hoped this would put him off. Maybe I shouldn't have brushed my teeth after being sick... that would definitely have sent him packing.

I needed some form of water to rehydrate me so I headed into the kitchen and grabbed a bottle of water from the fridge and headed back into the room reluctantly. The smell of alcohol clinged to every corner and that was just from me because Josh was sober.

'Good morning gorgeous, how are you feeling?', he said sitting up topless in my bed.

Oh no, he was awake! The beast had risen!

'I don't feel gorgeous.' I croaked.

'What's your plans today?' he asked, as he patted the other side of the bed, summoning me to sit next to him.

On a Saturday, I loved chilling on the couch and watching the football and putting a few bets on, especially when I was rough.

I would usually go to Uppercrust, the local sandwich shop which did the best baguettes ever, to get myself some stodgy hang-over food but I had to remind myself that I was a vegan, so this wasn't an option today, much to my sadness.

A chicken ferno was always a top hang-over curer, so God knows what plant-based treat was going to curb this feeling today.

I told him my plans and he said he would stay and watch it with me too.

Ugh, let me die in peace! I wailed in my head.

But he stayed and we moved into the living room on the couch and watched the football. He offered to go to Tesco Express and get us something to eat but I explained to him that I was vegan and that just Irn-Bru would be fine.

So off he went. I didn't even have the energy to text Caitlin and tell her all about this escapade.

One, because I felt like I was on the brink of death.

And two, because I was mortified to even be associated with him.

He gave me the highest case of the ICK ever known to woman.

The ICK is 'A dating term that means you get a sudden cringe feeling when you have romantic contact with someone and become almost immediately put off by them'.

It wasn't long before Josh quickly arrived back with two bags in his hands. He opened them up and handed me two cold bottles of Irn-Bru and also a box of vegan breakfast bars.

That was a nice thing to do, but still, he could have bought me a Range Rover at that point, and I would still not have changed my mind.

I noticed a wee bundle of clothes sat on the end of my bunker.

'Where did they come from?' I asked nodding over at the clothes.

'Aw, I had a spare change of clothes in my car from coaching so I thought I would bring them up.' He grinned, looking pleased with himself.

Was he telling the truth, or had he planned this?

Much to my hung-over delight (not), we spent the afternoon watching football. It was fine; he tried to cuddle into me a few times, so I just lay there like a sack of tatties and let him. I was too hung-over to care, and the attention was quite nice, but I just couldn't really bear to look at his face. It was terrible; he was nice enough, but I just couldn't get over myself making another godawful decision when drunk.

When he was speaking to me, I glimpsed at him and desperately wanted to find things that I liked. No harm to the boy/man, but all I could come up with was his teeth. They were perfect, to be fair.

Let's blame the vegan vision.

Time passed. I fell asleep on the couch and when I woke up, he asked me if I wanted to get some food.

Was he going to be staying here for much longer?

'Erm. If you want?' I said sheepishly. I was still feeling rough.

He told me that when I was napping, he had looked up vegan things to eat from takeaways and Pizza Hut had not long started doing vegan pizzas with cheese and everything. That was nice of him, I suppose.

My mouth watered at the thought. I'd been eating a plant-based diet for what felt like forever now and I hadn't yet had anything that made my tastebuds tingle – I was surprised I didn't have vegetables coming out my ears by this point.

So I agreed. I was so hung-over – this day was a write off anyway, so what harm would it do? Maybe I would grow to like him? The chances were slim or more so, non-existent.

Josh went out to collect it and when he came back, we sat on the couch and ate and watched a film. I was feeling better, it wasn't so bad when he didn't say cringe things, we could have just been two pals eating a pizza, but we kissed a few times, I couldn't not do it, it would be really mean if I didn't especially as we shagged (for two minutes) the night before.

Nothing else happened.

It was getting later, and I told him I was tired.

'Do you want me to stay again?' he asked, looking hopeful for round two.

'Naaa, not tonight', I said, the thought paining me.

'Another time then, for sure!' He smiled.

I smiled back, not saying a word.

So, he got up to leave and kissed me again. I didn't even see him out I couldn't really be bothered at all.

I heard the door shut over and was relieved. Thank fuck for that.

The next day, he bombarded me with texts. They included lots of heart-eye and kissy-face emojis – the ultimate ICK factor.

I replied to him out of politeness. I had the total Sunday fear that day and knew I had to blow cold for him to get the hint.

I decided that I would do it over a few days to try to soften the blow or he would know that it's because I think he is an absolute toad who wasn't up to much in the bedroom, don't get me wrong he seemed like a decent guy, but he was just too much for me.

When he was at my house, he told me that he was going to be moving back in with his parents so he could save to buy somewhere as his rent was too much.

Oh fab – a 38-year-old living with his mum and dad – how attractive!

When texting me that following week, Josh actually asked me if I wanted a 'flat mate' insinuating that he move in with me.

What?!

The texts went a little something like this:

Me: *Erm no. I like my own space.*

Josh: *Come on, think of the fun we could have, football and coupons on a Saturday and cuddles on the couch – I would pay my way! And sleep in the spare room if you really wanted me to.*

Me: *No. It's not going to happen.*

This was way too much; I'd only met him once!

After that, he would text me and ask when he could see me next, and I constantly made excuses.

He asked and asked and asked so frequently that I eventually told him that I wasn't interested, and he wasn't best pleased and even said: *I know I'm not the best in bed, but I promise I'll do better next time.*

There isn't going to be a next time, pal.

And that was it. He was angry and ended up blocking me.

Oh well.

But a year later, there was one more next time, another drunken mistake on my part, of course.

He ended up coming back to mine – again, I was drunk, and the same thing happened, he bombarded me with texts asking if we could go out on a real date and I told him nothing was going to happen and again he blocked me.

I don't know why I did it again for a second time. I think I was just intoxicated and horny and I think he popped up at a time I didn't have anything better happening but as soon as he got to mine, I already knew it was the wrong thing. In the words of Julia Roberts in *Pretty Woman* – 'Big mistake – huge!'

But it wasn't huge, Josh was a little problem that I couldn't wait to get rid of and when I finally did, I was so glad, what a needy bastard!

Josh was the first 'one-night stand' I had ever had, except a guy on my sixth-year holiday in Ibiza but holiday doesn't count – what happens in Ibiza stays in Ibiza – doesn't it?

But technically I wouldn't even count Josh as a one-night stand because he was there for like twenty-four hours. It was the longest one-night stand ever in history as he well and truly overstayed his welcome.

So, WHAT DID I learn from having the world's longest one-night stand?

1. Vegan's get drunk quicker apparently.

2. Carrots definitely don't help you see in the dark.

3. Broccoli doesn't ever belong in fajitas.

4. No one-night stand should ever last twenty-four hours, even if there is pizza involved.

Thank you, next.

7. Catching Flights and Feelings

It was now March, I'd successfully completed a month of being a vegan and had lost a stone in weight. I was feeling good but was enjoying stuffing my face with Kinder chocolate and Nandos and all the other things I missed over the last month.

Tinder had taken a backseat for a while, I just couldn't be bothered with it especially after Josh, he definitely put me off guys for a while.

Besides, in a few weeks' time I was jetting off to Singapore to meet my uni friend Rosie.

Rosie had moved out there not long after we graduated and had always urged me to come out and stay with her for a few weeks.

I'd been single for one whole year now. I'd still been working between the paper and Starbucks and had saved like mad to finally book up to go and see her.

I was going away for three weeks; it was literally the trip of a lifetime!

We would spend a week in Singapore before moving on to Bali for a long weekend then back to Singapore for a few more days.

After that, I would leave Rosie and go on to Dubai to meet my best pal Heather who was out visiting her dad who lives there, for five days.

I was honestly so excited I hadn't really been on any 'big trips' apart from New York when I was sixteen, so I was really looking forward to seeing a new part of the world.

The whole trip was honestly one of the best experiences of my life. It was so great to see Rosie, even though we hadn't seen each other in about two years, when we were together it was as if no time had passed at all.

We had an absolute ball, Bali was my absolute favourite part, what a place, it was out of this world!

It was stunning and it's safe to say, we were drunk the entire time.

We drank cocktails, went to beach clubs, got massages, went clubbing and when I was there, I ended up getting off with the most handsome Australian basketball player you had ever seen.

His name was Brett and that's all I know about him. He was so tall and so muscly. Dark hair with dark eyes – an absolute fucking babe and the only man who I would be OK with wearing basketball shorts.

I literally had the time of my life and when I was there, I actually considered moving out to Singapore, it was a different world and Rosie's life just seemed perfect – she was living the dream.

But reality was, I was a home bird at heart and I can hardly go a few hours without talking to Pam never mind not living in the same country as her.

I loved Dubai too. Heather and I went to bottomless brunches, drank cocktails from pineapples at the very famous Palm Atlantis and had breakfast at the top of the world – The Bhurj Khalifa.

I was just pure magical from start to finish.

But when my holiday was over, I came back to Glasgow with a bang. I arrived back on the Monday night and was straight back to work on the Tuesday morning.

I was an Arabian princess one minute and a junior journalist working for buttons the next. I was on a major holiday come down and I wasn't sure how to break out of my Bali blues.

After getting a banging tan and taking some fabulous snaps, if I do say so myself, uploaded all my holiday photos on to Facebook and Instagram and decided to put some of the good ones of myself on my Tinder profile.

This included the one I spoke about earlier, in the sea at the Palm, smiling with a low plunge swimsuit on, my small boobs did look great in it, so I decided to upload it and soon the messages came flooding in.

Now let me tell you something about Tinder, some of the opening lines I've received have been absolutely ridiculous. Some guys are honestly just shameless, but I must admit, some of them did make me laugh.

You look deflated, want pumped?

Hey, why don't you sit on my face and I'll eat my way to your heart?

You got Snapchat?

Or just, Hey. How's u. xxx

Majority of them I just ignore and unmatched as they were so bad. When someone asks for your Snapchat in particular, it means they're just really interested in sending you unsolicited dick pics – something I'm not a fan of in the slightest.

I'd been on a mad swiping spree since I got home from Singapore and had received lots of messages, but one really stood out to me for some reason.

Hey, is that Dubai you're in? In that last picture? What a place! I'm not long back myself, looks like you had a great time.

Oh, who is this? Clicking on to see what I was dealing with here; I went on to the profile for a quick nosey just to see if it was worth my while replying.

From his bio I gathered that his name was Chris, he was thirty-one and worked as a gas engineer.

I began scrolling through his pictures and much to my delight he was tall, had dark hair, brown eyes (huge tick) and was a Celtic fan.

Finally! A guy who supports the same team as me and was actually ridiculously handsome.

He looked really nice and very my type. His selection of pictures showed him at festivals, on holiday and at the football. It seemed that he liked doing all the same things I did, what more could I want? He ticked all the boxes at the first glance anyway.

So, I responded to him almost right away and told him I was just back from a trip of a lifetime.

And he got back to me and asked me all about it.

We chatted for absolutely ages that night.

He asked all about it and swapped holiday notes, we did the same kind of things when we were there.

It wasn't long before Chris asked for my number and straight away, without a doubt, I gave it to him, and we continued our conversation over on WhatsApp.

By now I already had 'Lewis – Tinder' and 'Josh – Tinder' in my phonebook, so I punched in 'Chris – Tinder', pressed save and we began to chat.

It was so easy to talk to him because we had so, so much in common.

He was really witty and shared my hatred for bad grammar.

He knew the difference between their/there and they're and I cannot tell you how much this pleased me.

Chris and I messaged back and forth that night until 2 a.m. He had loads to say and so did I, but I had to sleep for work and headed off to bed – with a smile.

This was the first time I was actually excited about someone from that bloody app.

I knew I'd only spoken to him for a night, but it was just easy, he wasn't like the other guys on Tinder he was genuinely interested in me and my life and that was so nice.

The following day I went to work feeling chirpy.

I told my work mate Leona all about Chris at our morning coffee in the office kitchen.

Shoving my phone in her face, I showed her some pictures from his profile.

'Oh, he's handsome! And a Celtic fan, get in there, K!'

'I know I've literally just started talking to him, but I've got a good feeling about this one!' I grinned, feeling optimistic.

I hadn't had a good feeling about any of the others I'd met on Tinder, I didn't have that excited feeling every time my phone buzzed with the others but with Chris, I did.

I had those butterflies I'd been desperately looking for and I hadn't even met him yet! Was it just too good to be true? Or would he shortly be depositing £300 in my bank in exchange of nudes?

I was in the middle of writing a story for work at half nine when I got a text.

Slept in for work, I'll blame you for keeping me up late with your good chat! xxx

I smiled.

He didn't send me soppy good morning texts and he didn't call me babe, and he didn't tell me I was beautiful every two minutes. He didn't do any of the things that made me cringe and I really liked that.

It was a far cry from the 'ICK' that I had with Josh.

A week went by and Chris started calling me on my way to work every morning.

It took me about 20 minutes to get to work from my house and it quickly became my favourite part of the day.

'When am I finally getting to meet you then?' He laughed.

'Well, I'm busy this weekend it's my pal Hayley's birthday so we're going out but what about the following weekend?' I suggested.

'Yeah, that's fine, we can go for drinks in Glasgow?'

'Sounds good!'

My heart skipped a beat.

I decided that I wasn't going to offer to meet him during the week like I did with Lewis, he could wait. If he was worth it, it wouldn't be a problem.

We'd finally set a date for a first date. My first proper date that wasn't a coffee date or in Next or in my house. Fuck, I better get a new outfit!

'OK, that's me just got to work, I'll text you on my lunch, have a good day!' I said, smiling like a crazy person.

I got into the office and turned on my computer and while I waited on it coming to life, I grabbed my mug and shouted over to Leona.

'Cuppa?'

Knowing fine well that I must have had some boy chat, Leona grinned back.

'Yeah sure!'

As we waited on our tea brewing, I told Leona that I had a date next week.

'Oh my God, that's so exciting! With that guy you showed me?'

I told her how we had been phoning each other every day and that I really felt like I was catching the 'feels' for someone that I hadn't even met yet – which is crazy.

'This sounds promising unlike the rest of the looneys you've met up with!', she said, sipping her hot tea.

I'd told Leona all about my crazy Tinder life and she was stunned at some of my stories, especially when I told her about potty-gate and the more recent twenty-four-hour one-night stand.

'Well, you can let me know how it goes!'

We sauntered back over to our desks and began working on putting together our local weekly newspaper.

I pulled my diary out of my bag, ready to input 'Date with Chris' when I noticed my page for next Saturday already had two things scribbled into the little box.

'Shannen's baby shower' and 'boozy brunch with Jodie and Rachael'.

Fuck! I'd double booked myself, twice!

What was I going to do? The baby shower started at noon so that wasn't a problem, but the Boozy Brunch was booked for four o'clock. Rachael, Jodie and I did the brunch every few months, I couldn't cancel on them, it had been planned for ages. Maybe I could do all three?

I text Jodie and explain to her that Chris wanted to meet me that day so I would go out with them first then meet him later on and she said that was fine.

Phew! I better not get too pissed; I didn't want to turn up in the state I was in at Angels – we all know how that ended!

At lunchtime, I text Chris and explained that next Saturday was going to be a busy day for me as I had a baby shower, a Boozy Brunch and our first date.

You better not stoat in the door! He joked.

I'll be on my best behaviour, I promised.

I was unbelievably excited, honestly, I hadn't felt like this in a long, long time.

We continued our phone calls and still texted each other until ridiculous o'clock every night. I felt like I was falling for him already, was that even possible for someone you hadn't met? I wasn't sure but it seemed to be happening.

I sat at my desk that day and sneakily messaged my hairdresser and make-up artist. I wanted to look my best, so I booked appointments for Saturday morning to get my hair blow-dried and my make-up done. I had three events that day after all, I might as well make the most of it!

I should really have been getting on with my work, but I went online to buy a cute black and gold blazer that I'd been eyeing up for a while. That would look nice with my leather jeans and Steve Maddens.

Sorted – roll on Saturday!

THE WEEKEND CAME and went, and I went out with my pals from school. There are seven of us, Caitlin (another one), Hayley, Heather, Lucy, Samantha, Shanice and me, also known as 'Gals, Gals, Gals'.

I'm not exactly sure why but that's the name of our WhatsApp group chat and has been for years.

We've been friends since high school, some of us since primary school and they're literally my best pals in the world, My OGs, my day ones.

Our night out had been planned to celebrate Hayley's birthday, which was two weeks after me but I'd been in Dubai for mine so this was the first time I'd seen them in a little while. It was so good to see them again and catch-up over dinner and drinks.

As we toasted to Hayley's birthday, I told the girls that I had a date next week and they were so excited for me. The majority of 'Gals, Gals, Gals' were all in relationships except me, Heather and Hayley – the singletons of the group.

I showed them pictures of Chris and they agreed that he was definitely my type.

The next day, it was the morning after the night before and I was feeling very tender.

How was your night then? xxx Chris had text me in the afternoon and I told him all about it.

We went for dinner and drank wine and now I'm lying on the couch, burst! Waiting on a Chinese xxx

We spoke for hours, I sent him some selfies of me looking like a burst ball and he sent me some back.

My God, he was just gorgeous.

I couldn't get over how good looking he was. He'd been on call at the weekend so hadn't been drinking. He said he went to the gym and a few hours had passed and I hadn't heard from him.

And the next thing, my phone rang.

'Hello?'

'Bloody got called out, didn't I? Nightmare! I'm just driving to Largs so I thought I would give you a phone and see if you were still alive since I can't text.'

We blethered away and it was just so normal. I honestly loved speaking to him, it was so easy. He had the patter, and it wasn't cringe.

We spoke about what we'd do on Saturday, and he suggested meeting in a bar called Citation at 8 p.m.

I'd never been there before but I just let him decide and I was so excited.

'Right, I better go, get some work done, I'll give you a text later!'

I hung up and smiled again. I really liked this guy. Could this be it?

Obviously, I was getting way ahead of myself, but I just couldn't help but feel excited.

I better let Pam know I had a date; she would be delighted.

So I called her.

'Oh hello, I was wondering when you would surface. How was your night?'

'Good yeah, I'm a bit rough. But I have some news which I'm sure you'll be delighted about. I have a date next week!'

'Oh my God! How exciting! Give me details, what are you going to wear?'

I told her a bit about him and told her what I planned to wear. She was coming to the baby shower with me on Saturday and I explained that I was meeting him after being out with Jodie and Rachael.

'Oh, Kirsten, that's not a good idea, I know what you're like when you're out with them, you always end up drunk! You better not turn up drunk – he won't want to know you!'

'I won't, Mum, calm down. I'm hardly going to stagger in steaming, am I?' I scolded.

'You better not!' I could hear her sigh over the phone.

My mum honestly gives me a hard time for my drinking.

Fair enough I do overdo it sometimes, or a lot, but it's just at the weekends – I'm young, free, and single and just having a good time.

No one is being harmed apart from the lining in my stomach.

IT WAS A quick week at work, the paper that I was working with at the time had just announced that they were going to be co-hosting a 10K run in September, so we had been busy setting up the campaign and getting photos taken. Of course, I'd agreed to run it to represent the work. Yeah, that's right, the girl who couldn't run for a bus, was running a 10K. This should be a laugh!

I told Chris all about it on the phone. He had run a marathon before – which was very impressive. He said he would give me tips and we could even go a run together. My God, he would never speak to me again if that was the case – I was so unfit.

Although I managed to keep the stone off that I lost being a vegan and I was feeling quite good about myself, I was still quite unfit.

But the main thing was that I was fitting back into my size 12 jeans, because after I split up with Dean, I totally ballooned but now I was eating healthy and feeling quite confident in my body for the first time in a long time.

I decided to run the 10K and raise money for a cancer charity which was pretty close to my heart – The Beatson. If I was going to do it, I might as well make it for something worthwhile!

My team at the office worked our socks off that week and launched the campaign in the paper on the Thursday.

It had been a good week all round and I knew I was going to have an even better weekend.

'Fat Friday' quickly came around too but I just opted for porridge, I wasn't vegan at this time, but I'd been healthy eating all week in a bid to look my best in my leather jeans on Saturday.

I'm really looking forward to meeting you tomorrow xxx Chris messaged as I slapped fake tan all over myself on the Friday night.

Me too. I'm really looking forward to it CB! xxx

I'd nicknamed him CB, as his second name began with a B and in return he called me KM – it was a bit lame, but I didn't mind it, it wasn't babe, after all, and was my way of showing affection I suppose.

I was having the ultimate pamper night on the Friday. I did my nails, a full body shave – except the grains, Lisa wouldn't be happy if I had, as I was booked in with her the following week.

I needed to look my best.

I went into my wardrobe and pulled out my new black date outfit and decided to pair it with a red clutch to add some colour. I honestly couldn't believe the lengths I was going to for a first date. Is this normal?

I called Caitlin, who wouldn't be at the Boozy Brunch with Jodie and Rachael as she had something else on and gave her the latest Tinder gossip and in return, she told me hers.

She asked what I was wearing like everyone else I'd told about the date and I sent her a picture of my outfit hanging up over the door – she also thought it was a good combination.

She then quizzed me about how I was feeling about it all and I told her I was excited and that I had a really good feeling about Chris.

'Don't get your hopes up too high, hen. You'll know better when you actually see him.'

What if she was right? What if the connection wasn't there? Like it was over the phone?

I put the thoughts to the back of my mind and got ready for bed, I had a big day ahead of me after all.

I text Chris.

That's me heading off to sleep. I'll see you tomorrow! xxx

I can't wait. Night! xxx

I woke up to the sound of my alarm. It was 8 a.m., and I had to head over to Airdrie for my hair appointment – I was getting my extensions topped up and a blow-dry.

I went for a quick shower to wash my stinking fake tan off, shoved a jumper on and hopped in my car.

I loved going to get my hair done, it was nice to catch-up with my hairdresser Nicoll – she was also more like a therapist than a hairdresser I always filled her in on all my gossip.

She knew loads about me even though I only saw her every few months. I'd been going to Nicoll to get my hair done since I was about seventeen, so I filled her in with my plans for the day.

'That's so exciting! Let me know how it goes!' she said as she held the mirror up to show me my fresh new locks.

Now on to the make-up.

I drove back to Motherwell to go to my local make-up artist Linzi O'Connor. She was brilliant at what she does so I was lucky to secure a Saturday appointment with her at such short notice.

As Linzi painted my face, she asked what the occasion was, and I told her I had a busy day ahead and explained the details – I was telling anyone that would listen about my date – was that sad? Probably.

'Aw amazing! Hope it goes well!' she said, applying pink gloss to my lips.

When she showed me the mirror, I honestly felt amazing. I told her I didn't want anything too heavy and to go for a 'soft glam' look and she did just that.

Racing against the clock now, I headed home and put my first outfit on of the day for the baby shower. It was a classic 'jeans and a nice top' occasion.

It was my unofficial cousin Shannen's baby shower. She was expecting a little boy with her husband David. Shannen's dad Peter is my godfather and I've known her my whole life, so she's my fake cousin. Every family has a fake cousin, don't they?

Her mum, Rosie, had organised the baby shower in her house and me and my mum said we'd go along for a couple of hours.

I decided to drive because if I started drinking this early on there would be no way I would get to meet Chris in a reasonable state, so I said I would drive Pam so she could have a few. Is it just a Scottish thing where people drink at baby showers?

I drove over to my mum's house to pick her up, but if you tell my mum a time always add on at least twenty minutes because that woman is always late.

I impatiently beeped my horn outside her house and sat for a bit, checking my flawless make-up in the mirror of my car. While I waited, I decided to text Chris.

Hey, just heading over to the baby shower now, what you up to? xxx

The next thing, my car door swung open and there she was, Pam, fifteen minutes late, as causal as you like.

'Oh, you look nice! Your make-up is gorgeous! How are you feeling? Nervous?' She giggled, kissing my cheek.

My mum had bundled in my car with about four bags, her handbag, a baby gift bag, and two bags of alcohol. Typical Pam.

I wasn't feeling nervous at this point, but I knew I would be later on. I tried not to think about it much because then I would overthink.

We pulled up at Rosie's house and gathered all the bags.

In true Rosie fashion, the house was decked out in pale blue balloons and banners, and she had an outdoor gazebo with a bar. It looked amazing!

'Hi!' Shannen smiled. 'It's so nice to see you both, thanks for coming!'

'Can I get you both a drink?' Rosie asked, taking our jackets.

'I'll join Shannen on the diet Irn-Bru, I'm driving,' I said.

Pam chimed in, 'Kirsten's got a date later!' She beamed.

Oh, for Christ's sake!

We'd only been in the door two seconds.

'Oh, Kirsten! Tell us all!' Rosie giggled.

I gave Pam a *look*. I might as well make my date front page news, because at this rate, everyone knew about it.

I think the last time I'd seen Shannen was at her wedding, and Dean was there as my plus one, so I had a lot to fill her in on, obviously she knew that we had split up but she didn't know what my situation was now.

'Just this guy I've been chatting to. I've never met him in person so I'm going into town later to meet him.'

Pam again. 'She met him on Tinder!'

'Right thanks for that, Mum!' I said hushing her, embarrassed.

We had such a lovely afternoon at the baby shower, Pam had a few vodkas, we watched Shannen open her presents, and all had a laugh. At about 2 p.m., we decided to head back to Motherwell.

We said our goodbyes and off we went. I was dropping Pam off then getting a lift into Glasgow with the girls.

We pulled up outside my mum's.

'Right, have fun, be safe and whatever you do, Kirsten – don't get too drunk or take him home with you!' Pam said as she gathered her belongings from the floor.

I rolled my eyes. 'For God's sake, Mum! I won't! I'll phone you tomorrow. Bye!'

She made a funny face at the window, and I dashed home to 'spruce up' and change my outfit. I pulled on my leather jeans and a black V-neck top and put on my new cropped black blazer, which came with a black belt with a big gold buckle. I loved it so much that I also ordered it in white too.

I didn't look too dolled up, but I thought I looked good if I did say so myself.

I doused myself in my trusty Chanel perfume and chucked it into my clutch along with my lip gloss, lip liner, my purse, a comb, chewing gum, and my menthol cigarettes and a lighter. I wasn't a smoker but was partial to a cheeky fag when I was drinking. I would have a few when I was out with the girls then use my perfume and chewing gum to cover it up before I met Chris. Some guys hate smoking and it's a big turnoff for quite a lot of people, I know.

Before I knew it, my lift was downstairs, so I grabbed my shoes and my bag, looked once more in the mirror and headed.

'So what time you meeting him at?' Jodie quizzed me as we clinked our first cocktail in Bar Soba.

'About eight I think?' I smiled. The nerves were starting to kick in now and I was getting 'nervous belly'.

'Where are you going to meet him?' Rachael asked sipping on her pornstar martini.

'Citation? I think it's up the Merchant City way?'

'We can head up that way after here if you want just so it isn't too far for you to walk on your own?' Jodie added.

'Perfect,' I said smugly.

We had come to Bar Soba for the Boozy Brunch as it was brilliant value for money, you get four cocktails each, a sharing starter and a main course for £25, we did it often, it was our favourite haunt.

At least I knew I would be lining my stomach properly this time, that was for sure and there wasn't a single carrot in sight – much to my delight.

As always, the three of us had a great afternoon, gabbing away, talking about Jodie's wedding plans and most importantly the hen party that Rachael and I were eagerly organising in Magaluf.

We sat in Bar Soba that long that the girl behind the bar came over and said they would need the table back in half an hour, by this point we had done in the four included cocktails and were on to our sixth.

I wasn't drunk though; I was merry and feeling pretty good.

I looked at my phone. I had a text from Chris.

Just out for a few drinks with my mates to calm the nerves, see you at 8! xxx

He's feeling nervous too? That's good, I was glad that it wasn't just me.

Jodie, Rachael, and I headed over to the Merchant City, an indoor square with lots of different bars.

The square was packed, and we weren't sure where to go but we found a little bar tucked in the corner that appeared to have tables, we needed somewhere with a seat, my trusty Steve

Maddens were letting me down for the first time ever and pinching my heels.

It was now 7 p.m., one hour to go until the big meeting!

Jodie suggested we get the shots in.

Oh no, was this a good idea? Shots always get me absolutely hammered, which I didn't want to be but obviously, I couldn't say no to a shot.

One thing was for sure though, there was no way I was doing sambuca, but Jodie met me halfway and suggested Tequila Rose instead. Tequila Rose is our drink, we always have it when we are out so I couldn't possibly say no, plus it was a little bit milder than actual tequila and definitely more pleasant than sambuca.

When the shot was placed down in front of me, I took a snap of it on my phone and forwarded it on to Chris.

Maybe I'll be stoating in to meet you after all xxx

And within seconds my phone pinged.

Good minds think alike! xxx he replied, along with a picture of some kind of red shot.

I smiled. I really couldn't wait to meet him, he just seemed perfect in every way.

It was now quarter to eight, I went to the bathroom one last time to touch up my make-up and hair and again douse myself in perfume to get rid of the evidence of the two menthol fags I chuffed on earlier.

'Right, that's me off, I'll let you all know how it goes!' I said as I blew the girls air kisses.

'Good luck!' they squealed in unison.

Citation was literally only a five-minute walk around the corner from where we were but due to the Steven Maddens, five minutes turned into fifteen.

The wind was blowing so hard that I held my clutch bag up to my head in an attempt to do some damage control.

As I turned the corner, I saw the sign for Citation and suddenly I felt sick.

I wasn't sure if it was the shots that I'd just tanned or the fact I was going to meet the guy that I'd been talking to morning, noon, and night for the last few weeks.

What if it's different?

What if he doesn't like me?

Fuck!

I was nervous, I don't think I'd ever felt this nervous before in my life.

I put my clutch bag under my armpit and climbed up the uneven concrete steps.

Oh, my fucking God, this is it, this really is it!

I took a deep breath and pulled open the door before stepping inside.

It was so busy, which meant I didn't spot him straight away so looked around, trying to suss out where he was, but the bar was so packed that it made it difficult.

It was a lovely wee place and each table was filled mostly with couples. The sound of laughter and general chit-chat filled the room and I continued scanning around to find him, when the most handsome guy I'd ever seen caught my eye, it was Chris.

Sitting in a little booth in the middle of the room, the first thing I saw was his smile. Oh my God, he is so fucking good looking! Even better than what I imagined or expected.

Grinning, he got up from the booth and walked straight over to me, probably because it took me longer to get to him because of the heels but I was stunned at just how gorgeous he was.

Smiling, he put his arms around me and kissed me on the cheek.

'Hi, you look amazing!'

I remember thinking that he smelt fucking incredible, he was wearing some really nice aftershave, which I love in a guy.

My heart melted a bit just looking at him.

Maybe it was all the alcohol that I'd drank throughout the day or maybe it was because I absolutely fancied the pants off him.

'Hi! Thank you, so do you.' I grinned.

He led me over to the table and offered to get me a drink. I asked what he was drinking as I looked at the half full glass in front of him.

'Jack Daniels and Coke.'

I hated Jack Daniels.

'Just a vodka and lemonade for me, please.'

He flashed those incredible teeth once more.

'No bother, I'll be two minutes.'

As he walked up to the bar to be served, I couldn't help but just stare at him.

He had opted to wear a crisp white shirt with jeans and smart shoes, not too over the top but certainly not causal. He looked fucking amazing.

As he faced the bar, I remember looking at his broad shoulders and just thinking *Oh my God, I fancy him so much.*

I still felt nervous, please let this go well! He's so my type.

Returning to the table, Chris sat a double vodka and lemonade down in front of me. A double! I was going to be pished by the end of the night, I could see it already.

'So how was your day then?' he asked with a glimmer in those big, beautiful eyes. Those deep brown eyes, I could just stare at them all day long.

I told him all about it, and that I'd drank more than I'd originally planned to but it that it really helped with the Dutch courage.

I was still nervous. As I sat and listened to him speak, I twiddled my hair in awe of his every word. I know I've already said it a few times but I couldn't believe how much I fancied him. There was this overwhelming attraction.

'Are you nervous?' he asked. 'You keep touching your hair.'

Fuck, was it showing that I was?

I thought about saying no but I'm a terrible liar, so straight away I just told him that I was and that I thought he was so handsome.

He smiled and gazed back at me.

'You have the most amazing eyes, like honestly.'

My heart melted again. Fuck, any more melting and it would soon be a puddle on the floor. I didn't usually take compliments well, look at Josh, but this was different this time.

I just smiled like a crazy person and in one moment we just looked at other and he leant in and kissed me.

Oh my God!

It wasn't like a big sloppy, wet one which I was glad of, but it really sent sparks flying and my stomach flipped – the knots had gone and I had those butterflies that I'd been seeking for so long.

We both started laughing. I said that I wasn't expecting to get a disco winch this early on in the night, he smirked and kissed me again.

I drank in every bit of him. He was the definition of perfect.

We chatted more and sipped our drinks.

'Another?' he asked.

'Let me get these,' I argued.

'Not at all,' he said touching my hand.

I rolled my eyes, 'What about equality these days eh?!'

He just laughed and made his way to the bar again.

Citation was extremely busy by this point with lots of thirsty people eager to be picked next by the barmaid.

I picked up my phone quickly and sent Jodie a thumbs up emoji just to let her know it was going well.

I put my phone back into my bag, ignoring the other million messages I had from all my group chats and of course one from Pam asking me how it was going, I would fill her in later.

I lifted the cocktail menu up from the table and began to browse when I heard a rowdy bunch enter through the front door, I glanced up and noticed a few guys laughing and stuff but took no notice and looked back at the menu… a Porn Star Martini, maybe I'll have that later!

I was flicking through the pages when I heard the rowdy group erupt in laughter across the room and I looked up again. What the…

Sat at a table with a group of random guys, the rowdy crowd was no other than bloody Jodie and Rachel waving like lunatics.

Oh my God, what the fuck are they doing here!?

I gave them the death stare of all death stares and mouthed at them to go immediately, but the two of them were feeling brave and just waved back and blew kisses over to me.

They mouthed to ask if the guy in the white shirt was Chris and I nodded.

I laughed, then I got mad again because, what the hell were they doing here!?

The both of them peered over at him and gave me the thumbs up and almost immediately Jodie stood up and went to the bar, and of course stood right next to him.

Oh my God! What on earth is she doing?

Of course Chris was too busy trying to get the barman's attention to notice a crazy drunken girl making funny faces behind his back.

Only shit like this happens to me. It's always me!

I'm sure at one point Jodie even asked him to pass her a straw.

I had a decision to make here and I had two options:

One: I tell Chris what the hell has just happened and he finds it funny or, Two: keep it to myself and completely ignore them and hope they don't cause a scene.

I decided on the latter, he'll think I'm absolutely nuts if I tell him my drunken cousin and her pal have crashed my first ever Tinder date, well… second…

I put my head back into the cocktail menu and was now studying the wine list in an attempt to ignore Jodie and Rachel so that they would get bored and go else where.

'Here you go!'

Another double vodka was placed down and front of me and Chris went back up to the bar to fetch two tequila shots, salt, and lime.

We had spoken previously about both loving tequila so he thought I would be a good idea to start on the shots on our second drink.

I smiled and was impressed that he remembered I liked tequila, many people absolutely hate it but not me.

We chatted some more just about life and the gigs we had both been to. Turns out we had both been to many of the same ones.

I just couldn't help but smile. I'd never felt this way about anyone before after just meeting them. I felt like I was smitten with him. I knew it was so early, but they say when you know, you know!

I was talking about something, I think it was that I'd taken up running when Chris leant in and kissed me. I kissed him back, this time it lasted longer than before and it was the best kiss ever.

I pulled away, remembering that I now had an audience.

I took another sip of my vodka and cast my eyes over to the gruesome twosome to see if they'd noticed our kiss.

'I'm just going to nip to the toilet', he said, kissing me once more.

He got up and walked across the room to the bathroom and the next minute I heard clapping and cheering.

Of course, it was Jodie and Rachel with their new group of random guy friends.

My face burnt red but I was getting quite well on with the drink now that I just laughed and gave them the middle finger.

Rachel toddled over quickly, like she was on some sort of secret mission.

'On yourself hen! He's handsome! And you kissed him!! How exciting,' she squealed.

'Yeah, I know. Now fuck off! He'll never want to see me again if he realises that you two have crashed my date.' I laughed.

'OK, see you soon!'

She shuffled back over to her table and I just tried desperately to pretend they weren't there at all even though I could feel eyes burning into the back of my head.

Chris returned from the toilet and sat down and put his arm around me.

It just seemed so easy to talk to him. I caught myself feeling a bit silly for being this happy about someone I just met but I couldn't help it.

I knew this wasn't the vodka or the tequila, it was me. I was opening up properly to someone for the first time since Dean.

As we drank more and more, I needed a pee, so I kissed Chris on the lips and made my way to the loo only to conveniently bump into Jodie in the toilets.

'How is it going?' she quizzed as she glossed her lips in the mirror.

'Amazing Jods, I really like him'. I smiled.

'Right let me know when you're home safe, we're heading now you'll be pleased to know.'

Oh I definitely was!

She gave me a hug and off she went.

Chris and I drank more tequila, and more vodka and Jack Daniels. We kissed more and chatted the night away.

And I couldn't help but wonder if we were that disgusting couple that kissed in public places that everyone screws their faces up to. I had a feeling we were.

It was half eleven by this point and the last orders had been called.

'Let's get one more and head somewhere else?' Chris said, squeezing my hand.

'Yeah sounds good!'

We slugged the last of our drinks and headed out the door. He took my hand and led the way and the second we got over the threshold he stopped in his tracks and pulled me in close and kissed me once again.

I put my hands on his neck and passionately kissed him back, it was honestly like something out of a film. The butterflies in my stomach were like no feeling I'd ever felt before.

I pulled away smiling, and he smiled too.

I smiled so much that my jaw began to ache.

Chris grabbed my hand again and off we headed to our next destination – a bar called 29 which was open until 3 a.m. Perfect!

As we walked along the streets of Glasgow, hand in hand like love's young dream, and extremely slowly at that due to the blisters my trusty heels had given me, Chris turned to me and asked me a question.

'Do you smoke?'

Fuck.

Had he tasted the two menthols from earlier on my breath? I thought I covered it with chewing gum. Oh fuck, lots of guys hate smoking so maybe if I say I do occasionally it may change things.

146

Oh Kirsten, just be honest with him it's not the end of the world.

'Em, only when I'm having a drink I do! But other than that, no!'

That was half a lie. Sometimes, if I was stressed out when working in Starbucks, I would go out to the bin shed and chuff five fags in a row, but I was always stressed when I worked there. So basically, yeah I did, but I couldn't tell him that.

'Oh, that's good. I'm the same. Do you want one?'

He pulled out a crumpled packet of cigarettes from his pocket and offered me one.

I laughed and nodded. It's like we were the same person. I was glad I didn't have to hide my filthy part-time habit from him and could be my absolute self.

We made our way to 29 and as we walked up to the bar, I told him that I was buying the first round as he hadn't let me get a single drink in Citation, so I paid for two doubles and two shots of tequila.

By this time, we were both very well on and were just having such a good time. We chatted and kissed and drank and laughed.

It wasn't long before we headed out on to the terrace to have another cheeky fag.

Slipping into a picnic table, we lit up a cigarette. It was nice to be able to speak to each other without the music blaring in the background too.

We were lost in each other's chat, when a girl with a hen night sash stumbled over to us and asked if she could borrow a lighter. I nodded to Chris and he passed her one.

'Oh my God, your eyebrows and eyelashes are just amazing, doll! You're a lucky guy, how beautiful is your girlfriend?'

I smiled at her awkwardly, feeling a bit odd about the girlfriend comment, before butting in.

'Actually, tonight is the first night I've met him.' I laughed.

Chris piped up.

'Yeah, it's the first night we've met up, but yeah, they are beautiful, aren't they?'

'What do you mean? Like your first date together?' she asked, surprisingly as she sparked up her fag.

'Yeah, we're on a Tinder date.' I nodded.

'Oh, my fucking God! How exciting. I hope it all works out for you both, you're a fucking stunning couple by the way! All the best to you!' she said as she threw the half-smoked cigarette on the floor and stubbed it out with her sparkly heels.

She stumbled back into rejoin her hen party and when she was out of sight, we looked at each other and giggled at her comments and had yet another kiss.

I can honestly say with my hand on my heart it was the best first date I've ever been on. It really was perfect.

Even when the bar was shutting, we were the last to leave and were winching like a couple of teenagers outside after it closed in the archway at Royal Exchange Square.

I'd somehow managed to rope Gals Gals Gals Cailtin into picking me up at that stupid hour – what an angel!

'I don't want you to go. I don't want this night to end already,' he said, kissing my lips.

But it was 3.30 in the morning. We were both quite drunk, but there was no way I was going home with him and he knew it. I liked him and I liked him enough not to… a first for me?

My phone pinged and it was Caitlin to say she was around the corner, I told him I had to go. He kissed me then let me go, then pulled me in again, it was really sweet.

'Right, I need to go I don't want her waiting any longer!'

'Let me know you get home safe!' he whispered.

I kissed him one last time and walked to Caitlin's car, grinning like the cat that got the cream.

'Well? You look happy!' Caitlin squealed as she clocked the smile plastered over my face along with me caressing my red chin and top lip from Chris's beard.

'Oh my God! The date was amazing. I really like him Caits. Really, really, really like him.' I grinned, melting into the passenger seat.

I told her everything as we zoomed over the motorway and back to Motherwell.

Before we had even made it home, I checked my phone and found I'd got a message from Chris just minutes after I left him.

I really like you. Thanks for such a good night. Definitely the best first date I've ever had. Get home safe xxxxx

My heart literally fluttered. I couldn't believe how good I was feeling about it. I felt I was so happy that I started to wonder if it was too good to be true.

Things surely can't be this easy?

I told Caitlin this and she said that I shouldn't let what Dean or Dave had done in the past affect my thoughts or feelings on anyone else and she was right.

When I finally got home, I text him straight away.

Thanks for such a good night. I had a really good time. Hope you got home OK xxxx

That night, or early morning, I couldn't sleep for excitement. All I could think about was Chris and how he had unleashed this feeling in the pit of my stomach, but what was it? It was something I'd never felt before. I think I was definitely catching the feels.

Surprisingly, I woke up the next day hang-over free. Chris had called me as soon as he woke up and we chatted for ages and ages. I was like a teenager again pacing about my flat as I was on the phone to him, hanging on to his every word.

He said that he had such a good time that he wanted to book dinner for us in Glasgow for the following weekend and I agreed.

A second date! I was absolutely buzzing.

The whole week, I walked about with a spring in my step and a real smile stuck on my face and I truly believed this was it and that he was 'The One'.

I told my work colleagues all about it, Christ I think Pam even had her hat looked out for the wedding. Not really but I told her I had a good feeling about it and she was pleased for me.

One thing that didn't really tick my box though was that Chris stayed about 40 minutes away from me which wasn't really ideal so we decided that he would drive over to mine first for a few drinks, we'd get a taxi into town and he would come home with me.

It was a no brainer, I was happy to sleep with him on the second date given that we had spent so much time speaking beforehand and of course on the back of our amazing first date.

The week was full of phone calls and texts and Saturday rolled round soon enough.

I'd just taken the last roller out my hair when I heard the buzzer go.

Dashing over to it – no waiting around this time like the others – I eagerly picked up the phone.

'Top floor!'

I skipped back over to my dressing table in my room and quickly spritzed Chanel all over me, I believed it made me go from a 5 to a strong 7, it really smelt amazing.

The door knocked and he was here.

I remember thinking he got upstairs quicker than the others had in the past, but then it was only about 6 p.m. and he hadn't had drink yet so maybe that's why, but this guy was fit, he ran marathons for God's sake!

I pulled back the door and smiled.

'That's a lot of stairs you've got there!' He laughed carrying a fresh blue shirt on a coat hanger over his shoulder.

I rolled my eyes and laughed at the familiar comment.

'Come in!' I said moving to the side to let him squeeze by me.

He stepped in and shut the door behind him and right away pulled me in for a kiss. I honestly don't know how to put it into words but there was just this spark, there was something there and I was extremely happy about it.

'I just need to put my clothes on then I'll be ready so go in and help yourself to a drink.' I chirped, kissing him again.

When I finished work on Friday, I'd headed over to Lisa to banish the grains as I knew I had a big weekend, I'd been saving them for a few weeks to get that perfect wax.

I also told her all about Chris how our first date went and she was also excited for me.

After I was grain free and red-raw – it really is a horrific experience getting all waxed down there – I went to Asda to buy pre-date supplies. Vodka, pink gin, and a bottle of tequila, you know the one with the little hat? All got chucked in my basket.

At least we could have a few drinks before we left and once we got back.

I quickly pulled on my white blazer and made my way into the living room. Chris was sat on the couch drinking a gin and I went to pour myself one too.

Despite being caught up in all this sexual tension, I was really stunned when there was a weird awkward silence. I didn't want to ask him how his day was because I already knew how it was as we had been texting all day.

The ice clinked as it hit off the glass as I walked over to sit down next to him and complimented his shirt.

We had this crazy strong connection like I wanted to rip his clothes off there and then but I felt like at times we had spoken so much throughout the day that we had ran out of new things to talk about, so there were quite a few silent spells.

The journalist in me always came up with new questions to ask him although I was really clutching at straws.

It wasn't long before we finished our second drink and our taxi arrived to take us into town.

As we left my flat hand in hand, I felt like I was in a couple already, he opened the door of the taxi for me and also helped me out it when we arrived. I'd never had that before. I was lucky even if Dean offered to pay for us to get a train into Glasgow never mind hold a taxi door open.

Chris had booked a table for us at the Thai restaurant Chaophraya in Glasgow, I'd been once before with my mum for my birthday but never on a date. Dean wouldn't eat this type of food anyway, Nandos was about his limit.

The meal was lovely, I had some sort of coconut chicken rice thing and he had a curry.

I downed about three large glasses of rosé and he had a few pints. As we ate we spoke about family and deeper things like that, I asked about his previous relationships and stuff and he told me all about how he had not long moved out of his mum's and into his own two-bedroom house.

I was impressed, he seemed to do well for himself and it was apparent that he lived for the weekends, a bit like me – or a lot.

I got the impression he was always up for a bit of a mad one with his pals, he told me of times he went out on the Thursday and didn't come home until the Monday.

I'd done that once and needed about two weeks to recover but I found it a little strange that he still acted like that in his thirties but he seemed to have his head screwed on otherwise.

After I was full to the brim with food and rosé, we had a few more drinks and Chris asked for the bill before moving over to the next bar for more drinks.

Grabbing my hand after we stepped out of the grand doors of Chaophraya, we made our way over to Mitchell Lane, but before we got there, Chris tugged at my hand and pulled me in for a kiss.

Of course he didn't let me contribute anything towards the bill, which must have been a fortune so I thanked him and said that the rest of the night was on me.

Argyle Street was busy but not as busy as it should be for a weekend but there was still a nice buzz about the place.

One busker sang his wee heart out to Deacon Blue's Dignity and I chucked a fiver in his guitar case as we plodded down the street.

Just as I was eyeing up where we were headed to next, Chris had stopped me in my tracks and put his arms around me and leant in for another kiss.

Before I knew it, we were kissing passionately in the doorway of clothing shop Pretty Green, classy I know but there was just something about him, I couldn't keep my hands off him.

I'm pretty sure Liam Gallagher would be appalled that we were basically dry humping in the doorway of his shop but I just couldn't care less.

Eventually realising our surroundings after getting caught up in the moment, we pulled ourselves together and headed into another bar, and another bar and another bar after that.

I had another amazing date with him and what topped it off was waking up to him the next day.

When we got home, we had a few more drinks and went to bed.

I'll spare you the details but it was good. Not amazing, not terrible but good. I think I just enjoyed it more because I had a feeling for him that I hadn't had with anyone else before.

In my opinion, drunken sex is always better sex because you feel more confident and more adventurous than you usually would be sober – except for in Josh's case – ugh, I still shudder at the thought.

The following week, we decided to do something a bit more casual and went to the cinema, then for a Five Guys burger and then back to his house to drink.

We continued to talk, and I would stay at his most weekends. I had such a good time when I was with Chris. We would watch films, listen to music, chat and drink tequila together.

Chris didn't have shot glasses in his house, and we always ended up tanning tequila from tumblers so I bought him his own shot glasses the next time I saw him.

When he stayed at my house one weekend, he opened my fridge and complained that I drank too much bottled water after seeing my top shelf was packed with plastic bottles. I point blank refused to drink tap water. Call me weird but I think it has a funny taste.

When I stayed at his he would always give me a glass of water before we went to bed from one of those Brita filtered jugs. I always laughed and said it was a lame thing to own but he was adamant that it just tasted the same and that I should get one.

I disagreed anyway.

Chris honestly did make me laugh and I just loved being in his company. We chatted less through the day which I preferred as it gave us things to talk about when we were with each other.

It was the height of summer; a glorious July and the highlight of the month was Glasgow's music festival TRNSMT.

We were both going on the Saturday with our friends so I stayed at his the night before and we got drunk.

Around 10 a.m. the next day, I drove home to get ready with a day in the sunshine with my pals.

I was extremely hung-over from all the tequila we drank the night before, but when I was inside TRNSMT I actually spotted Chris standing with all his friends.

I didn't have a signal to text him and say that I could see him and I decided not to march over and say hello in front of his friends. If he spotted me then he could say hi.

We never did cross paths that day but I didn't hear a peep from him for three days after that. He must be out on one of these benders he spoke of.

It was Tuesday when I eventually got a text from him. He said he was so hung-over that he missed his work on the Monday. That wasn't wise at all but I decided not to give him a hard time about it.

It was my brother Jonathan's birthday in a few weeks and as I'd always mentioned that most weekends I was with Chris, Jonny had suggested that I bring him along to his birthday BBQ.

It was a whole different kettle of fish – meeting the family.

I wonder what he would say to that?

We had been going on dates for a little while now so this might give me a better idea of where I stand if I asked him as we never actually had the conversation.

So I forwarded on the text from Jonny to Chris, this way I wasn't directly asking him.

I've got something on that weekend, sorry xxx

No worries! Just thought I would ask! xxx

I can't lie when I say I was gutted. I really wanted him to meet my family because I was crazy about him. But maybe he was just busy or maybe it just was too soon.

It was understandable.

Chris was going to a gig with his two pals and he did mention it a few weeks ago, to be fair to him.

It seemed that things were a little different now, the morning phone calls got shorter and shorter and the texts got less frequent.

On the night of Jonny's birthday BBQ, I was the only singleton there and after a few drinks, the inevitable happened and my family grilled me on my 'new man'.

'He's not my man, I don't know what's happening,' I snapped.

I had a nice night regardless of being constantly quizzed about my love life, I was used to attending these family gatherings on my own with no plus one, so it wasn't anything new to me.

At about 10 p.m., I arrived home feeling confident after a few wines and made the silly decision to text Chris as bold as brass.

Hey, hope you're having a good night! That's me just home. I was just wondering, what's actually happening with us? Like is this going anywhere? Obviously, I really like you but just not sure where I stand xxx

The minute I hit the send button I threw the phone across the couch with nerves.

Fuck, what had I done?

About five minutes went past and my phone remained silent, so I picked it back up to make sure it sent.

That's the beauty of WhatsApp, it tells you when a person was last active, when your message was delivered, and what time it was read at.

I looked at the message and saw two blue ticks – oh my God! He's read it!

I sat and stared at my screen, now with a sick feeling in my stomach.

I searched the top for the *'Chris is typing...'* but it never appeared.

Three hours passed by and still nothing.

I shouldn't have mentioned it at all. What the fuck was I thinking?!

But the thing was, I just hated not knowing where I stood.

I went to bed that night feeling uneasy, I had a feeling something was wrong, was I right after all? Was he too good to be true?

Sunday morning rolled around and still nothing. So instead of waiting about and letting my mind go into overdrive, I decided to keep busy.

I went and met Jodie for a coffee and we went a four mile walk like we usually did on the Sundays that we happened to be fresh.

I explained the story to her and she said I shouldn't worry; he was probably out enjoying himself and was more than likely still in bed nursing a hang-over.

Maybe she was right?

But she wasn't.

It was about six o'clock when the message that I'd been anticipating from Chris arrived and it wasn't the answer I was looking for at all. I had a horrible feeling in my stomach so I opened it the minute I got it.

Sorry for ignoring your text last night, I was just going into the gig and I don't know if I could have got into things. As much as we have fun, I don't see it going anywhere to be honest. Do you? xxx

My heart sank, tears filled my eyes, and I threw the phone back down.

My little bubble had been well and truly burst.

How could I not have seen this coming? How had I let myself feel so deeply for someone when I didn't know they felt the same?

The only two words I could use to describe how I was feeling was confused and gutted.

I'll admit, I cried. I know it hadn't been long but I felt more upset about this than I had after my six-year relationship with Dean ended.

I wasn't even crying over a relationship here; I was crying over a situationship.

Something that didn't even have a fucking label, and I let myself think this could actually go somewhere.

I was ugly crying like Kim Kardashian when she lost her diamond earring in the sea, and I was fucking heartbroken.

What actually upset me more was the fact that I was so blind to him feeling like this, it totally knocked me for six.

He was still showing affection and having sex with me and texting me all through the day. So to be honest if he was showing these signs and 'not feeling it', he was giving me mixed signals.

I was angry so just decided to reply.

Ah, OK. That's fine. That's a shame as I really liked you x

He replied saying sorry and I left it at that, I didn't reply.

I still feel silly for saying this, but I honestly was devastated.

The next few weeks went by in a blur. I lost my spark and my work began to suffer, it's crazy how the whole thing just shifted my mood.

I remember lying in my bed most nights that week crying because I was so distraught about it, how could I feel like this after such a short period of time? I wasn't his girlfriend. Get a grip Kirsten for fuck's sake!

But I couldn't. It was all I could think about, I would literally think about him all the time.

At work, on the drive to work, at the football, in the shower, any time I gave my head space or I wasn't thinking about anything in particular, he popped up.

Every time I heard Oasis or Kasabian, I thought about him too. My favourite songs were now tarred with memories of him because it's what we mostly listened to when we got drunk in his house.

I didn't tell my friends right away about what had happened with Chris purely because I was embarrassed that one minute, I was raving about this amazing guy who could potentially be 'The One' to then saying that the same guy had effectively dumped me over text.

I couldn't talk to anyone about it.

Three weeks after this all happened, I still hadn't heard from Chris, I wasn't expecting to really.

As much as I wanted to text him to see how he was, I didn't and it really did pain me.

I felt that same emptiness that I had after Dean, going from all to nothing.

A few times I caught myself secretly snooping on his Facebook on my lunch break to see what he was up to, that's really how bad it got.

To add to my series of unfortunate events that month, I found out when I got home from work one day that someone had smashed into my car again for the second time this year while it had been parked up in my car park.

The first time it happened when I was in Singapore and someone drove into my car and abandoned it. The front of my bumper was buggered but it was soon fixed.

And now, while parked in the exact same spot as before, some other fucker had done the same thing.

I broke down, it really did tip me over the edge.

Taking to Facebook to rant about my ordeal and to appeal for any information, I posted a picture of the mangled bonnet.

I was raging, I just really felt like it was one bad thing after another.

I decided to just get my head down and try to forget about Chris and my car.

I threw myself into work and one day, I was sitting at my desk, knee deep in a news feature when my phone pinged.

It was him.

My heart sank even seeing his name flash on my screen.

I had to check and make sure I was seeing this properly. Chris? What did he want?

I didn't open it for about half an hour as I didn't want to seem bothered.

But when I did, I was extremely shocked.

Hey. Hope you're well. I saw someone crashed into your car again, that's annoying! I left a wee present for you outside your door to cheer you up xxx

What. The. Fuck!

8. The One That Got Away, Twice

My jaw was literally on the floor.

I just sat there staring at the screen blankly in complete and utter shock.

A present? What the hell?

The last time I had something delivered to my doorstep, it was those godawful glittery apology roses from Dean.

Had he left me flowers? Were they 'I'm sorry for being a dick' flowers?'

I was so confused.

I decided to reply. Curiosity got the better of me.

What? You're at it! x

I decided to keep it witty, I didn't want to be gushy because I didn't even know what it was yet, plus I didn't want to look like I was pining for him, because I definitely was.

BUT I WAS honestly baffled, for a few reasons:

1. Because Chris stayed at least forty minutes away from me, so why was he in my postcode?

2. You don't leave presents for people who you 'don't see it going anywhere' with, do you?

3. Why fucking bother?

4. Talk about mixed messages?!

It wasn't long before he replied saying he was 'passing with work and decided to drop it in' and that I 'better use it'.

Instead of announcing it to the whole office, I forwarded on the text to Leona… who was sitting at the desk behind me and aptly put: *'WTF?'*

Wow, what the hell?' she replied back over our work messenger.

I really wasn't sure what it was but I had an idea it might be flowers? Time would tell.

It was only twelve o'clock in the afternoon and I didn't finish work until 5 p.m. How was I going to be able to wait all this time to find out what sort of present graced my doorstep? The suspense was killing me.

I thanked him anyway for the impromptu gift and that I would let him know my thoughts on it when I got home.

He continued the chat through text which I thought was a bit off, asking how I'd been and what I'd been up to.

Had he changed his mind about us?

I just replied saying that I'd been so busy with work that I didn't have a minute which was a total fucking lie but I couldn't let him think I was moping around and missing him.

We chatted some more, and you really wouldn't think anything had ever went wrong between us, it was like nothing ever happened, just as it was before he said he 'didn't see it going anywhere'.

I knew I shouldn't have but I continued to talk to him.

It soon hit five and I don't think I've ever rushed out the office quicker in my whole life. I promised to let Leona know what the 'present' was as she was as intrigued as me.

I zoomed home and legged it straight up the stairs of doom, faster than any fella had before.

I pulled the fire door open that let you into the landing of 'the penthouse' and saw the 'present' sitting there on my 'Don't come in unless you have gin' doormat.

I burst out laughing.

It wasn't flowers.

It was a bright pink, fucking Brita filter jug.

Fucking hell.

Then I flashed back to the time that he told me I drank too much bottled water after noticing a crate of bottles in my fridge.

Had he really travelled all this way to give me a fucking filtered water jug?

I text him and thanked him for my not so useful present and we continued to message back and forth.

I really had mixed feelings. I started to wonder if this was his way of saying sorry without actually saying it. But he kept the conversation going and I took that as his silent apology.

I used the water jug a few times but let him think I used it all the time, I don't care what anyone says, bottled water tastes better. End of discussion.

The hot pink jug sat in the door of my fridge and every time I opened it, all I could see was Chris, which was an odd thought in itself.

It wasn't long before he asked me if I wanted to go over to his at the weekend and I accepted. Was I stupid for not playing a bit harder to get?

Yes.

Did I care?

No.

I really, really liked this guy more than anyone I'd ever liked before and I thought everyone deserved a second chance. Plus, surely he regretted it or he wouldn't be asking to see me again? Unless he was just horny? I certainly was.

It was Saturday, and after an impromptu fanny shave over the sink (sorry Lisa) I headed over to his and spent the night with him.

It was just the same as any other Saturday I'd spent with him.

We listened to Oasis and the Stone Roses and drank gin and shots of tequila, we smoked menthols in his garden, and while it might not be everyone's idea of a 'romantic night in', I was just happy to be spending time with him once again.

A FEW WEEKS had passed, and things seemed to go back to normal with us.

He wasn't quite as affectionate as he had been previously, but I just put it down to him not wanting to be too forward after everything that had happened.

I spent the Friday with Chris then I'd planned to go to the pub with my friends Lucy and Heather on the Saturday.

I told them all about the situation and Lucy right away told me to be careful.

'Has he told you he made a mistake?' she asked sipping her vodka.

'No, but nothing says I'm sorry quite like a hot pink Brita jug does it?' I laughed.

But it did make me think. What were his intentions here?

Did he actually like me or did he know that I really liked him and had nothing better on the go?

It was nice to catch-up with the girls again, and even better that the pub had started to do venoms by the pint.

As the night went on, I necked more venoms and shots, and what Lucy had said really played on my mind.

Drunk me decided 'fuck it' and that I was going to text Chris and find out once and for all what was really happening with us, even if it wasn't what I wanted to hear.

What's actually going on here? With us? I'm getting mixed messages from you?

It didn't take long before I got the reply that at the back of my mind, I knew was coming.

It hit me right in the gut.

I really like talking to you and yeah we have a good time when we're together but I don't see it becoming anything more than whatever it is now. I haven't really been thinking about it to be honest. I've just been happy to talk away to you because it's so easy which is probably unfair on you because obviously you've been wondering what's happening xxx

Once again feeling my heart shattering, I replied.

No shit. Thanks for wasting my time, again.

He got back.

I know I'm sorry, I would never intentionally waste your time. I found it hard to stop talking to you a while back but maybe should have just left it xxx

And just like that I was heartbroken once again.

I know I shouldn't have given him a second chance in the fucking first place, but I was falling for him and if I didn't ask him, there would always be this 'what if' cloud hanging over my head plus I didn't want to waste any more time on someone who doesn't feel the same way I did.

I knew that I went fishing for an answer that I didn't want but I needed.

That's the thing with us girls, we go snooping to find things we don't want to find. We break our own hearts to save someone else doing it for us.

I cried into my vodka, I cried so much that my strip eyelashes crumbled off into the tips of my fingers. I went outside to smoke but couldn't stop the tears trickling down my face. I felt silly for crying because really, I'd brought this on all by myself.

I was that girl you see outside on a night out with mascara-stained cheeks, smoking about six fags in a row after she's just fallen out with her boyfriend. I was that mile out.

After being dumped by text again, from him, again – I didn't hear from him after that.

I actually took it upon myself to delete him from Facebook because I found myself having a snoop through his profile more and more frequently to find any evidence of any new girls on the scene.

It helped a lot, out of sight out of mind kind of thing.

You'll be pleased to know that I got rid of the water jug too.

I'd kept it in the cupboard for a while but only last year when I was moving that I came across it again and I didn't want to think of him every time I opened the fridge so it went in the same place that Dean's roses went – the bin!

Sometimes when I think about him, I smile at how he was the first person to make me truly happy, but then I remember how he was the only person who truly broke my heart even although it hadn't been that long at all.

I used to wonder if he was Mr Right but at the wrong time.

But I don't think he was, and I simply think he was Mr Right Now, well, back then.

One thing is for sure though, he'll always be remembered as 'Mr Water Jug' to my friends and 'The one that got away, twice' to me.

MY SITUATIONSHIP WITH Chris taught me a few things:

1. Time doesn't mean anything – you feel how you feel and that's it.

2. Don't cry over boys who drink tap water.

3. Stop bloody drinking!

9. Ten Top Tips for Coping with Heartache

INDULGE

Consume lots of wine and/or pizza (both together is a solid 10/10 recommendation from me). Go out for dinners, order in a takeaway, give your body what it wants!

KEEP BUSY

Go on walks, listen to music, or read a book. Spend less time on your phone, time on your phone makes you want to snoop on them.

DELETE HIM

Get rid of every trace of him. Facebook, Instagram, Twitter, LinkedIn, and also WhatsApp.

We're all guilty of going on to check when they were last active, or if they're online, let's be honest. Let go and get rid, girl. It'll be the best thing you can do. This also avoids drunk texting him telling him you miss him. Delete his friends and family too for added zen.

GET UNDER SOMEONE ELSE

Controversial advice but it's sometimes good to have someone to keep your mind off them even though you end up comparing them to your ex.

PAMPER

Shave your pits, put on some fake tan, go for a blow-dry and get your claws painted.

Feel your best for you and no one else and post that banging selfie on Instagram (even though he won't see it because you deleted him, remember? Maybe delete him post banging selfie upload).

TREAT YO'SELF!

Buy the shoes, get new make-up, and order some new lace undies.

CLEAR OUT

Get rid of things you no longer need. Sell every single thing they ever bought you on Depop.

And see those Valentine's Day cards from then that you've been hoarding in that drawer next to your bed? Burn them (recycling is also an environmentally friendly option!).

GO ON HOLIDAY

It may be an extreme piece of advice but honestly, a holiday with your girlies is exactly what the Dr ordered!

Just like when Carrie Bradshaw takes her pals on the honeymoon of her jilted wedding – just make sure no one shits themselves from accidentally drinking the shower water.

EXERCISE

After you've indulged, you'll the want to go on this mad fitness journey in a bid to get that revenge body.

I highly recommend the app 'Couch to 5K'.

NIGHT OUT

Really let your hair down with your friends. Whether it be dinner, drinks, both, or a weekend away.

Plan a fabulous night out where you get all dolled up and dance until your heart is content! End up being that girl walking with her heels in her hand at the end of the night!

10. The Awkward Encounter

It was August 2018, and I was finally starting to get over Chris.

I kept reminding myself of what Pam always said.

'One way to get over a man, is to get under another' and I was determined to put this into practice in order to get over him once and for all.

But I'm not even joking when I say this. Online dating is absolutely draining, soul destroying, and beyond deflating.

I desperately wanted to meet someone while I was out rather than on an app but it never really happened.

I'd gotten a few numbers before in a few bars in Glasgow, but no one had the 'Chris affect' on me.

In fact, one night out in the town, I'd had a few drinks and was chatting to this guy, but when he messaged me the next day and I looked at his WhatsApp picture, I almost couldn't believe it was the same person. He was nothing like what I remembered he looked like, it must have been the beer goggles. So I swiftly ghosted him. He had text me about five times in a row – nobody has time for a needy guy!

Being on Tinder was like searching for a needle in a haystack, but my friend Claire, the dating app expert, had suggested trying an app called 'Bumble' because apparently the guys were more 'upmarket'.

The difference with Bumble was the girl had to message the guy first twenty-four-hours within matching with them.

Once you did that, they had twenty-four-hours to reply to you or they disappeared.

That sounds interesting, at least that way a conversation would definitely take place because sometimes you matched with people on Tinder and never spoke to them. Bumble had the same lay out as Tinder where you swiped left for the ones you didn't like and right for the one's you did.

So of course, out of curiosity, I downloaded it.

IT WAS ANOTHER Sunday and another session of senselessly swiping.

I was back playing my game, getting through as many as possible.

I'll admit I did give a few sympathy swipes but as soon as they started talking, I got the 'ICK' because the chat was just so bad and I couldn't even be arsed to entertain it.

Sometimes I would get a flurry of matches and other times not a bloody peep.

Looking through several profiles, I honestly wanted to give some of these guys a shake.

They clearly didn't know anything about good angles or how to take a decent selfie, it's not hard!

I was almost on the verge of deleting the app when I came across a guy called Jordan, his profile picture was of him in a kilt and I'm sorry if a man in a kilt doesn't do anything for you, there's something seriously wrong!

Jordan was tall, dark and handsome-ish.

I mean he wasn't bad, but not really my usual type he had a sort of dorky-ness about him but his bio seemed to be witty so that was good enough for me.

I sent a cheesy message asking if he was a true Scotsman or not and that was that.

He replied something along the lines of 'you'll have to find out for yourself' and we went from there. Jordan seemed to have the chat. He sent great replies, loved a bit of cheeky banter and he seemed all right. No socks were blown off but what was I expecting, really?

So we chatted, and like the rest of them... moved over to WhatsApp.

Jordan was entered into my phonebook as 'Jordan – Bumble' which was a nice change from all the 'such and such – Tinder' names.

It turns out I have a thing for people called Jordan, Jamie, and Sean as I had a few 'doublers' saved in my contact list.

Jordan was so quick and witty with everything he said, it was like he didn't even think about what he was saying, it was totally effortless.

I liked that about him, but I don't know, I didn't have that excited feeling every time he text but I went along with it because he was the best of a bad bunch effectively.

He told me about his job as a stand-up comedian and it made me think that he must be so easy to get on with.

His texts honestly had me chuckling and I thought he would be a total hoot to go out with but still I wasn't bothered if we did or didn't.

We soon arranged a date for drinks somewhere in Bothwell but since I wasn't really jumping for joy about this one, I ended up going out the night before with the girls and got absolutely steaming drunk and felt extremely hung-over the next day.

I really could be doing without going out on a date on a Sunday anyway so in an attempt to cancel, I pulled the poor me card and told Jordan that I was feeling beyond rotten.

But instead of him being understanding, it backfired, and he suggested coming over to my flat and 'chilling' with me rather than us going out for drinks.

Ugh.

When I explained that I really wasn't a sight for sore eyes, Jordan was pretty persistent in 'looking after' me as I was rough so I agreed.

Who else remembers when I promised myself after Josh that I wouldn't invite a random to my house again for the 'first meeting'?

Apparently not me, but I think I was probably still drunk, so it wasn't long before I awaited his arrival.

It was the same routine as the previous contenders. Wait on the buzzer going, then wait about five minutes after that on them climbing up the stairs of doom, and about 30 seconds before opening the door after the knock.

I'd really nailed it by now and timed his arrival in my head to perfection.

And soon enough, I heard a faint knock at the door.

It was so faint that I had to ask myself if it actually knocked. Weird.

I wasn't even that nervous at all, I couldn't really have cared less if I was totally honest, I'm not sure I even brushed my hair for the occasion either.

I pulled back the door and there he was. All 6 foot 2 of him, skinny and extremely awkward.

He held his zipper over his arms and just stood there and said 'Hi'.

The way that zipper was draped over his arm gave me the ICK.

That was it? 'Hi'?

No complaint about the stairs but I could tell by the look on his face he struggled.

He stood there awkwardly, and I just looked at him. 'Well, are you coming in then?' I laughed, thinking he would give me one of his quick and witty responses.

'OK.'

Ouch I was not expecting that at all.

I closed the door behind him. He certainly looked the same as his pictures but Jesus Christ, had he forgot to bring his personality along with him? This guy was a stand-up comedian, make some joke about rescuing the princess from the tallest tower or some shit.

I instantly just knew this was going to be a disaster. Did he lie about his job? Did I misread what he said he did for a living?

He just stood there as I shut the door, like a shy schoolboy waiting to be taken into the headmaster's office for a row.

'Just through there,' I said, pointing towards the living room.

Jordan gave the tiniest wee smile and headed in after taking off his Adidas Gazelle trainers and sat them neatly by the door.

Was I that bad? Maybe I should have brushed my hair!

It was so bizarre because he just stood there in front of the couch as if he was waiting to be told to sit down.

'Take a seat, make yourself at home.' I smiled before offering him a drink.

No thanks,' he said shyly.

My God, this was going to be like pulling teeth.

I grabbed myself a can of Irn-Bru from the fridge and sat down beside him on the couch and began to start the conversation.

He didn't really have much to say at all so I kind of pretended I was at work doing an interview and asked him question after question, a bit like that time Chris came over before our date.

I remember when he gave me one of his longer replies, actually looking at him and just dying inside.

Even the way he sat on my sofa made me cringe. He didn't even sit fully on it, he perched on the edge with his hands clasped between his legs, and his shoulders bent in the way – it was really off putting.

Was he nervous? Did I make him nervous? Did he not like me as much as I didn't like him?

Who knew but he had only been here for five minutes so I already knew it was going to be a long night.

It really wasn't long before the conversation got so boring and dry, like there were only so many questions I could ask him, so I had to think quickly.

I had a decision to make here, I either just punted him out my house after ten minutes or I make things a bit more interesting.

I decided to take one for the team and lean in and kiss him, I thought it would maybe kill the awkward silences, but in all honestly, he was just as terrible at kissing as he was at talking.

As my lips touched his, it was as if a switch had been flipped and things took a turn.

You wouldn't believe that the cheeky wee 'shy' sod tried to slip his hand down my leggings, but I quickly pushed him away before he could get anywhere near the grains. I continued kissing him and redirecting his wandering hands up from my southern region.

He tried again and again, and again and again; I rejected his wandering hands.

It had been a while since anyone had touched down there, and I wasn't prepared to break the seal for this weirdo, those boney fingers weren't getting anywhere near me, that was for sure!

I felt too awkward to ask him to leave so I put up with his terrible kissing technique and creepy-crawly wandering hands for another hour or so before telling him I was too tired and would be heading to bed soon.

I swear to God, I can't even explain what he did but he slapped his hands on his thighs then got up from the couch and headed into his hall and I silently sniggered to myself – he just was just ICK-ing from left, right and centre.

I towered over him as he tied up the laces of his shoes in the hallway.

After he secured the second double knot, we said our goodbyes with another terrible sloppy kiss and I shut the door over behind him.

When I sat back down on my couch I just burst out laughing, then it just dawned on me… I'd been personality catfished!

I couldn't believe the same funny guy who had been texting me for weeks was the same awkward beanpole who came to my house like a terrified lamb to the slaughter.

Maybe he just didn't like the look of me and that's why he acted like a weirdo? To be fair, I was like a burst ball after my big night out with the girls but still, he could have at least faked it, or left immediately, but maybe he was just better at chatting over a phone? Who knew, but I didn't hear from him again and he didn't hear from me.

It was an awkward encounter that still makes me cringe to this day whenever I think about it, and once again, I vowed to myself that I would never invite a guy over to my house for the first meeting.

But did it happen? Of course it didn't.

THINGS LEARNT FROM the beanpole:

1. Stop fucking inviting strangers to your house.

2. Stop drinking so much.

3. Not all stand-up comedians are funny.

11. Always Lock the Door!

So it would be fair to say that my luck with dating apps wasn't very good at all so I once again made the decision to come off them to focus on myself – those famous last words, eh!

But it was true, I was reading more books, eating healthily and exercising way more than I ever had before, I was finally looking after myself for the first time in a while, I even laid off the booze for a bit too.

Caitlin, Rachael and I made it our thing to go walks around Strathclyde Country Park with Caitlin's dog Reggie.

The park is about a four mile walk, so it let us get our steps in and always have a blether and a gossip with each other.

Jodie would sometimes join us on these walks, but that girl is so bloody bad at replying to texts in our group chat that sometimes we had been and gone before she finally got back to us.

'How's the Tinder going Kirsten?' Rachael asked as we strolled one Saturday morning.

'Ugh, I haven't been on it since my awkward encounter.' I laughed as I painfully reminded myself of how bad that situation was.

'Let us have a go at finding you a man,' Caitlin chimed in asking to see my phone.

I rolled my eyes.

It was always some chuckle letting your pals 'play' on your Tinder, without a doubt they would always match you with the most grotesque men on there with the hopes of a flirty conversation. One night we even connected my phone to the TV and sat with a few glasses of prosecco and giggled as we swiped left and right.

I handed my phone over to them and let them loose to swipe until their hearts were content.

The two of them were in fits of laughter as they swiped right for almost everyone until they came across one…

'Oh my God! That's Christopher's pal!' Rachael laughed.

Christopher was Rachael's then boyfriend and now current fiancé, they hadn't been going out that long, but it was clear to anyone that the two of them were absolutely made for each other.

'You need to match with him he's hilarious!' she added.

And before I could even look at the guy Caitlin squealed, 'It's a match!'

Oh God.

I grabbed the phone out of Rachael's hand to investigate my new match…

Euan, he was absolutely everything opposite from anyone I'd went for before and I probably wouldn't have looked at him twice in the street, but we were now brought together by Tinder.

I screwed my face up and put my phone in my pocket and we continued with our walk, discussing every single one of my dating disasters to date.

Caitlin was new to the Tinder life too, so it was nice to hear other stories other than my own. Caitlin went on a date with a guy to the Christmas markets, only to find out when she was wanting to buy a German sausage from one of the stalls that he was in fact a vegan.

We still laugh about it to this day because I picked them up from the date that night and dropped him home, and the minute he got out the car Caitlin made me take her to the McDonald's drive thru for a double cheeseburger and chicken nuggets.

She didn't hear from him again either and I don't think she was fussed in the slightest.

During our walk we organised another night out at Angels for two weeks time, our usual and I was so looking forward to it, I needed some girl time and I was pleased that on this occasion, I would be able to pick anything I wanted off the menu and not have to opt for broccoli and carrot fajitas.

But before our night of madness, I decided to have a quiet night in this weekend, a sober, chilled one would do me the world of good.

IT WAS SATURDAY night. I was sitting on my couch watching *Sex and the City* (classic single girl TV) when I got a notification on my phone from Tinder.

186

It was Euan.

Rachael had text me earlier saying they were all in the pub and he was there and she told him he'd matched with her friend.

I opened the message from him, to find three.

Hello.

Stop texting Rachael.

Haha.

I text Rachael saying he had replied, and she told me to say.

Heard you're the skinniest boxer in Lanarkshire, what's the truth in that?

So I did, obviously oblivious to what kind of slagging he gets from his friends.

And literally two seconds later he replied.

I heard you've nearly completed Tinder Lanarkshire, what's the truth in that?

I laughed.

I loved a witty guy who could have a joke, as we all know, and I knew how to give it back, so I replied again.

Yeah, it's true, just all the stragglers left to get through, ya know?

He got my sense of humour right away.

Haha, sooo, we've cleared up the fact you're clearly texting Rachael so fancy just texting me? I'm nicer than she's probably made out.

He added his number too and that was it, we began WhatsApping.

'Euan – Tinder' was really funny and made me howl with laughter over text, but I'd been down this road before with Jordan, was he this funny in real life? That was the question.

We continued to text and chatted about life and other things, he was easy to talk to and quite the giggle.

It was the following weekend and I got my glad rags on for our girl's night in Angels.

When we got there, the tequila shots were flowing, and we drank cocktails all night – I expected nothing less.

I always loved a night out with the Spoon sisters, they weren't shy of a good bevy and that's probably why we got on so well.

They quizzed me on my conversations with Euan and I told them that we had been texting and Rachael said that he was out tonight with her man and that we should go meet them in the pub later on.

And that's exactly what we did. We set off to the Camphill, a tiny wee pub right in the middle of Bothwell but it was always good any time I'd been there.

We were pretty drunk when we arrived but we got more drinks and met up with Rachael's man and his friends and of course, Euan.

We sat in a small little booth and it wasn't before long that he was over like a shot.

This was a weird first meeting, as my pals were there too and so were his, but it wasn't too unusual for me because Rachael had already been on one of my first dates before, remember?

188

He gave me a huge cuddle and sat down next to us and chatted away.

Euan seemed just as witty and cheeky in person as he was in text but looks wise, he just wasn't anything like my type, or even close.

But his personality was attractive, and I got on well with him.

As the night went on and we got more drunk, the pub was shutting and we all decided to go back to Christopher's flat for more drinks.

You know what it's like at an after party, you end up drinking whatever is going and it this point I was drinking whisky and Coke which was never going to end well for me, it never does.

We all sat in the living room and sang and drank some more.

I went into the kitchen to pour myself another drink of whatever I could find in Christopher's cupboard, and it wasn't long before Euan followed me in.

We stood for ages just talking and before I knew it, he planted a kiss on me.

I was taken by surprise but the tequila shots that I consumed earlier that night had caught up with me, it was nice but again no butterflies or fireworks.

Throughout the night as more and more alcohol was consumed, Euan began to annoy me, following my every move.

I was sure he was just being nice, but he started to bug me and I got the ICK a bit. I think he sensed this and after a while of sitting in the living room, someone asked where he went, and it turns out he had left.

Well, that was rude.

I took the huff a bit in my drunken state, you know what us girls are like, I didn't want him then but when he left, I was annoyed, absolutely no logic behind it at all.

And then, in true Kirsten fashion, I went and took it upon myself to kiss not one but two other people that night.

Nothing else happened but a kiss, but I woke up the next morning in the spare room with my head absolutely bursting, with a hang-over and with The Fear – a fear like no other.

I didn't really like Euan that much. I suppose I hadn't really given it a chance, but I definitely had fucked it now after winching not one but two of his friends.

Aw man. I put my head in my hands and begged for the ground to swallow me up whole.

Why do I get myself into these situations?

He left though, so let's blame him.

I text my pal Molly and ask her if she could come and collect me from Christopher's asap as The Fear had riddled through me so much and every thought I had in my head made me want to die inside.

Like the great friend that she is, she was outside waiting to take me home within about fifteen minutes.

I pulled open Molly's car door with my shoes in my hand doing the ultimate walk of shame and she laughed at the sight of me.

'Good night then?' She shook her head, knowing fine well there was some sort of drama to tell.

'Ugh, I don't even want to talk about it.' I sighed.

Molly managed to prise it out of me that I winched three guys in the one night, in the same house – who were all friends.

'Oh my God! You dirty stop out, Kirsten McStay.'

I threw my head back in my seat and grabbed the bottle of water I asked Molly to bring with her, I rolled the window down and hoped that the gustily wind would help shift this awful feeling... but of course it didn't.

I once again climbed the stairs of doom in my flat stopping at every floor landing to consider throwing myself down them all to take away this pain in my head and also the shame of being a wee slut the night before, slut is a harsh word but that's how I felt.

I stepped in the shower in a bid to wash all three of my sins away and let the mascara run down my face even further than it already was but nothing I did could make me feel better about what I'd done.

I knew I hadn't done anything terribly bad but I knew that I would soon be the subject of the guys group chat and that's what bothered me the most.

I got out of the shower to find that I had a text from Euan and my heart stopped slightly.

Fuck, did he know what I'd done?

Hey, sorry about last night, and sorry for getting up and leaving, was I a mile out?

I replied telling him not to worry about it and that I was also extremely drunk.

Fancy hanging out sometime?

He didn't know by the looks of it, but I knew he soon would.

Yeah, maybe once I'm back from Tenerife.

I was jetting off to Tenerife with Pam the following day for our annual girls' holiday. We had done it ever since I was at university, and it was so special to spend a whole week in the sun with my mammy. She was and still is my best friend in the world. I usually do tell her most things, but fact that I winched three guys at the same house party, was not going to be one of them.

The heat hit me square in the face as we stepped off the plane and into the glorious sunshine, it literally took my breath away and it was great to get away from Motherwell and all the terrible decisions I'd made.

I needed time to chill out and forget all my man troubles.

I began to wonder if I would ever just meet someone that I clicked with right away.

Euan continued to text me for the full holiday, so I wasn't sure if he knew about the extra two kisses I gave out that night or if he did and had decided to ignore it.

We chatted and even Pam knew about him, I would tell her what he would say and by his witty patter she liked him, but for me there was still something missing.

Even though he was now old news, I wondered when the time would come where I would stop comparing everyone to Chris. I rarely even thought about him now but when I did, it was when I was comparing my initial feelings for him to others and still nothing topped it, Euan was no exception.

I had the best time in Tenerife, sipping cocktails, reading books and having such a laugh with my mum. It was just what I needed.

I got a nice tan and was feeling so refreshed.

Since I'd been away for a week and was dying to see my friends, I arranged to go to the Edinburgh Fringe Festival with Caitlin on the Friday. I'd never been before and neither had she so we decided to make a whole day of it.

It was dress down Friday at work, so I got ready that morning for going out after. I finished at twelve and met Caitlin at the train station armed with two bottles of wine for the journey.

Due to the last-minute plans, I had to cancel my pre-planned appointment with Lisa, not that I would need it anyway, it was a girls' day and there were no men on the scene – that I knew of anyway.

Texting between me and Euan had kind of fizzled a bit but we spoke every now and then in dribs and drabs.

I was so looking forward to a day out in Edinburgh because I hadn't really been in the city since I left uni and it definitely had a special place in my heart.

Before we met for the train, Caitlin and I agreed that we'd fill our hip flasks to take with us, not because drinks were expensive but trying to get a drink at bars in Edinburgh was sometimes mission impossible.

I was going to be taking it easy-ish too because I had a full-day wedding the next day but I figured that because it was an early start that it would also be an early finish so I would be fine – I must praise myself for the initial thought because there was absolutely no early finish that night.

Caitlin and I visited almost every bar in Edinburgh – slight exaggeration but not really.

We went to see shows, did shots in between and at one point we even had buckets of vodka in our hands. We were absolutely smashed but we were really just getting started.

It was now about 7 p.m., and for one of our last stops we made our way to the Three Sisters to listen to a band sing when I got a text from Euan, he'd seen from our Instagram posts that we were in Edinburgh and said he was also here with his family.

I told him where we were and put my phone back into my bag, not thinking much of it at all.

Caitlin and I got talking to these guys who I think were in the Navy and I ended up winching one of them while his pal grafted Caitlin.

Me disco winching once again? I really needed to get a grip.

It's no shock to hear that we were both absolutely plastered, I'm aware that many of my stories stem from the consumption of alcohol – it really is the enabler.

At one point I remember we were singing Tom Petty's 'Free Falling' at the top of our lungs while sneakily topping up our bought drinks with our hip flasks which absolutely did not help matters.

It was now 9 p.m., we had been on the sesh for nine hours – that's like a whole day's work and the commute home! It was no wonder we were absolutely sozzled.

Before I knew it, I felt a tap at my shoulder as I swayed on the dance floor, it was Euan along with his family in tow. Luckily, I'd managed to sneak away from the Navy guy before Euan spotted us, I didn't want him to know I was kissing other guys, I had previous for that.

When I say his family were there with him, it was like his sister, brother-in-law, and a few others.

It was somewhat awkward that he was there with his family but at the same time, I was too drunk to care.

More drinks were ordered at the bar, and we danced some more, literally like we were the only people there.

I remember being in the toilet with Caitlin at one point, she was sitting on the sink attempting to sort her hair in the mirror while I was hovering over the toilet doing the longest pee in the world.

I was mumbling about my dilemma to her, I couldn't take Euan home after because I'd cancelled on Lisa when I probably shouldn't have and we were both so drunk we just started hysterically laughing into the tiny sink while attempting to put lipliner on each other, it's a wonder why anyone wanted to winch us that night.

Heading back out to the bar for yet another drink, I quickly glanced at my watch, and it was almost 10 p.m., the last train home to Motherwell from Edinburgh is at about eleven so we decided we better head to get it.

With Euan and his family in toe, we made a quick exit because we didn't want to miss the train, I didn't fancy paying for a taxi back home!

Euan and I stoated at the back of the crowd heading towards Waverly Station so we could have a cheeky kiss.

When the others were a little further ahead of us, we took the opportunity to eat the face off each other in the street like a couple of teenagers and because I was so drunk, I didn't care who saw us, plus it was Edinburgh, the chances of us running into anyone we knew were pretty slim.

The last train home from Edinburgh on a Friday night is always absolutely packed but it was even more rammed because of the festival so we ended up sitting on the floor.

The train was jam-packed with merry people eating chips and cheese, singing, some arguing and then us, kissing on the floor – how classy.

As we approached Motherwell, Caitlin had a wild idea that as soon as we got off the train we should go to Skoosh.

Skoosh is the shittiest nightclub ever known to man, previously known as 'The Point' – more like 'the point of no return' as no good decisions are ever made from going there and tonight was absolutely no exception.

It is literally a stone throw away from Motherwell train station and of course that's exactly what we did.

The wedding I had the next day at no point crossed my mind, or the fact I had to be up at 8 a.m. to get my hair and make-up done.

But we toddled up to the steps of Skoosh, which was dead, there was literally about seven people there and I don't really remember much from up apart from necking shots of tequila and staggering out to the taxi rank with Euan.

I blacked out again.

The loudest thud I'd ever heard echoed through the room.

What time was it? I didn't care, I was at death's door and Euan lay beside me, almost in a coma.

My eyes shut over again until I jumped from the sound of my bedroom door swinging open.

It was Pam.

'KIRSTEN! What the hell! You have a wedding in two hours! Why aren't you answering your phone?! Your keys were still in the front door, how stupid!'

By the time she realised I had a guest in my bed, I could see the wrath in her eyes, and she turned on her heel.

Oh my God, was this really happening?! Was my mother really standing in the doorway when I had a guy in my bed?

I pulled the covers up to underneath my nose in utter shame and embarrassment. I must not have locked the door and well, according to her, I'd even left them in the lock, I was so drunk, I don't even remember.

Luckily, Euan was kind of buried under the covers already, but I've never wanted the ground to swallow me up more than I did at this moment in time, not even the kissing three people in one night came close.

I was most definitely still drunk.

My phone wasn't on my bedside table, maybe I'd lost it?

My feet have **never** moved faster and the minute I heard the door slam shut, I sprung out of bed, in a frantic search to find my phone.

At my bedroom door, I was met with a trail of clothes (deja vu much), shoes and Euan's belt all on the floor. The trail led me to the front door where my bag had been dumped, along with my phone and an empty hip flask.

Picking it up, I clicked the button. Fifteen missed calls and six messages. Fuck.

I've never felt a hang-over like this since the day I took Chris home from the football and missed my work and this one had the potential to be worse than that.

I looked around in the kitchen and noticed Pam had left me a can of Irn-Bru to curb my hang-over. She was always so thoughtful even when she was mad at me.

I went back into the room to see Euan who was still lying half under the covers. He was awake by this point, fuck I would be too if I'd just got a wake-up call from the girl I was talking to's angry maw.

We definitely didn't go the whole way, I know it, the grains stood in my way thankfully, but I was still mortified about what had just happened and the fact my maw burst into my house AND bedroom when I had a guy in my bed, doesn't get any worse than that does it?

'Do you think she was mad?' he asked as he popped his head up from the covers.

'She'll be fine, but I better go get ready for this wedding. I'll phone you a taxi.'

Due to my long shift of getting on it, I'd obviously missed my hair and make-up appointments meaning I would have to do it myself and I winced at the thought.

Euan gathered his spread-out belongings and left. I still wasn't overly enthused about him, but I didn't really have time to think about it at that moment in time, I had a full-day wedding to get ready for and also my guts to spew up in between.

I sat down in the shower, like I had many times before in my terrible decision-making ways, but this time I actually had to hang my head over the bath and be sick into the toilet, my aim wasn't the best either.

I felt like the pits of hell and the last thing I wanted to do was go and watch one couple on the happiest day of their lives.

My eyes were so blood shot and I literally looked like death. The pictures from that day show it, I looked like I was dragged through a bush backwards, twice.

The original plan was for me to go to my mum's beforehand to get a drink before we headed to the church and I was meant to drive down there but due to being hung-over/still drunk, I got a taxi.

'Where ye off to today, hen?' the driver asked.

Fucking hell. Wasn't it obvious? Did the badly placed fascinator on my barely brushed hair not give it away?

I couldn't really be arsed with small talk in the fragile state I was in but to be polite I just said it was my brother's best pal's wedding and nothing more, I was fighting the urge to be sick in this tobacco fumed Skoda.

I arrived at my mum's house and the dread filled my belly as I made my way up to the steps knowing the look of judgement that would be sprawled across her face.

Just as I was walking in my sister-in-law Paula arrived too, phew, at least this way it would soften the blow.

'Hey! How was the Fringe?' Paula asked, looking like a dream in a peach dress.

And there was me bedraggled and looking like I was returning from a weekend in the cells and not going to a wedding.

'I'll fill you in later.' I sighed, still nursing my banging headache.

My badly placed eyelashes highlighted the redness in my eyes and accentuated my lack of sleep bags despite the copious amounts of concealer I'd plastered over them.

My mum opened the door to welcome us, and I let Paula take the lead.

Pam wrapped her arms around Paula to greet her and shooed her in the house, and then when it was my turn, there it was, the look I knew I couldn't avoid.

I felt fifteen again, being told off after being brought home by the police for drinking cider and blackcurrant down the park.

'Hi.' She frowned giving me a cuddle. As she pulled away, she looked at me and gave a half smile before whispering, 'Dirty stop out!'

I let out a laugh before, the hang-over wave hit me once more.

I ran to my mum's bathroom and once again relieved the bile of tequila and vodka that festered in my stomach from my Fringe Festival Fuck-up.

I was spewing so much that my eyes watered, ruining the half-arsed eyeshadow job I did earlier. I can't believe I even had the cheek to attempt to stick false eyelashes on, it was like sprinkling glitter over a turd – useless because no matter what you did to it, it was still a shite.

This was going to be the worst day of my life.

As I sat in the church and wished my life away. I was constantly battling not to be sick.

I dodged the videographer at all costs, I really was not the ideal wedding guest to be capturing at this moment in time.

My brother was the best man, and I could see him parading around in his kilt as we all waited on the bride making her big entrance.

Don't get me wrong, she was absolutely stunning, out of this world in fact but I would rather be in my bed suffering than be here right now.

After the lovely ceremony, we made our way outside when my cousin Jodie came up to me as I withered away in the background of happy guests tossing confetti all over the place.

'What happened to you last night then ya minx?' she said patting my shoulder.

I filled her in, and she just burst out laughing, she wasn't surprised by my antics and asked how I always got myself into these situations.

Who knew, really?

Our friend Julie came over to chat too and offered me a few pain killers she'd tucked in her Mary Poppins bag.

It was the worst idea ever, taking pills on an empty stomach. I hadn't eaten a thing because one, I didn't have time and two, I couldn't face it.

The reception was about a forty-five-minute drive away so we all climbed on a bus to make the journey there, and again it was something I could have been doing without.

I sat with Jodie and her fiancé Paul as they cracked open cans of alcohol for the journey as I slept with my bird's nest head against the window.

Jodie even took a fly picture of me that day and what a state I was.

To make matters worse the bus took the wrong turn and got stuck in a ditch and after many attempts to get out, the motion brought on another round of spewing for me.

Just before I showered the rest of the guests with vomit, I jumped off the bus and once again projectile spewed at the side of the road with all the guests laughing at my misfortune.

It was a total disaster, I got my heels stuck in the grass and had Jodie holding my hair back, to be honest sick in my hair may have been an improvement. I could hear my mum tutting from the bus and everyone whispering, 'look at her spewing!'

What an embarrassment.

But the series of unfortunate events didn't stop there, the minute the meal was put down in front of me I took one smell of it and ran to the toilet. Julie was sitting across from me at the table and had been suffering toothache so she had these Solpadine soluble tablets in her bag so she popped one into a glass of water for me and it did square me up a bit to be fair but still it was the worst day of my life.

After the first dance, I called one of my pals to come collect me urgently, I needed to get home to die quietly, dramatic yes but that's how I felt, my stomach was in tatters and my head still pounded.

I didn't really chat much to Euan after, I messaged him to say he had left his belt in my house that night to which he said he wasn't wearing a belt so that kind of killed the vibe.

I don't know if it was really Pam who killed the whole buzz or if it just wasn't really there to begin with.

I'll put it down to the vodka on that fateful night at the Edinburgh Fringe, but I wasn't too fussed. He wasn't really my cup of tea to begin with but that was OK.

Turns out the belt was his but he was just trying to be funny, which made me look like a bit of a slag.

Caitlin was absolutely buckled when I told her about the whole escapade and I'm pretty sure I was once again the hot topic of the guys' group chat.

And her maw walked in!

I could just picture the amount of laughing emojis there would be in the WhatsApp conversation, how would I ever live this down?

I even heard a rumour about it just a couple of months ago that someone said we were 'doing it' and my mum walked in which totally wasn't the case and truth be told we didn't even do anything, maybe some bits but definitely no notches were made on the bed post and I'm so thankful for that.

LIFE LESSONS FROM Euan:

1. Never date anyone connected to your inner circle – the drama will haunt you forever.

2. Never go on the heavy sesh the day before an all-day wedding – even if it is an early start.

3. Always lock the bloody door!

12. The Ultimate Wing Woman

My boozy ways landed me in all sorts of trouble more times than I care to count so it was time to cut back for a bit and refocus.

Feeling fresh on the Monday morning was certainly quite pleasant and something I thought I could maybe get used to.

I sipped on my coffee at my desk when my phone rang, it was my landlord saying that someone was coming to service the boiler and that would I be in this afternoon around 3 p.m.

'Em, no but I'll ask my mum if she can pop round and let them in?'

I text Pam and asked her for the favour.

Of course. No problem xxx

I didn't think much of it then until twenty past three, when I got a text from her.

My screen flashed.

Shame u had to work. He's hot! Xxx

When I opened the message, she had attached a picture of this guy up on my kitchen worktop working on the boiler.

I laughed, that's so typical of my mum.

I sent her back some laughing emojis and that was that, until…

My screen flashed again.

Mum: *1 image attached*

What the hell?

When I opened the text, I immediately burst out laughing.

There standing in front of the front door to my flat was a young guy posing for the camera.

The message read.

I showed him ur pic. He thought u r gorgeous. He says he's gonna look for you on Facebook. His name is Ryan and he's from Glasgow. Had a girlfriend for 9 years but they've fell out just now.

Oh, my fucking God!

As if my mother is trying to set me up with the man who is in servicing my boiler and she'd taken a picture of him standing outside my house!

I erupted in laughter to the point tears were actually blinding me and everyone in the office wondered what was going on.

'You guys are never going to believe this. My mum has actually stood and took a picture of the man who is in servicing my boiler in a bid to set me up with him! She's not real!' I howled.

'You're kidding! Let's see!' Leona giggled, hovering over my phone.

Honestly, my mum was desperate to marry me off, and I admire her boldness but Ryan the gas engineer never revealed himself in the end sadly.

EVEN THOUGH I never physically set eyes on this guy, the scenario taught me:

1. Your mother is your best wing woman – fact.

2. You CAN have fun without alcohol.

3. Avoid gas engineers in future.

13. The One Who Had It All

It was now just coming up to November, I'd spent the last three months training for the 10K run for work.

I put all my time and energy into that and hadn't given Tinder or Bumble or any other pretentious dating apps much attention, a few messages here and there but I just couldn't face that God fucking awful dry chat.

Hi, how are you?

Good weekend?

What is it you do for a living?

It really sucked the soul right out of me and I ended up more or less just copying the same conversation to everyone I spoke with.

And as it came into the winter months, I really started to miss having a boyfriend.

I missed going to the Christmas markets, Christmas shopping and all the other festivities you take part in with your other half and of course, the shagging.

Christmas was always a lonely time, it's always about couples, and my social media feeds were rammed with 'Oh look what my boyfriend bought me' or 'the boy did good' and quite frankly, it made me sick – much like Valentine's Day did.

It was a Saturday afternoon, and I was feeling bored as always, everyone was busy with their other halves and the single ones also had other plans.

Most people pick up a book or indulge in a new TV programme when they're bored and have nothing to do but not me, I decided to re-explore Tinder because after the 'Fringe Fuck-Up' I'd avoided it for a while.

I actually enjoyed being off it for a while but the boredom, as it had done before, had kicked in and I was ready to take on a new victim or in this case, become the victim.

After blethering to a few duds, I matched with a local guy called Jack.

It transpires that we lived about ten minutes away from each other.

He looked quite nice, he had dark hair, a nice smile and was a Celtic fan – my ideal type as we all know.

He had a proper cringe paragraph in his bio which made me wince a bit, but I had to stop being so judgemental and start giving people a chance, what if I'd swiped past the love of my life? I mean I highly doubted it, but you just never know.

I always give myself a silent nudge when I start to think about these kind of things – get a grip Kirsten!

But as soon as that big *'You've got a match!'* banner flashed across the screen, he messaged me right away. Like almost instantly.

I can't really remember how the conversation went but I remember thinking *'this guy isn't shy'* and that he seemed like a bit of a twat but a likeable twat, so I gave him the benefit of the doubt.

We chatted for a while that day, he told me he was an engineer in the army and had just returned home from Kenya for Christmas.

He said he was spending some time with his family and that he was close to his mum, sister, and nieces and nephews.

I really admired that, a guy who is close to his family. Isn't that what every girl wants? Absolutely!

We chatted for what seemed like ages on Tinder before Jack asked for my number, he said he didn't want to be seen on Tinder in public so it would be better for him to text me instead.

I thought this was just a typical cheeky guy way of asking for my digits, so I agreed and we continued constantly texting back and forth.

'Jack – Tinder' was input into my phone.

As the text messages flew back and forward, I noticed that this guy used a hell of a lot of emojis, again cringe but who doesn't in this day and age?

There I went again nitpicking silly things like the use of emojis – lord above!

I remember some of the stories he told me of his time in the army being very farfetched but what did I know about the army? Absolutely hee-haw.

It was obvious that Jack loved his job from the way he spoke about it. Again, it was nothing I knew anything about, he could have told me he was the sargent of the moon mission and I would've believed it because I was clueless. I took his word for it anyway.

He seemed really passionate about what he did and said he worked long hours as he just absolutely loved his job.

Fair enough. A guy who really loves his job, and has a dedicated profession? How could I complain?

He also told me that he had just bought a house on his own, but it needed a lot of work done, and that he would be spending all his time renovating it over the next few months.

This guy really seemed to have his shit together and I admired that a lot about him but there was something about Jack that was off, and I just couldn't put my finger on what it was but I thought I was just doubting him because he was so nice, and this always seemed to bite me in the arse (see previous chapters).

But the chat got better and better and we spoke all day, every day. He would always text me at the crack of dawn when he woke up right up until late, say one or two o'clock in the morning.

I began to wonder if the guy was superhuman as he never seemed to sleep, he was always awake!

He said it was due to being in the army and being used to no sleep, God I couldn't imagine the things you have to do in the army, it really did sound horrific.

Jack was always asking me questions about my life, about what I did and about my previous relationships.

I didn't think this was necessarily a bad thing at all that he wanted to know and thought it was nice that he was so interested.

With Christmas coming up and yet again my diary being filled with many nights out, just like Lewis the previous year, it was impossible for us to agree on a day for a date.

But I wasn't overly fussed as I had a lot coming up, like the following weekend it was my annual Christmas jumper day out with Jodie and the Spoons and it was always my favourite night out of the year.

I continued to text Jack the whole week and it wasn't long before my night out arrived.

I donned my sequin skirt, thigh high boots and my red 'Prosecco Ho Ho Ho' jumper and I went out to paint the town red like Santa's Little Hooker.

Like every other story I've told previously about being out with that lot – a lot of alcohol was consumed.

We did a local bar crawl and shots were downed at every single pit stop, we really do love a shot, don't we?

As the night went on, we laughed and danced on the sticky floor of every single grotty pub in Motherwell.

Giving them the usual 'dating debrief', I'd told the girls about Jack and they seemed excited for me, I even caught myself smiling as I told them all the details and how we seemed to get on so well despite never actually meeting.

Again, I would tell myself, 'we've been here before, so don't get too excited'.

But I felt I was half kidding myself on because in the pit of my stomach I knew for a fact, he wasn't 'The One'.

Back to the 'when you know, you know' patter. I don't know what it was I just didn't see myself being with him, it's weird how you just get a vibe, isn't it?

We really did jingle all the way that night, feeling merry and well and truly 'gin-gle bellsing'.

The pubs were shutting and as we all hung about outside waiting on taxi's, I pulled a packet of crumpled menthols out my bag and put one to my lips, I really needed to quit this stinking habit.

Leaning against the wall with the pom pom of my Santa hat flopping over the front of my face, Caitlin came bouncing up behind me.

'Soooo... are you going to get him round?' she said swinging the pom pom around my head.

I rolled my eyes.

'Hmmm, you know what happened the last time I invited a guy round to my house the first time.'

We both laughed as Caitlin teased, 'What time was that then?'

214

Cheeky bitch.

I kissed my besties goodbye, smudging festive red lipstick on all their cheeks and by this point, one of my thigh highs were slumped down at ankle and I definitely looked like Santa's Little Hooker now.

I jumped into the taxi on my own, the others were heading back the other way, so it made sense.

'Where ye off to the night darlin'? The North Pole?'

I giggled as I fought with the seat belt in the back.

'Aye, please.'

It had been over two years now since I moved into my top-floor flat, so I pretty much had mastered the mammoth stairs, both full of bevvy and sober.

If I've been drinking, the trick is to take the heels off at the bottom but of course the hooker boots didn't make this easy, so I plopped my arse down on the first step in the stairway and tugged at them. The one that was already at my ankle didn't take much effort to get off but the other one was a struggle. Finally, after admitting defeat to the tug-of-war with the stubborn one, I toddled up the stairs with one still on and the other tucked under my arm with my bag.

I don't know why I never fish my keys out while I'm still in the taxi, every time, without fail, I end up dumping the clutch on the door mat and unloading its contents until successful.

After prizing them from the lining of my bag, I pushed the heavy door open, dropping said bag by the door along with my

Santa hat, and the remaining boot which I had to sit on the floor to get off.

In true drunken Kirsten fashion, I didn't bother to even take a make-up wipe to my face and just flopped into bed, the way I imagine Santa would after a busy day at the office.

Checking my phone with one eye open, I realised Jack had messaged me four times.

Four messages? Fucking hell.

Hiiiiiii. How's your night? xxxx

You home yet? xxxx

Fancy a visit? xxxx

Let me know, I'm out with the boys the now but heading home soon! xxxx

Jesus, he wants to come here?

It didn't end well the last time I did this and the time before that and the time before that, which I kept trying to remind myself.

But as we know, sober Kirsten and drunk Kirsten are both two completely different people, with different moral compasses.

And right now, drunk Kirsten said yes.

No questions asked.

It never once crossed my mind to say 'why don't we wait until next week' or 'na not tonight' just yeah, OK, Jack, here's my address come on over stranger.

I was once again playing stranger danger Russian roulette and I was more than happy to take the risk because we all know what happens when a guy comes over after midnight on a Saturday and my God, it had been a while.

I punched in my address in a text message and waited on him arriving.

Who the fuck do I think I am inviting guys from Tinder over at this time?

You always hear these horror stories about girls who are murdered by a Tinder date, but at no point did this cross my mind. It was pretty fucking irresponsible looking back at it now.

I was sprawled across my bed still wearing my Christmas jumper and sequin skirt with a pair of sports socks when the buzzer echoed through the hall – a sound I'd heard oh so many times before.

Falling off the bed, I stumbled into the hall and held on to the wall as I picked up the phone and pressed the button to let him in.

I hadn't even bothered my arse to check what I looked like in the mirror before the late-night stranger arrived, but I knew I was an absolute mile out and I didn't really care, he was here for one thing and one thing only and the sooner I accepted that, the better.

My drunk mind just kept thinking about what me and Caitlin always laugh about and it's the phrase 'Y H Y H', which crudely means 'yer hole's yer hole'.

Besides, I was better just acknowledging now that in the morning, I would be feeling terrible about myself for shagging a guy on the first meeting, but I mean it's nothing I've not done before, is it?

Fuck it.

I waited the standard 4-5 minutes (you know the drill by now) and there it was, the chap at the door, the chap I'd also heard so many times before.

I swung it back, 'Hiii.'

'God they stairs! Hey!' he puffed.

'Come in then!' I whispered, not wanting my neighbours hear my late-night guest.

The only light on in the flat was the one from the TV in my bedroom I wasn't even going to have the courtesy to take him into the living room for a 'drink', so it was straight to the bedroom, to get right down to business.

I looked at him as he led the way and I locked the door behind him, (it's common practice now after Euan) and assessed the situation in front of me.

He was shorter than I thought, he had big shoulders and arms but the skinniest wee legs ever, Christ I think if he put on my thigh high boots, they wouldn't even touch the sides.

When he took his jacket off, and unveiled a tracksuit sort of thing, it became evident that he definitely wasn't 'out out' with his pals.

He sat down on my bed, and I sat down too. I was surprised by how un-awkward it was. This wee bastard was a blether and to be honest I wasn't really up for talking at this ungodly hour.

But he went on and on and on.

While I let him babble on until his heart was content, my attention was drawn to his hands – they were fucking tiny.

They were like T-rex hands, I couldn't believe how wee and stubby his fingers were when I noticed that on his right hand, he was wearing a PINKY RING.

What in God's fucking name is that?

'Is that a pinky ring you're wearing?' I asked savagely.

'Yeah, it's got my initials on it,' he said, showing the piece of gold off proudly.

'But, why?' The tequila made me brave.

'My mum got me it when I was younger,' he said as he twisted it around his abnormally small finger.

I was glad he wasn't looking directly at me when he said it because my face couldn't lie – it was fucking awful.

A pinky ring? A fucking pinky ring? I thought I'd seen it all being a full-time Tinderella but a pinky ring? My papa wore a pinky ring and he was in his 80s.

I tried my absolute best not to look at it, but I just couldn't stop. It was horrific.

I was thankfully distracted by how good he smelt, he was wearing Hugo Boss aftershave, which I only know because I asked him.

And before I could be put off by anything else, he pulled me in and we started kissing.

It was passionate and intense and in all honestly, I enjoyed it.

Jack was clean shaven, not usually what I went for, but I was glad I wouldn't have that awful kissing rash you get when you winch guys with stubble.

He was a pretty good kisser to be fair, and what lead after that was decent, too.

It didn't blow the hooker boots off me, but yeah it blew off the cobwebs let's just say. I think the first time with someone is always rather disappointing for some reason?

I woke up slightly hung-over. I deserved to feel worse.

My head buzzed a bit, but there was no urge to spew, and that in itself was a result.

As I fully began to open my eyes, I could hear Jack next to me already awake.

I clicked my phone to check the time. It was eight o'clock in the morning. Why the hell was he up so early? It was a Sunday.

As he saw me turn to face him, he put his phone on the bedside and put his arm around me.

'Good morning', he whispered, kissing my neck.

Jesus, this wasn't like any other one-night stand I'd had before.

'What's your plans for the day then?' Jack asked as he pulled me in closer.

I kind of wanted rid of him soon, so I lied.

'I'm going down to my mum's and we're going out shopping,' I said, trying to sound as honest as possible.

One thing I noticed was that Jack was very affectionate, to the point I wasn't sure if I liked it or not.

I'd never been in a situation before where I wasn't really sure of a guy. I either really liked him or really didn't.

But with Jack I just didn't know if he made laugh or cringe. It was a serious mixture of both but at this moment in time, I couldn't wait to get rid of him and probably never see him again.

I started dropping hints left, right, and centre that I probably should get up soon and start getting ready. Jack took the bait and got his brother to come and get him.

It wasn't long before I was kissing him goodbye in the hallway, dodging last night's clothes and boots on the floor as I waved him off.

I slumped back on to the bed and FaceTimed Caitlin.

'Ohhhh, hen, check your hair!' Caitlin said as our cameras connected.

'Hi to you too, hen.' I laughed, ruffling the matted beehive on top of my head.

'So how was your night then?' she asked, referring to my night after I left her at the pub.

'Em, aye. Interesting. Slept with him, probably won't see him again. So, aye, another one bites the dust.'

I filled her in on the juicy details that every single girl tells her best pal the morning after the night before and explained that I wouldn't be fussed if I did or didn't see Jack and his pinky ring again.

I was taken by surprise though, when I got a text message from him just one hour after he left my house that day, thanking me for a good night and saying that he hopes we can do it again soon.

Was he blind this morning? Did he see the absolute nick of me? Do 'it' again? 'It', sex? Is it just sex?

I think I would maybe be OK with that. I mean, I definitely don't see myself marrying a guy with a pinky ring so…

I mentally check myself for even talking about marriage after only sleeping with a guy I hardly know anything about, get a fucking grip, Kirsten.

So I text him back.

Yeah, that would be good! xx

You free on Thursday? xxx

Yeah! xxx

I stewed away on my couch for the rest of the day, texting Jack back and forth.

He said he had a busy week at work and Thursday was the only day he had free.

That suited me. I was working 9-5 at the paper Monday to Friday and then Monday to Wednesday 6-11 p.m., I was in Starbucks.

Working fourteen hours a day wasn't ideal, but I lived for the weekends and going on holiday, so it was the only way I could afford to live the life that I did.

I was bloody knackered, but it was always so worth it.

It was a long week, and I busted my arse at work. It was always so busy around Christmas time with everyone taking holidays to get their Christmas shopping done.

Most people's works wind down towards the festive period but not for us. The news never stops.

That week I was out at a house fire, a council meeting, and a charity event.

It had just been one of those weeks; I finished my shift as a journalist then headed down to Starbucks to start making coffees, again as this was my second job, I didn't really give a shit.

But it was soon Thursday – my favourite day of the week.

I loved it because when I finished at 5, that was me for the night and on the Friday, I only worked until twelve, so it was pretty much a breeze after that.

When I was at work Jack had texted me to ask if I could pick him up that night as his brother needed to borrow his car for something.

I said that was fine and to just send me his address, but he said he stayed in a wee 'hard to find' scheme so to make it easy for me, I could pick him up at the shop around the corner.

Em, OK? It was a bit of a strange request.

Jack suggested bringing over some red wine for us to drink, which evidently meant that he was staying the night at the penthouse.

When I drove over to get him, I sat outside the grubby wee corner shop and began to wonder if there was a particular reason that I was sitting here and not outside his house.

He said he had his own house and his mum stayed round the corner.

Was it to make sure she didn't see him leave and not return?

I wasn't sure to be honest, but I wasn't that interested in him to investigate the actual situation.

Don't get me wrong I was happy for the company, it was better than sitting in on my own.

Waiting for his arrival, I flicked through the Instagram app when I saw his short figure cross over the road in front of me.

He had come from the complete opposite direction, that's weird.

I squinted my eyes and examined him as he got closer and closer.

He had an Adidas zipper on with a pair of teal blue shorts on and a pair of Adidas Gazelle trainers.

Is this guy really wearing a pair of shorts in November?

I noticed that clutched in his tiny hands was a plastic Tesco bag, presumably carrying the promised red wine for us to have on our first sleepover together.

Jack's pace picked up after noticing my car parked, waiting on him.

I felt a very familiar feeling creep across me... the ICK.

I couldn't help but watch his every move as he opened the door and hopped in the passenger side.

The wine clicked beneath the bag as he pulled the door shut and from the minute he clicked the seat belt in place, he wouldn't stop talking. This guy loved to chat and totally oozed confidence, but it was a bit too much for me.

Before I could get a word in edgeways, he was halfway through a story about his day at work, and how something was broken and it was going to cost his company thousands of pounds but because of him it was fixed and he was the hero.

I remember yawning in my head when he was telling me this tale of being a knight and shining armour.

Did it even happen? Probably not, but I let him have his moment while I silently regretted picking him up.

We soon arrived back at mine and the two bottles of wine clinked in the bag as we climbed the stairs together. Two bottles of wine on a school night? I was definitely going to have a sore head at work the next day.

I pulled the cork from the bottle and poured the dark liquid into two large glasses.

I made my way over to the couch where Jack had already made himself at home and popped myself down next to him.

'That's nice wine!' I said sipping on the rich, warm notes.

'Yeah, I read an article somewhere that recommended that one, it's good, eh?' he said, rather pleased with himself.

I hadn't really been a red wine drinker until I went to Singapore to stay with Rosie, and we drank it on roof top bars on the daily and I was converted ever since.

The one Jack had brought was the Casillero Del Diablo wine, the one that's on the TV advert where the big seductive voice says, 'Wine from the Devil's Cellar.'

I'd never tried it until now, but it was actually really nice.

As we made our way through the first glass, Jack turned to politics talk and I couldn't have rolled my eyes anymore if I tried.

I absolutely hate everything about politics. As a journalist, it should really be something I show even a slight interest in, but it doesn't. I remember when I started working as a news reporter I was sent to cover a local election and it was honestly one of the worst days of my life – slight exaggeration but it's just not something that really interests me at all if I'm honest.

Jack proceeded to say that he always watched *Question Time* on a Thursday night.

Question Time? What the fuck is *Question Time*?

That shows you how much I knew.

Question Time was an hour-long topical debate show where politicians and the media answer questions by the public.

Fuck's sake, that sounds like my idea of hell!

We were in the middle of watching a film, when it soon approached the hour and Jack was quick to tell me to change the channel.

What? Is he serious? I thought he was joking!

226

But he wasn't joking, and the channel was turned over and I could see a smile creep across his clean-shaven face.

I began to down my wine in serious boredom as Jack's beady eyes became engrossed in Fiona Bruce and her special guests.

'Is this boring you?' he asked, as he noticed me getting up to pour my third glass of wine.

'Erm, yeah it is.'

'Sorry, I'll give you more attention then.' He grinned, putting his teeny wee hand on top of mine as I topped up his wine and plopped myself down beside him once again.

'I'll give you more attention then.' – ICK!

And true to his cringey word, he put his arm around me and pulled me in for a kiss.

Before I knew it, we were kissing passionately to the point I nearly spilled my wine over on the carpet.

I could taste the tang of the wine on his lips as they touched mine softly.

He ran his small hands through my hair and cupped my chin. Jack was a pretty decent kisser, I couldn't deny that at all.

'Should we go to bed now?' he whispered, evident that he had lost all interest in his shitty politics show.

'OK,' I said, getting up from straddling over his fucking teal shorts.

They really were horrendous; I don't even think they would be nice if he was wearing them on a beach, but we move.

I had the wine buzz. I always did when I drank red wine. It was a warm fuzzy feeling when you're not drunk, but you feel light and giddy.

I blew out the candles in the living room, turned off the TV, and headed into my bedroom. The fairy lights around the headboard on my bed glistened.

'Hold on I need to go and brush my teeth,' Jack said as he plugged his phone in to charge and sat it face down on the bedside.

'Erm, OK,' I called back, thinking that brushing my pearly whites was the last thing on my mind right now.

He pulled out a green toothbrush from his zipper pocket and headed to the bathroom.

At least he cared about his oral hygiene I supposed, but did he really just pull a toothbrush out his zipper?

Almost ten minutes later, he reappeared, put his toothbrush back in his pocket and jumped into bed beside me.

'I used your face stuff that was at the sink to wash my face.' He laughed.

'My Clinique face wash?' I said puzzled.

'Yeah, I just saw it and thought I would use it, feel how good my face feels!' He smiled taking my hand and rubbing it across his cheek.

So that's why he took fucking ages, what a bizarre thing to do.

Jumping into bed, we cuddled in and he spooned me and obviously you know what spooning leads to…

I opened my eyes in a sleepy daze to Jack kissing my neck and making his way round to my face. What time is it?

I was like a half-shut knife, was he really insinuating sex, right now?

Reaching over to my bedside, I looked at my phone, it was 3.30 in the fucking morning.

He really was insinuating a shag at this ungodly hour.

We had literally just done it, but OK…

I rolled over after our late-night session, and was confused to feel soaking wet sheets against my skin… I was lying in an absolute puddle of sweat.

What the hell?

It wasn't like we had done anything outrageous, but Jack seemed to be absolutely pishing sweat from head-to-toe. This wasn't normal.

'Maybe you should change your bottom sheet, it's wringing, and I think I'll go have a quick shower.' He panted.

At this time? It was half three in the bloody morning!? He was right though, the bed was absolutely soaked like I'd never seen before, it literally looked like someone had just hosed it down.

He headed to the bathroom, and I could hear the shower come to life.

I mean, I'd been with a few guys in my time, but never one that produced as much sweat as he did… weird.

Rubbing my sleepy eyes, I fixed the new bottom sheet to my king-size mattress and tossed the heavy wet sheet in the washing basket.

I couldn't quite believe I was doing this at this time in the morning but I was so tired that I just jumped straight back into bed and didn't even wait on him returning before falling back asleep.

It was the morning, and as I woke from my broken sleep, I could see Jack from the corner of my eye lying with his face in his phone.

'Morning,' I croaked.

'Good morning,' he said cheerily, sitting his phone down and pulling up the covers to bring me in for a cuddle.

I still had crust on my sleepy eyes when he started kissing me again and initiating round three?!

Again?

Who am I to say no to morning sex?

After the deed was done, I sat up to check my phone, it was only 7 a.m.

I was hardly ever awake at this time. I was so unbelievably tired, but I had to pull myself out of bed and get into the shower and wash away the three rounds of sins I'd committed in the last ten hours.

I stood and let the steamy water run over my head, massaging the soapy lather into my hair and assessed last night's events.

Does that guy actually ever sleep? I thought.

I never actually witnessed him sleeping at all last night, he's definitely superhuman… but again maybe that's something to do with being in the army?

Had we really had sex three times? That's a superhuman quality too… I wasn't really complaining but truth be told, I was fucking shattered.

I poured the piping hot water from the kettle into two mugs filled with heaped spoonfuls of coffee for us both, this should wake me up a bit.

With a towel wrapped around my freshly washed hair, I toddled over to pass it to him as he sat on the couch watching the morning news.

In an attempt to put some life into myself following my sleepless night, I gulped down my coffee, blow-dried my hair and got ready for the day.

I realised that before work I would have to drop Jack home first so I flicked on my mascara in a hurry.

'Just drop me here. That's fine, saves you turning and you can just go straight up that way,' Jack said, pointing over to the pavement.

'Aw honestly it's no bother,' I replied, secretly wanting to see what his house looks like.

'Naa it's fine, I'll just get out here,' he was quite adamant.

He kissed me quickly and pulled open the door and I headed off for work.

I had a weird feeling about everything that happened that morning and the night before, but again I told myself it was because he was a nice guy, who possibly just had an outrageously high sex drive, that I was doubting it, and I need to stop overthinking everything.

IT WAS THE work's big Christmas night out.

The week leading up to it, it was all we spoke about in the office.

'What you wearing?'

'Are you getting your make-up done?'

'What you doing your hair like?'

These types of conversations flew back and forth over our small office, to the point the guys started taking the piss out of us shouting over to each other, 'What you wearing Andy? Think I'll dig out my sequin dress!'

Sequins are a given for Christmas time, so are red lips and nails and sparkly eye shadow.

I'd bought a glittery gold and black midi dress especially for the occasion and I felt really good in it.

Christmas songs echoed in the festively decorated bar, the drinks were flowing, cocktails, shots, halves, and pints. We ran our company kitty money dry within a few hours and all chipped in again to get the rounds in.

I introduced my workies to Tequila Rose, and it really was going down a treat.

We were in the Slug and Lettuce on St Vincent Street, not my place of choice but it suited our mixed company.

Jack was also out in the town with his work that day, he had text me a few times throughout the night saying his do was shit and that he was dying to leave.

I told Jack I could maybe meet him later before I headed home, and he could come with.

Why don't I come meet you just now? xxx

I'm out with my work pals though! Plus, it's still early xxx

It was only about 9 p.m., we'd been out since 4 o'clock-ish, I was drunk but not like being out with the Spoon's drunk.

I had a text.

Yeah, that's fine, I don't mind meeting them xxx

WHAT?

This was only the third time I would have met him, surely, I can't bring him to my work's night out?

He was pretty adamant though, but this showed me that he was keen, it could only be a good thing, right?

I was a bit mortified telling the remaining of my workies that Jack, a guy I'd met from Tinder only three times, would be joining us on our WORK night out but they were too drunk to properly care.

Perching over the bar, I was ordering number God knows what, round of tequila shots when felt a pair of hands snake up my thigh and around my waist. It was him; he was really here.

233

I turned around and greeted him with a smile, he did look quite handsome, with a crisp pink shirt, jeans, smart tanned shoes and navy trench coat – a far cry from those bloody teal shorts.

He looked the part so I was more than happy to introduce him to my work wives Shirley and Stef.

'This is Jack,' I cheered as I shooed him over to our table.

Everyone smiled and said 'Hi' as I went around the table and rhymed everyone's names off to him.

He didn't look fazed at all, he looked more relaxed in fact.

Jack sat next to Shirley and Stef and began to engage in deep conversation with them, I turned my head to my other colleagues and started to neck my drink nervously.

After about half an hour, Jack excused himself to the toilet, and I took his absence to quiz my work mates on what they thought of my new 'acquaintance'.

'He seems nice,' Stef said, sipping her strawberry daiquiri.

'Yeah.' Shirley sighed, not so convinced.

'Yeah… what?' I piped up, slightly worried.

'I don't know there's just something about him, I can't quite put my finger on it.'

Shirley was usually always right about everything, but I ignored her uncertainty and put it down to the amount of alcohol she'd consumed.

Let's be honest, I was never going to marry the guy, but he would do for now.

Jack returned from the loo and we had more drinks. The general consensus of the night was that we'd get the last train home, by this point it was literally only me, Jack, Shirley and Stef left, everyone else had bowed out in dribs and drabs.

The four of us were all very drunk as we staggered to Glasgow Central Station for the last train back to Motherwell.

Shirley and Stef decided they wanted to go for a Burger King with just ten minutes to spare for a drunken scran, so Jack and I ditched them at the kiosk and headed to the train, I definitely didn't want to miss it and have to get a taxi.

Jack grabbed my hand and we made the mad dash to the carriage.

As clutched his hand back, I could feel that hideous pinky ring rub beneath my finger, it was still as awful as I initially remembered it.

Like some sort of Christmas miracle, Shirley and Stef made it by the skin of their teeth into the packed train, clutching their brown Burger King bags and giggling like a pair of schoolgirls.

Jack and I got up from our seats to give them both somewhere to sit and eat their burgers and we moved over to the side of the door and squashed together into the corner.

I looked at Jack standing there, looking all dashing in his smart coat and I smiled, you know, maybe this could be something.

Could it? Or was this just the alcohol talking again? I know how much it deceived me…

Back at Motherwell, we waved off Shirley and Stef as they bumped into people they knew at the station and decided to head to the Tavern for 'one for the road'.

The Tavern is a nice wee pub just around the corner from the station, it's actually quite near Skoosh too but I definitely wasn't going there with him, I still had PTSD from being there after the Fringe. Anyway, the Tavern's got a good atmosphere, better than some of the other shit-holes tucked into the corners of the ML1.

Jack and I ended up ordering Jager bombs, before the bar man rang the bell for last orders, so we got a vodka each, tanned it and headed for a taxi.

The pair of us staggered up the stairs to my flat giggling and kissing at every landing stop.

I hung from his neck as we spun in circles occasionally banging into the brick wall. God if my neighbour, Gordon, saw us, he would've been mortified but I didn't care, Jack was really growing on me and now he had met my work pals, it seemed to be going in the right direction.

Like I've mentioned before, drunken sex always seems to be the best because you don't really give a fuck, so much so that, by this point, I began to wonder if Gordon downstairs could hear my bed squeak vigorously.

Even though we didn't get in until maybe 1 a.m., I was once again woken up at 4 a.m. by Jack to do it again. I mean, I love a good shag as much as the next person, but I also love my sleep. Why does he keep doing that?

Should I really be complaining about a guy who just wants to have sex all the time?

I continued to see Jack every week, Caitlin and I branded our meetings Wine Thursdays since all we used to do was drink red wine and shag.

Occasionally, Jack would bring over pizza for us or something else to eat, which was cool but on a Friday in work I was always shattered because I got no sleep on Wine Thursdays because every single time, I got a 4 a.m. wake-up call.

I didn't ever see Jack at the weekend because I always had plans and to be fair, so did he.

Jack was turning thirty a few days after Christmas and I was stuck in this dilemma, do I buy him a birthday present or not?

I liked him, but I didn't like him enough to buy him anything crazy expensive and we hadn't been seeing each other that long so I turned to the girls in the work for advice.

'What the Tinder date you brought to the work night oot?' My boss Bob teased as I toyed with the idea with parting with my hard-earned cash for a gift for a guy I had only been seeing for a month.

'Yeah, that's the one, I don't know what to do.'

I still hadn't lived down the fact that I brought a date to my work Christmas do, but I decided to embrace it anyway.

After much deliberation me and my colleagues decided that just a minding would be fine.

Jack and I shared a love for Hendricks gin, so I picked him up the gift set that came with a wee teacup. I also picked him up a men's Clinique skincare set since he always used mine when he stayed over and as a laugh I bought him a set of cheap fairy lights for his house when it's done because he always said the ones wrapped around my bed posts were daft.

Jack told me he had ripped his house apart, tore up floorboards and knocked down walls, he was doing a full renovation and often sent me progress pics, or lack of.

It did look a mess and that's why he always came to my house because his was a building site which was covered in dust, or so he said.

It was one week until Christmas, I was sitting in work when Jack text me asking how my day was.

It was a pretty slow day news wise so there wasn't a lot going on.

He said he was out shopping and sent me a picture of his purchases.

Jack said he and his sister were very close and she'd been through a hard time recently, he didn't really say why but that she needed cheering up.

Alongside a picture of a Gucci gift bag Jack messaged me saying, 'I'm the best brother ever'.

Oh my God, he bought his sister a Gucci belt? Me and my brother Jonny give each other a tenner in a card each Christmas if even that, so I was pretty gobsmacked that he spent that much.

The one thing that really ticked me off about Jack was that he always bragged about having money, I really disliked it.

He was always asking how much money I earned a month, and what my salary was, I never told him exactly because I thought it was a bit rude and also, none of his fucking business.

However, he always made sure that I knew he had money, even going as far as to show me his bank balance and payslips.

One night we were sitting on my couch sipping the 'devil's wine' when he showed me his bank account with £25,000 in it.

I don't know if he expected me to be impressed but if anything, it did the complete opposite.

It's never about money for me, never has been and never will be.

When I went out with Dean, money was no object, he didn't have a bean to rub together and neither did I, I loved him for him not for his money or lack of.

It was another 'Wine Thursday' and as we sat on the couch together, I reached behind the arm of the couch and pulled out a green gift bag and passed it to Jack.

He went a bit red in the face, I don't think he expected me to get him anything but seemed pleased with the daft bits that I bought him and even laughed out loud when he pulled out the box of fairy lights.

'For when your house is all done up!' I joked.

'Aye, that'll be right! It'll be a manly house! Thank you though, that was really kind of you,' he added, kissing my red wine lips.

I saw him the day after his birthday as he went out for dinner with his family. I saw the pictures on Instagram of him huddled around a cake with his nieces and nephew at that Cook and Indi's World Buffet in Motherwell, which surprised me as I didn't think people still went there, never mind have their 30th birthday dinner in it but each to their own I suppose.

'How was your birthday then? What did you get?' I asked taking a large gulp of my wine.

But before I'd even taken the glass back from my lips, I had to pick my jaw up off the floor when he pulled back his sleeve and revealed a chunky gold chain dangling from his wrist.

What the fuck is that? I thought.

'My mum got me this, it's nice, isn't it?' He smiled showing it off like a proud dad to a newborn baby.

This was the type of thing you saw total bam pots wear or like Mr T. It was fucking horrendous, and my face couldn't hide it.

The pinky ring was bad enough but a matching gold BRACELET?

Fuck me.

NEW YEAR CAME and I went to my pal's for a party as usual.

My school friends, the 'Gals Gals Gals', always spent New Year together it was like a tradition where we'd all unite along with partners if you had one and congregate in the pub and then back to one of our houses.

This year, we went to the Jack Daniels, our local, and brought in the bells there.

It was a brilliant night, we drank copious amounts of booze and welcomed in the New Year.

10, 9, 8, 7, 6, 5, 4, 3, 2, 1…

HAPPY NEW YEAR!

We kissed and hugged each other as the bagpipes imploded the room, many rejoiced with joyful cheers and drunkenly slurred about how good the year ahead of us would be. And I did too, I had a really good feeling about 2019.

My next thought turned to Jack.

He had gone to the Edinburgh Street party with his pals to enjoy the famous celebrations in the capital.

So, I text him, one minute after midnight.

Happy New Year J! Hope you've had a good night. I'll see you tomorrow xxxx

Happy New Year to you too! Yeah, it's been really good! See you soon xxxxx

I smiled at the thought of a new year and a new start and also that I would be spending New Year's Day slobbing out with him.

Maybe this would be the year that I settled down and had a boyfriend. Jodie was getting married, maybe I would finally have a plus one for her wedding?

I was the only single bridesmaid out of all six of us so it was a running joke with us that I was on a mission to be coupled before the big day.

I know I'd previously written off Jack for the pinky ring, the bracelet, the shorts and also the smallest hands in the world, but was he really that bad?

After bringing in the bells in JD's, we drank about four more rounds of drinks before staggering back to the after party at one of our houses.

This year we went to Samantha's, she'd not long moved in with her boyfriend Craig, and the year before we went to mine, so I was off the hook for after party duties.

We were all absolutely steaming drunk, as you would expect on New Year's Eve. It got to the point in the early hours maybe about 4 a.m., we all started dropping like flies and when Elton John's 'Your Song' started playing, that's when I knew it was time to go home.

I had drunk so much that I knew a spew was coming my way, my stomach was churning like a washing machine on the spin setting and I just wanted my bed, or my toilet to hang my head over.

I called a taxi, but the girl on the phone told me it would be a two-hour wait.

TWO HOURS? I couldn't hold on that long, I tried a few other companies who said the same thing.

Fuck.

I rubbed my head, feeling the hang-over set in already, I needed to go home, and I needed to go home now.

Before I left for the pub that night, I stuffed a pair of flip-flops into my clutch bag knowing fine well we'd have to stoat to an after party and that my 6-inch Steve Maddens weren't going to make it easy to do so.

I was certain that if I told my pals I was going to walk home at this ridiculous hour on my own, they would try to stop me. Half of them had fallen asleep on top of each other on the couch and the rest were absolutely destroying whatever song came next on Samantha's Spotify playlist, so I decided to slip away quietly to avoid being lectured about walking home on my own.

The cold January air pinched my nose as I began my journey into the darkness of the early morning.

The bitterness of the air nipped my toes as my flip-flops padded along the icy pavement beneath me. I tucked my heels under the arm of my coat and headed off on the half an hour walk home.

The streets were quiet, with a few muffled laughs in the distance of drunks making their way home from whatever party they'd been to.

I walked past Mega Bar, a nightclub I spent many weekends in when I was in my sixth year at school, and it was now empty. They shut up shop a few years ago due to no one going anymore.

I smiled as I reminisced about all the times, I'd stood at the front door with someone else's ID praying that the bouncer didn't question the unlikeness of my picture.

I'd even gone as far as to remember my false star sign in case the bouncer tried to catch me out, oh to be young again!

I let out a giggle as I remembered the time that me and Shanice got thrown out for being too drunk and sat at the bus stop outside eating chips and curry.

That place, as much as it was a total dive, held so many fond memories of my early adulthood.

Continuing on my journey home, I walked up past the Indian Villa and noticed my phone only had about 3% battery. As I quickly checked my filled inbox to see the many Happy New Year messages, a shadow caught the corner of my eye and I looked up to see a guy walking towards me.

I moved to the side a bit to let him past, but his shoulder brushed mine ever so slightly.

'You OK?' he muttered, taking me by surprise.

'Yeah, thanks,' I said as I scurried past him.

I continued walking and so did he.

It was a bit strange, but I assumed he was just a drunk being polite.

I walked for a further ten minutes, taking in all that happened that night.

My stomach was brewing up a hearty spew, I could feel it simmering away.

Walking faster as the cold of the January night stung my body, I was just desperate to get home and put my head straight down the toilet.

I was now about ten minutes from my house when I heard a voice shout from behind me.

'Do you want me to walk you home?'

Confused, I turned to find the same guy who had brushed past me ten minutes before, now walking in my direction.

I froze on the spot.

Without even realising that I was doing it, I clutched at my heels in case I needed to use them as defence, the size of them surely could do some significant damage.

Why had he turned around?

I examined his face. Did I know him?

The man in question wore glasses, was maybe in his late thirties, and had dirty thinning hair.

I tried to remember as many details about him as possible in case I would speak to the police later, God, I really was thinking about the worst.

I'd seen this on *Crimewatch* before, so I tried to remember as much as possible.

A pale grey 'jail tracksuit' hung off his tall skinny frame, and as he took long strides towards me, I felt a shudder run down my spine, I wasn't sure if it was the cold air or the fear of not knowing what was about to happen.

'No, thank you,' I said politely as my heart thumped beneath my satin black dress.

'Where do you stay? Where's your boyfriend?' he asked.

'What? No thanks.' I stuttered, starting to walk briskly ahead.

'C'meer, you. I'm talking to you.' He snarled.

By this point I was frightened, shaking in fact.

'No. Please go away.' I could feel my voice start to crack.

As if in slow motion, or what seemed like it to me, he reached out to put his hands on my shoulders to grab me and I quickly thrust away in front of him.

'NO!' I screamed as I began to cross the road in a desperate bid to get away from this frightening stranger.

He crossed the road too, and I felt sick, the sick that was brewing earlier on might just be making an appearance earlier than anticipated. I tripped over my flip-flop…

14. Radio Silence

I stumbled a bit as my flip-flop got stuck in a dip in the road beneath me, but I managed to hold my balance and not fall over.

I felt the bile rise in my throat, that awful sour taste washed over the whole of my mouth and nipped my tongue.

Panic was really setting in, I was shaking with fear.

I fought the natural urge to wretch, I couldn't be sick now, because being sick makes you vulnerable… a position I really couldn't afford to be at this moment in time.

It was all happening so fast.

Where did he come from?

This creep was right behind me, and the thoughts running through my head were absolutely wild.

I thought of news headlines like the type I wrote about in work.

'WOMAN ATTACKED AFTER NYE PARTY'

'GIRL RAPED ON WAY HOME FROM NYE CELEBRATIONS'

'MURDERED ON DOORSTEP'

The words rang in my head as I wondered which one I was going to be.

I decided to bolt across the road again, in an attempt to escape my would-be attacker when, as if by some perfectly timed miracle, a car pulled around the corner.

'KIRSTEN?! GET FUCKING OFF HER!'

This person clearly knew me, but I didn't care who it was. I ran over to the black Fiesta and rattled the locked handle until I gained entry.

The creep ran and scarpered into the darkness.

I couldn't breathe, my body shook violently.

I was having a panic attack.

'It's OK, you're OK, what happened?'

I looked up at the driver, I knew his face.

Then it dawned on me.

It was a guy called Jamie who I used to run about with a while back ago but hadn't seen him in over seven years.

Words failed me, I couldn't speak, I was breathing faster than I ever had before in my life, my chest was tight, and my heart felt like was going to explode out of my low-cut dress.

'I... I... t-t-t-taxi... w-w-walked... he... f-f-f-followed,' I tried, before bursting into a flood of tears.

I was hysterical.

'Where do you stay? I'll take you home.'

Jamie had always been a nice guy, always looking out for others, and I can't believe at the moment I needed someone, anyone, he just happened to be my knight and shining armour.

Someone was definitely looking over me that night.

I sat in Jamie's car for about 15 minutes until I came out of my state of shock.

He parked up outside my house and we talked for a bit, and I explained everything that happened.

'You should never have walked home on your own! That was stupid Kirsten.'

'I know it was, I'll not be doing it again.'

'I don't drink, so here's my number, if you ever need a lift just phone me and don't be bloody walking again!'

'I won't, I promise, thanks so much Jamie, you literally saved me.'

'Any time. Take care!'

I gave him a tight hug, I was so thankful for what he had just done for me, I owed him big time.

Jamie and I were good pals, I'm sure we winched a few times when we were about fourteen but after that we just realised we were better off as friends.

I couldn't believe he spotted my struggle and stopped to help.

As I shut the entry door to the flat over, I let out a sigh of relief as I heard the lock click into place.

I was safe.

Every step I took up the stairs was slow, as the thoughts spun in my head of what could have happened to me earlier on.

Could I be lying in the ditch outside the underpass?

Or worse?

Could I be dead?

I couldn't stop thinking about it, or the impeccable timing of Jamie's arrival, it was absolutely unbelievable.

I climbed into bed still in my dress.

The earlier events had sobered me up but still left a sicky feeling in my stomach. I lay on my crisp white bedsheets and the room spun around me and seconds later I ran to the toilet and relieved the expected spew.

I grabbed the spare basin from under the sink, bought specifically for hang-overs, and retired once again to bed, I felt broken.

My phone buzzed.

I was woken by the vibration of it against my glass unit, it continued to buzz until I had no option but to check it.

It was twelve noon, and I had about sixty messages and three missed calls.

One was from Jamie, asking how I was.

About six of them were from Jack and the rest of them were from my Gals Gals Gals group chat, my mum and the Spoon's and Jodie group chat.

I couldn't even find the energy to explain my ordeal to them all just now, so I tucked my phone under my pillow and went back to sleep.

When I eventually told people what had happened, everyone was angry at me.

My mum, my friends, and Jack.

'How could you be so bloody stupid, Kirsten? You could have been killed!' Pam screeched down the phone to me.

'I know, I'm sorry.'

Kirsten! Why did you walk? You could have stayed at mine no problem! Please don't do that again! Samantha said, when I told the group chat the whole story.

And Jack wasn't best pleased either.

'Anything could have happened to you! If I was there, I would have killed the fucker.'

I rolled my eyes.

Would he though? That specky guy would have probably annihilated Jack but it was nice to know he cared.

What annoyed me most though was really was it my fault?

Why couldn't I walk home in my hometown? The place I'd lived since I was born?

It's OK for men to walk home, so why not women?

Even though I was angry that I was getting a hard time about it, I still promised that I wouldn't do it again.

That night, Jack came over to mine as promised.

I couldn't even face a wine with him though like we usually did, I was too ill.

My stomach was in absolute tatters, I couldn't even bear the thought of the steak pie that my mum had first footed me with either.

In all honesty, I just wanted to curl up and go to sleep.

It was nice to have someone to have hang-over cuddles with though, we lazed about all afternoon and even fell asleep on the couch.

I enjoyed the fact that having Jack was like having a boyfriend, without the grief.

He just slotted into my life when I wanted (mostly a Thursday) and that suited me to a T.

Things were fine, I was happy enough to keep doing what we were doing and so was he, or so I thought.

IT WAS A Saturday towards the end of January. I was so skint after Christmas and the several nights out that came with it, so I offered to do an overtime shift in at our Glasgow office.

The money was good and it kept me out of the pub.

Jack had text me saying he was out for breakfast at a local café.

He sent me a picture of his full English in a bid to make me jealous as I'd started my 'January diet' like everyone else.

Looks good! What's your plans for the rest of the day then? xx

I finished my shift at five and had still heard nothing back from Jack.

Not. A. Peep.

That's weird, he was usually pretty quick at replying.

A few hours turned into a few days, and a few days turned into three weeks.

Total radio silence.

What had I done wrong?

It surprised me at how unbothered I was by Jack's actual absence, I'd been seeing him since November and now it was the first week in February.

I wasn't missing him, but if he wasn't feeling whatever it was that we had, he could have just said.

That week, I went to a spin class with my pal Heather. We had made it a regular thing and I was actually really enjoying trying to shift that festive podge that most people got over Christmas.

The sweat was pishing off me as I jumped off the bike and picked up my keys and phone from the floor, I clicked the lock screen, to see I had a text from Jack.

Hey, sorry I've not been in touch. I've been busy with other stuff to be honest like mega important stuff x

That's it?

I was fucking pissed off because he could have at least been a bit more apologetic and come up with a better excuse.

So I replied, short and snappy.

OK then.

One minute later my phone buzzed again.

My mum has a lump in her stomach and has been to the doctors and stuff so we're waiting on a scan.

Fuck. Now I feel bad.

I'm sorry to hear that… Is she OK? You should've just said that though, rather than dropping off the face of the earth.

Seconds later…

Dunno waiting on a scan.

He was cold. I knew something wasn't right.

If that was the case, you would've just said, 'Listen, I've got stuff going on at the minute,' or something along those lines, but to go completely off the radar after sending me a picture of a full English breakfast? It's just odd.

After that, he explained that he had been let down by builders and other tradesman for his house, so that was also stressing him out, but again, just fucking say that.

I don't know why, but this situation totally flicked a switch on with me and I had my guard up.

He was hiding something from me and I knew it.

I decided to keep him at arm's length but he didn't appear to get the hint.

I missed you if I'm honest. Want to hang out on Thursday? xx

He wants to 'hang out' now?

After going MIA for three weeks?

Any normal girl would've just told him to fuck off, but because, as we know, I'm not a 'normal girl', of course, I said yes.

I was bored and wasn't talking to anyone else, the same reason as all my bad decisions, but this confirmed for me that I didn't like him, I just liked the company.

Jack told me that he was heading to Newcastle the next day to see one of his friends from the army and would be back for Thursday and couldn't wait to see me.

He text me the whole time he was away, saying him and his pal were heading out for dinner, and even sent me a picture of their dinner receipt to show how much red wine they ordered.

Jammy bastard, wish it was me! I thought.

I was looking forward to seeing him again though, it was a lonely few weeks, I needed some form of attention.

He came over that Thursday and it was nice, he told me all about his trip and what him and his pal got up to, and again all the stories about his house and how the builders were giving him grief and it was going to take a lot longer than he initially thought.

'I can't wait to see it all done!' I said, reassuring him that it wouldn't be long.

I wouldn't see Jack the following Thursday because it was Valentine's Day which fell on a Thursday which meant Celtic were playing in the Europa League against Valencia which Caitlin and I arranged to go to together.

Since we'd be together, Caitlin and I said we'd celebrate 'Galentine's Day' instead and go to the football, drink pints, and live our best single gal lives.

I say single, because Jack didn't even wish me a happy Valentine's Day so that really told me where I stood with us, plus after his little disappearing act, it was fine by me.

If you're not in a relationship, being single on Valentine's Day is awful.

It's hard to see Instagram and Facebook flooded with girls posting soppy tributes and sharing the bouquets of red roses they get delivered to their workplaces.

It just made me feel like utter shite if I'm honest but in order to keep our minds off it, we headed into Glasgow straight after work.

Caitlin and I went to a wee pub next to Celtic Park called the Real McCoy before the game and drank pints of venom (venom is a drink of spirits and bad decisions in my opinion, no good decision is ever made after you drink one) before heading in to Parkhead to watch our team beat Valencia 2 – 0.

It was an amazing night and since we were in the celebrating mood, we decided to head into the city centre after for more drinks after the game. Plus given the day, any single guys would be out drinking so maybe we'd get a few phone numbers, we usually did when we went to the football.

Heading back out through a sea of green and white, we managed to grab an Uber with two guys we bumped into that Caitlin knew from school and headed to an Irish bar called Malones in the city centre.

We heard there was a live singer on until late, so it was perfect. Absolutely no fucks were given that we had work the next day, we were out to have a good time.

I quickly chuffed a fag before we went up the stairs into the crowded bar filled with a green flurry of happy Celtic fans, when my heart stopped beating for what felt like a lifetime.

Chris.

There he was standing in the corner with his pals holding a pint.

Oh my God. I didn't think I would see him again.

And before I could make an Irish exit (literally), we clocked eyes and he smiled.

'Look who it isn't!' he said, reaching his arms out to give me a hug.

Caitlin looked at me, giving me the 'Is that him?' eyes.

I quickly introduced him, and Caitlin held no prisoners.

'Oh, Chris. I've heard a lot about you.' Caitlin sighed.

'All good I hope?' he said taking a sip of his pint.

'Mmm… not quite. Are you thee Mr Water Jug?'

His face went red, he obviously hadn't admitted to his friends about his 'romantic' gesture and just laughed it off.

We stood for a while chatting about the game and Caitlin spoke to his pal.

'Want to go outside for a fag?', he asked nudging me with his elbow.

'Yeah, OK.'

Caitlin wasn't a smoker and every time we were out, she didn't fancy going outside into the cold to watch me clog up my lungs.

I nodded and he led the way.

We stepped out into the cold February air, and I pulled a packet of bashed cigarettes from my bag.

'How's things been?' he asked as he leant on the wall beside me.

'Yeah, great, really good. What about you?', me again with another lie.

I wasn't really great, or really good. I hadn't gotten over our two month 'situationship' which ended over seven months ago, but he didn't need to know that.

'Yeah, I've been good. I've missed you though', he whispered as he held a lighter up to the cigarette hanging off my lips.

Aw fuck. Here we go, here he was in my life again for two minutes and already pulling at my heart strings.

After I inhaled my first draw and let the smoke escape from my lips, he leant in, and again, just like that first night in Citation, he kissed me.

And muggins here, of course, kissed him back without a second thought – I told you, no good decisions happen when you've been drinking venoms.

The butterflies were back. The feelings were back although I'm not even sure they'd gone anywhere in the first place, but they were here again and more intense than ever.

Pulling away, realising that it was pretty grim to be winching while smoking, we finished our cigarettes and went back inside where I was met by Caitlin and her 'what have you been doing' eyes.

That girl can say a lot just by giving you a certain look and that's why I love her. She was always honest, even if the truth hurt.

We drank some more, sang along to Celtic songs, and of course, tanned more tequila.

Caitlin suggested that we go and get a kebab before getting a taxi home and considering the state that the two of us were in after drinking since 5 p.m., that was a good idea.

I turned to Chris and said goodbye.

'We're going to go get food and grab an Uber home. Was nice to see you.'

'Aw, we were just going to do the same, we will get you down.' He smiled before knocking back the dregs of his pint.

Great. He's coming with… he better not try anything funny.

So, Caitlin, me, Chris, and his two pals sauntered down Sauchiehall Street.

Caitlin even ended up on one of the guy's shoulders, the other pal wandered off ahead to phone his girlfriend to tell her he would be home soon, and Chris and I tailed behind everyone.

We stopped and kissed a few times and again, I felt the feelings I felt back in April last year, but at the same time, I felt sad. Sad because I knew deep down, I wasn't what he was looking for.

He asked if he could come back to my house and stay, and I declined.

I had work the next day and in general I just didn't think it was a good idea because we bumped into each other by chance, not by choice.

We found ourselves outside 'Best Kebab', if you're from Glasgow you'll know all about this place, I'll say no more.

Caitlin was willing to dice with her health for the sake of some chips and cheese and I waited outside with Chris as she ordered.

We kissed a few more times outside the kebab shop as classy as ever and Chris asked once more if he could come back to mine.

After politely declining, our taxi pulled up outside and I thought that once again, I was closing the door on my Chris chapter.

Guilt riddled me the next day, but I liked Chris way more than I liked Jack and I couldn't help how I felt.

Jack had been texting me throughout the game too, but after a few pints, I didn't really care at all.

But in order to make myself feel a little better, I kept reminding myself that Jack didn't even get me anything for Valentine's Day so that spoke volumes.

I just tried to forget about it all.

A few days after that, Jack and I were texting when he said, 'Can I ask you something?'

Oh my God, he must know!? I thought in a panic.

But my heart rate came back down ever so slightly, when Jack asked me the question every girl dreads.

How many people have you slept with?

Aw fuck.

Why do guys want to know this information? Why is it relevant?

I told him a number, not the real number, but a number, and he didn't make me feel good about myself at all.

Really? I can count mine on one hand, so less than you, he replied.

One hand? Five or less?

That's kind of unheard of for a guy, I was actually quite shocked.

Not that it's any of his fucking business how many people I'd been with, I'm not embarrassed by it in the slightest but the fact that he was trying to make me feel worse because he had slept with less people than my fake body count.

Jack had told me a while ago that he'd booked to go to Mexico with his family in March and that he would be missing the Old Firm game, you know, the one that just happened to fall on my birthday?

'You want my season tickets to go? That can be your birthday present from me,' he said one night as we sat down to our usual glass of wine.

'Oh my God, really? That would be amazing!' I said, excited for another big day oot with Caitlin.

'Are you sure? Do none of your pals want it?' I added, the tickets were really hard to get.

'Na, they've all got tickets, so I'll give them to you.'

Old Firm tickets are like gold dust, and unless you have a season ticket, they're almost impossible to get a hold of.

I told Caitlin that I managed to get my hands on them for us and she couldn't believe it either.

'From Jack? Radio silence guy? He gave you his tickets for the game? He must really like you!'

I wasn't so sure about that, but I was grateful that he gave me them.

It was the last 'Wine Thursday' before he left for Mexico.

The way it worked out, he would only be home for three days then I was away out to Singapore to see Rosie, so this would probably the last time I would see him for over a month.

He brought over a wee feast for us.

Two bottles of 'devil's wine', a Marks and Spencer pizza, crackers, hummus, and cheese.

The way to every girl's heart, through her belly.

We both got quite drunk that night as we tanned every drop from the two bottles of wine. I was pretty drunk that I even tripped over my own two feet and scaled my glass over my grey carpet which left a huge stain, which is probably still there now.

But it was nice just to let our hair down, knowing fine well that we wouldn't see each other for a few weeks.

As always, that night, or should I say that early morning, I got my 4 a.m. wake-up call and again before work.

We had coffee and toast in bed that morning and watched the news, it was like we were a normal couple doing normal things, except shagging at ridiculous hours of the morning.

It was still early so I didn't need to get ready for a while yet.

'Oh, before I go, here's the season tickets!' he said, grabbing his Louis Vuitton wallet from the bedside table and handing me the two green cards.

'Thanks so much for that, I'll see you before I go to give you them back,' I said kissing him.

We cuddled in bed for a bit before I waved him off at the door and that was it, he was off to Mexico tomorrow and I was off to the fitba.

It was the morning of my birthday, a Sunday and Old Firm day.

Every 'Old Firm' match falls on a Sunday, I think, to supposedly minimise the drinking, so fans don't overdo it and cause riots.

Caitlin decided to drive this day and since it was my birthday, I was going all out.

I downed a bottle of rosé wine before we even set foot in the stadium for the twelve noon kick off, which was definitely a bad idea.

Speaking of bad ideas, on top of that, I even tucked a hip flask filled to the brim with vodka down the side of my padded bra and drank every drop before half time.

I waited on the 'Happy Birthday' text from Jack, but it never did arrive.

He had text me a few times when he was in Mexico showing off his fancy hotel and the incredible view from his balcony, it did look amazing but then after that it was radio silence once again.

What's this guy's problem?

I was really pissed off. I hadn't heard from Jack at all that day, but it was my fucking birthday, how long did it take to type out 'happy birthday' and hit the send button? There was absolutely no excuse.

I also noticed that Jack had posted on Instagram that day a picture of him at the beach wearing a Celtic top, so by this point I was fuelled with wine and hadn't made any terrible decisions so far and decided to write on his picture.

Looks amazing! Cheers for the tickets again!

But I heard nothing back.

One person who did message me on a happy birthday, was Chris, much to my surprise.

Just as we were walking into the stadium, I opened the birthday message from him and replied to him asking if he was heading to the game too, he said he was, and I said I might see him after.

Chris, who I hadn't seen in months had text me, and Jack, who I had been seeing for months, hadn't and for me that spoke volumes.

As we walked up the stairs to our seats, a few rows in front of me was a guy I'd met years ago and had slept with (way before Dean's time) and he noticed me and gave me a cuddle.

'How ye doing?'

'Aye, good thanks, steaming right enough! How are you?

'Aye, not bad thanks. Happy birthday by the way!'

'Aw, cheers!'

I had this guy on Facebook, so he had obviously seen that it was my birthday, which was nice of him, eh?

The sun was shining over Celtic Park, the game was brilliant, we ended up winning 2-1 so it was cause for double celebrations all round, for the score and also for turning twenty-five.

Caitlin wasn't so keen on going out after and said she'd take me wherever I wanted to go so I text Chris and he said he was in a sports bar round the corner from where we had our first date.

I told Caitlin to take me there.

'Are you sure? Maybe you should go home? You're pished, hen!'

'It's my birthdaaaaaay. Take me there, driver!'

She rolled her eyes and started up the engine.

Looking back the sensible thing would have been to have gone home but it was only 3 p.m., the night was still young, in fact, it wasn't even night yet.

Reluctantly, Caitlin dropped me where Chris was, with all his work mates, but I didn't care at all, I swanned in there as bold as brass obviously due to the wine and vodka giving me the confidence boost that I would not have had sober.

He introduced me to his pals just as Kirsten. They were all pleasant enough and one even offered me a drink.

We knocked back a few more drinks in the sports bar and then ended up moving to my favourite Irish bar, Grace's which was literally around the corner.

Let me tell you about Grace's. It's the best Irish bar in Glasgow with live music, and venoms by the pint but at £12 a pop, they weren't cheap.

Every time I've been to Grace's I've had a great time, but I've made some terrible decisions after drinking in there and today was no different.

It was just me and Chris by this point and about 200 delighted Celtic fans.

Jack never crossed my mind once.

At the bar, I bought four pints of venoms and swiped my contactless card to pay for them along with two tequilas – for old times' sake.

In my drunken state, I was also texting another guy that I'd matched with on Tinder that day, telling him to come meet me in this bar, even though I was with Chris – I'm not sure who the fuck I thought I was, but it was very bold, even for me.

Forgetting about him, I shoved my phone back in my bag and ordered in more drinks.

Chris and I met some randoms that we palled about with for the rest of the night and I'm pretty sure (my memory is very hazy) that me and him were winching in the middle of the pub, again, like old times.

He didn't say he missed me this time or anything like that because I would have remembered that, but we just chatted about the football and drank.

Really the only thing we had in common now.

We must have been there until about 7 p.m. and I told him that WE were leaving.

I booked a taxi, God knows how, by this point I was miraculous, and we headed back to mine.

I don't even remember the taxi home to be honest, I obviously hadn't remembered that it had been about three weeks since I last visited Lisa, so I definitely had 'almost grains', not a good look but I was so drunk I didn't give a fuck.

I remember kissing him on the couch, we were both absolutely sozzled, so it wasn't even passionate it was more of that fumbling about way, but I remember we ended up going into my room, and of course, without a doubt, we had sex.

Something felt different this time and I could feel it even in my drunken state, not about the sex as it was just average but about the connection between us, he was different now, colder and the spark was absent.

I really don't know how I could sense this as, my God, I was the drunkest I think I've ever been in my life.

Once the deed was done, I got off him and lay there naked before dosing off…

I WAS SCARED to even open my eyes. Because I knew right away that I was going to be sick.

My stomach churned and my head was splitting like no hangover I'd ever experienced before, it's hard to believe I know.

I lifted my head from the pillow and turned to see Chris, naked beside me.

I had deja vu because this wasn't my first rodeo…

Oh fuck, what have I done?

I shut my eyes again for a minute and scanned my brain to try to remember what level of stupidity had taken place that night.

I remember the football, Caitlin dropping me off, the bar, Grace's, the venoms, booking a taxi then not much else after that.

I looked at my phone. 8.45 a.m. Fucking hell, I was supposed to be working in fifteen minutes. Fuck, fuck, FUCK!

I got up and sat on the edge of the bed and put my head in my hands and I heard Chris stir behind me.

Clearly hung-over too.

'You OK?'

'No,' I replied too frightened to open my mouth in case spew escaped.

It was about as much as I could manage.

'I'm going to need to phone in sick. I can't go in like this,' I added, rubbing my forehead.

Now, here's the problem…

I'd previously asked for this day off as a holiday which was rejected and now I was going to have to phone in sick – they were going to know I was hung-over.

There was no way I could drive. Drive? There was no way I could be a professional today. I was fucked – mentally and physically, in all aspects.

'Yeah, I'll need to do the same,' he croaked.

Before I could say anything back to him, I got up from the bed and ran to the bathroom to be sick and it was the worst spew of my life, again pure yellow bile from the lining of my stomach because I didn't have anything to eat at all yesterday except half a pie at the football, it was no wonder I felt the way I did.

The sick didn't stop, it was pure green, like the venoms I'd been putting away one after the other like it was my last day on earth, part of me wished this day was my last on earth because I felt beyond horrific.

I think I was still drunk because I staggered back to my room and bounced off the walls in the hall with my glass of water going all over the carpet.

Back in my room, I sat down on the edge of my bed and looked at my phone.

I had sixty-four messages, five missed calls, about 100 Facebook notifications and the rest but not a single one from Jack.

It was just about to turn nine, so I told Chris I was going to have go into the living room to phone my boss and tell him I wouldn't be in.

He asked me to bring through his phone which was in there, it must have fallen out his pocket when his clothes were being ripped off.

I was nervous, I'd never phoned in sick before, ever so I didn't even really know what to say.

It rang and after about three rings someone picked up, it was Shirley – fuck!

'Hi, Shirley, is Bob there?'

'Eh… yeah, sure.'

Ah Jesus, even Shirley knows I'm still fucking pissed, this isn't going to go down well.

'Hello?'

'Hi, Bob, it's Kirsten. Listen I'm really sorry, I'm not going to be in today, I can't stop being sick since yesterday. I'm so sorry.'

There was a silence.

The fear was creeping in on me from all angles. I couldn't handle this, my palms sweated as I waited to hear his response.

'Oh, OK. We'll see you tomorrow then. Get well soon. Drink plenty of water.'

He knew. I was already riddled with dread for going into the office tomorrow.

Had I really just done that?

It was better to be off sick than to go in drunk.

I sat on the couch for a minute and re-evaluated my life.

It's done, forget about it for now and worry about it tomorrow, I told myself.

As I stood up I looked around at the trail of clothes on the floor.

My bra, his jeans and the contents of his pockets sprawled out on the floor, two Celtic scarves and trainers all scattered between the hall and the couch.

I looked for his phone among the pile of belongings to take in to him, and there it was sitting face down on the arm of the couch.

As I picked it up it was ringing in my hand.

Incoming call from Laura...

I stared at the phone, who is Laura?

When the call stopped ringing, I noticed that she'd tried to call him seven times.

I was confused and then it hit me, Laura was the new me.

The morning phone calls, it had to be.

My heart sank, but not as much as I thought it would. I knew things weren't the same between us but it still hurt to know there was someone else on the scene.

The palm of my hand sweated as I clutched the phone tighter.

Getting up from the floor, I staggered once again back into the room and chucked his phone on the bed.

'There you go,' I said sternly.

He sat up and looked at his screen and it wasn't long before he went chalk white.

His tune quickly changed.

'Maybe I should just go into work late or something. I feel bad.'

He was a terrible liar. He didn't feel bad about the work, he felt bad that he had a fucking girlfriend and was in someone else's bed.

I decided not to ask him anything about it because quite frankly my headache was extreme already without this added drama.

We lay in the bed on our phones, and you could literally cut the atmosphere with a knife.

He knew that I knew, and the guilt was ripping from him.

'Do you think you'd be able to give me a lift home in about an hour?' he asked quietly.

'Yeah, you'll need to give me time to sober up though, I'm in no fit state to drive right now.'

Looking back, I should have told him to get his shit and get a fucking taxi, but I just couldn't.

In an attempt to 'sober up' I went for a shower.

I stood under the hot tap and just stared at the floor, I felt so sick I could faint. I held on to the wall and let the water run over my hair which smelt like a fucking ashtray, and I cried silently as the water ran over my face and ran last night's mascara all down my cheeks.

My heart hurt. Again.

Here I was, crying in the shower over a man.

I think I stayed in there for about twenty minutes with all sorts of things running through my mind.

1. Was I going to get the sack for phoning in sick the day after an Old Firm?

2. Was he lying in my bed texting her lies about where he was?

3. Did he want to come back with me or was it the alcohol that made the decision for him?

4. Am I going to be sick again?

5. Was it even worth it?

6. What about Jack?

The day was worth it, but I should have just gone home after the game. Why didn't Caitlin drag me home by the ankles? She probably tried to, but I was a woman on a mission that day.

Caitlin will absolutely kill me! I thought.

I ran a comb through my damp hair and stared at myself in the mirror, resembling something from a horror film.

I stood naked in the bathroom and just looked at my ghostly white reflection staring back at me.

Why was I doing this to myself?

I began to well up. I felt worthless and it was all my fault.

The only feeling I can compare to this was after a weekend stint at T in the Park and having that first shower once you got home, you're still blazing and no amount of cleaning yourself can make you feel any better.

'Ready?' I said as I pulled an old jumper over my wet hair. I didn't have the energy to even towel dry it.

'Yeah,' he said as he knotted the lace on his trainer.

It was the longest forty minutes of my life.

As I was driving, we made some small talk, I mentioned that I'd booked Magaluf for Jodie's hen and he said he had a few stag dos coming up this year.

I don't even remember much else about our conversation as my stomach was going like a washing machine filled with acid – they don't call it 'venom' for nothing.

But he didn't once mention having a girlfriend.

I took a right turn to arrive at his house and pulled up my handbrake.

We sat for a minute both knowing that he thought what happened last night was a huge mistake. He took off his seat belt, leant over, and hugged me and said thanks for the lift.

And honestly? I felt nothing. I don't know if it was because the incoming call from Laura knocked me for six or the fact that I just knew there was nothing left between us. No spark, no crazy sexual connection, absolutely nothing.

I drove home feeling like utter shit though, but as I scooted down the M74, I made a vow in my head that it would not happen again.

I closed the chapter on Chris once and for all.

I PHONED MY mum who was absolutely livid at me for missing work, as was Caitlin as I filled her in on the long drive home.

I spent the rest of the day, lying on my couch spewing and crying, I felt so low.

At one point I decided to check my bank balance to see what damage I'd done and winced when I realised that I'd spent over £200.

I'd parted with £90 alone in Grace's all in with four different transactions.

Fuck. I was ill, skint, and feeling worthless once again.

I had The Fear all day but the thing that played on my mind the most wasn't Chris, it was what was going to happen tomorrow at work.

My eyes were opened before my alarm had gone off. I hadn't had a great sleep at all, because I was so worried.

I made sure I got in earlier than usual just to make a point, but I was absolutely riddled with The Fear.

Of course, Leona was straight over at my desk before I even took my coat off, asking where the fuck I was yesterday.

I shrugged as I clutched my head, which was still thumping from my two-day hang-over and I told her everything.

'Oh, he wasn't happy with you yesterday,' she said, sipping her tea.

'Oh great, make me feel worse than I already do, thanks for that, L,' I muttered back.

Ten minutes later, Bob strolled in, took off his coat, made himself a coffee and said those dreaded words I knew I couldn't avoid.

'You want to step into my office, Kirsten?'

Fuck.

I followed him into the office at the side of the building and decided that I was going to be honest and not try to make up some bullshit story about having the shits or eating a dodgy curry.

We sat down and I cuddled my cup of coffee close to my chest. I was nervous.

'What happened to you yesterday, then?'

'You know, Bob, I'm not going to sit here and lie to you or make up any excuse about why I wasn't here. I buggered up, I went out, Celtic won, it was my birthday, and I had too much to drink, I was sick and I'm sorry, it won't happen again.'

He said that he appreciated my honesty, but the guys in the office had to work harder by picking up all my stuff too, and it wasn't good enough.

I agreed with him that it wasn't and assured him it wouldn't happen again.

He gave me a verbal warning and decided to draw a line under it, and I was so thankful.

I was more than happy to draw a line under the whole weekend and more importantly, Chris. I really hoped I would never clap eyes on him again.

ONE WEEK WENT past since that sinful Sunday and I hadn't heard from Jack or Chris.

I felt so guilty that Jack had kindly given me the tickets and I ended up in bed with someone else. I tried to keep busy to stop myself thinking about it, but I had to remind myself that he wasn't my boyfriend. He hadn't even wished me a happy birthday for Christ's sake!

Nonetheless, I'd thrown myself into work in a bid to make up for the fact that I phoned in sick on the Monday, so didn't even have a minute to think about anything.

Jack was due home the following day, so I thought I would go snoop his Instagram to see if he had posted anymore holiday snaps.

I typed his name into the search bar, and nothing came up.

Not nothing pictures. Nothing Jack.

He was gone, totally disappeared.

That's bizarre? Had he deleted me?

I phoned Caitlin and got her to check it out.

'Yeah, hen, he's still got Instagram. Looks like he's blocked you!'

Blocked me? Why? What the fuck?

I text him in a rage.

Have you deleted me from Instagram?

Two days went past and still nothing from him, and I knew he was back home, so I text him again.

Actually, I don't know why I'm even asking if you've deleted me because I know you have. Text me your address and I'll post your tickets through your door because I can't be arsed with your shite.

It took him a whole day to reply.

Just back. That's fair enough. I'll get the tickets at some point the morra if that's OK.

Why did you do that? Dick move once again from you.

He got back instantly.

What delete loads of people, why not? Why's it a big deal?

Is this prick fucking serious? A big deal? I'd only been sleeping with him for the last five fucking months. The bastard!

I honestly don't know what your problem is. I've not got time for your stupid games. I don't deserve to be treated like that. Send me your address now and I'll post them through your door.

OK. Can you post them to my mum's? I'm going away for a while.

Cool.

And that was it.

Going away? Going away where? Back to the army? Jail? Hell? I didn't care enough to ask, as long as it was away from me.

I posted the tickets and deleted his number.

Prick.

A FEW DAYS later, it was finally time for me to jump on a plane and forget all my man drama.

I sat in the airport with a large goblet of pink gin, waiting to board my flight to Singapore to see my gal Rosie once again, and I honestly couldn't wait. It was the break I needed. This time we were going to Thailand together too, then I was going on to Dubai to meet Heather again. I was excited about another adventure and to see more of the world.

I treated myself to some Mac goodies in duty free and was sipping away at my second gin when I got a text from an unknown number.

Jack.

I nearly spat out my gin when I read it and my blood began to boil. Fucking wanker!

Btw. I may as well be honest.

You have slept with one of my close mates that I didn't know about a wee while ago. I'm no going into who or that as it doesn't matter.

Like it's no big deal, just think pals would be a better option for us, as I have nothing against you. Your really sound and stuff, so if that's ok way you? Like it's a wee bit awkward, but I don't want it to be.

HOW. FUCKING. DARE. HE!

He is an absolute narcissist!

I was absolutely fuming. I swear I could feel my blood boiling away in my veins. Who the fuck does he think he is? Who I've slept with? I think I know fine fucking well who I've slept with. Is he implying otherwise?

The fact that he used the wrong 'you're' also really riled me.

Oh my God, I was about to unleash on this fucking prick.

First of all, how fucking dare you? If I've slept with 'one of your good mates' then I'm sure you won't have a fucking problem telling me who it is? I know fine well who I have been with and who I have not, and none of them are your 'mates'. So see you? Get yourself so far to fuck, fucking arsehole.

He point blank refused to tell me who this supposed shagging companion was.

The only person I thought it could be was the guy I bumped into at the football that wished me a happy birthday as he sat a few rows in front of Jack's seat. Even at that, that was when I was sixteen so it couldn't possibly be him, plus after searching on Facebook, they weren't even friends, so it definitely wasn't him.

So, I just text him and told him where to go.

Fuck off then.

I boarded the plane and left my Jack and Chris drama behind, although when I met with Rosie, I told her about the whole saga over a few lychee martinis.

She couldn't believe it either.

'He sounds like a nutter! Boy, bye!' she said as we cheers'ed to the single life.

I had the best time with Rosie, catching up on a year's worth of gossip, going for dinner and seeing new places.

Singapore was absolutely beautiful, and I loved it more and more each time I went and was sad every single time I had to leave.

I had the total holiday blues when I got back once again as I sat at my desk back in the office and stared at the Polaroid pictures which now graced my computer screen.

I was skint, depressed, and single.

Great.

I'd been back home for a few days now and was just starting to get into the swing of things when once again I got another text from another unknown number.

Hiya, just a quick message to say I apologise for the way I acted when we stopped chatting. It was childish and you deserve better than that. I'm no trying to be best pals or that but I felt I needed to say sorry and apologise. Hope you had a great holiday.

Aw here we fucking go. It was my time to shine…

When we stopped chatting? No we never 'stopped chatting' you started spouting absolute lies, see if you didn't want to see me any more just fucking say it.

I was absolutely furious. Why did he keep doing this to me? The wanker!

I'm sorry. It was a shit thing to do. I have about a billion things going on at the minute and just needed to cut everyone out for a wee bit to try to sort my life out with the house and work, and my mum, it's all getting too much to juggle and that. I apologise for the way I done it. It was shit and I'm sorry.

Again with the excuses, what's that about?

I just text back *OK* because I couldn't be bothered entertaining him anymore.

I was well and truly deflated by the whole scenario. Finding out Chris had a girlfriend, Jack basically slut shaming me over text message, and to add to the carnage, a few weeks later, the whole Dave/hotel room saga occurred.

281

I was on an actual rampage, off the rails. I was drinking every weekend and just making a string of terrible decisions, and it had to stop.

I was back on Tinder, talking to everyone and anyone who would listen.

After everything with all the guys previously and constantly allowing them to treat me like shit, I just didn't feel like I was worthy of a relationship or anything with meaning.

Most people could see that I was in quite a dark place, it was obvious.

My best friend's David and Darren would come over to make me dinner as at one point I was so low I was changing out of pyjamas and into new ones.

The two of them are complete godsends, my husbands, I'm practically an extension of their marriage whether they like it or not basically.

David is always nice about everything and tends to look at things from both angles, but Darren on the other hand is so brutally honest, a bit like me and told me I needed to give myself a shake.

I was blaming every terrible decision I made on Mr Radio Silence and Darren was having none of it.

'Are you really letting someone with a pinky ring who is gas-lighting you make you feel like shit? Get a grip, wash your hair and remember who the fuck you are.'

That was it, it was the wake-up call I needed, Darren was the voice of reason and he was right, my hair was fucking greasy and

I was letting myself go over a guy who I didn't particularly like anyway.

They always picked me up and dusted me off after I had a wobble.

I decided that instead of moping around, that I had to get on with my life.

I continued to Tinder and Bumble and speak to an array of different guys that I wasn't in the slightest bit interested in.

It passed the time and kept me slightly occupied when one day, I got a text from the unknown number again which I recognised as Jack's.

Hey, fancy grabbing a coffee sometime?

A coffee? For real?

I entertained him put of pure boredom, but I never trusted him after the whole 'you shagged my mate' bullshit.

Of course, Darren and David weren't pleased when I told them I was chatting to him again.

They were over for a Chinese one night when made the announcement after shovelling a forkful of noodles in my mouth.

'Tell me you're joking! You're talking to that devil dick again?'

'I don't even like him anyway!'

The both of them rolled their eyes.

'Well, don't come crying to us when he goes radio silence on you again!'

I knew they were right.

Truth be told, it was never the same with Jack after our fall out. We would talk some days, then go weeks and even months, without a single word but he always seemed to pop back up.

It was now July, I had another brilliant summer with loads of different nights out and weekends away but in all honesty, I loved all these events with my pals, but see when I got back home? I was miserable.

I was single and miserable, and I hated it.

This was when I made the mistake of letting Jack back into my life and into my house.

Wine Thursdays were back on, much to David, Darren, Caitlin, and everyone else's disapproval.

Jack even left a green toothbrush at mine now for when he stayed over, it had escalated greatly considering it was only a few months ago that I told him to fuck off.

'You're seeing Jacko again? Hen, come on, you know how we all feel about this,' Caitlin huffed on the phone.

'It's purely just wine and sex, I know that. I'm the one that's using him this time.' I reassured her.

'Only if you're sure, but you know I hate him, he's a bastard for what he has done to you.'

'Y H Y H.' I laughed.

'Yer Hole's Yer Hole! I'll give ye that!' she chuckled back.

Jack was on a steady streak, we had been texting for about three weeks solid with no radio silences, was he feeling all right?

Can I ask you something? he text.

What? I replied.

See since like, we first met? Have you, like, been with anyone else?

FUCK. He knows. He knows about Chris and Dave. He must know. Why would he ask otherwise?

But I didn't owe this prick anything, so I lied.

No, why? Have you?

Naaa, how could I? I have no time. I hardly have time to eat never mind go with anyone else. I'm working flat out.

Hmm, true, he always seemed to be working.

Jack asked me this a few times, he always asked about sex, about things like 'when I last done it before him' and about what we did together and if I had done certain things with different people before I met him. It was all very strange, but he was strange, and the more time went on I began to realise he was just a fucking loser, him and his fucking pinky ring.

One night he even left the gold bracelet on my bedside table and I FaceTimed Caitlin to show her it.

'Oh, my fucking God, you weren't joking, were you? That's fucking awful, oh my God, wit's he playing at? Wit are you playing at? Going with someone that wears that bloody monstrosity!'

We howled with laughter.

AUGUST 2019

It was soon Jodie's hen weekend in Magaluf, nine of us set off for four days of absolute carnage.

We packed inflatable willies, devil horns and hen night sashes in our cases and prepared for a weekend of chaos.

I couldn't believe that after a year of planning, it was finally time to celebrate our girl getting hitched.

I knew majority of the girls on the trip but some of them I'd only met briefly, and they loved hearing all about my terrible dating stories and the fact that I was still sleeping with a guy I really wasn't that into.

We were by the pool one day sipping cocktails, when Jodie probed me to tell everyone the story about the 'water jug guy' and how her and Rachael had crashed our first date.

I was more than happy to oblige to the bride's request and sat on the edge of the pool and told the girls all about it, even down to waking up next to him the day after the football.

'He left you a water jug on your doorstep? Even after he said he didn't see it going anywhere?' Julie asked.

'Yes, the prick!' I said swirling the ice in my strawberry daiquiri around with my straw.

Later that day, half of us had planned to go into Santa Ponsa for the day to watch the football.

Celtic were playing St Johnstone and Santa Ponsa was known to some as 'little Ireland' as it had many little Irish bars so we decided it would be best to go there for the day.

Some of us went there to watch the game and the rest went to get their hair blow-dried – the hen party really was a mixed bag.

We agreed to all meet in one of the Irish bars later on as they had a live band playing after the game and it was a little bit different to the busy Magaluf strip we had been on every night since we got here.

A life-sized inflatable of the groom also tagged along with us and we played games and dares and I honestly laughed so much that my sides ached for days.

Just before the band were about to start, we sat at a table outside and continued to play 'Never Have I Ever' where a cheeky statement is read out and if you've done it, you take a drink.

'Never Have I Ever, shagged someone outside.'

Majority of us lifted our glasses and took a sip before laughing uncontrollably, then went round the table to find out where, when and with who.

A table of two guys next to us joined in.

One guy was in his thirties and the other in his forties.

We got chatting to them and it turned out they were on a stag do but the rest of the guys were too hung-over from the night before to make it out for the football and would be joining them later. We knew the feeling; it was impossible to get everyone out at the same time.

We found out more about the guys, their names, what they did for work and where they were from.

It turns out they lived in the same town Chris was from.

287

I decided not to ask if they knew him, because it was quite a big town plus, I didn't really have much to say about him, I couldn't exactly say, 'Do you know my ex-situationship?' Who I last saw back in March? After sleeping with him then realising he has a girlfriend? So, I just left it.

The guys explained that the live band who were due to play that night were actually from there too.

As the sun started to set, the other girls returned from the hairdressers to meet us and by this point, the football lot were all pretty well on.

We ordered more shots and cocktails by the jug before moving inside so that we could dance to the band when they started.

By luck, we managed to get a table with the two guys and as soon as the music roared, we were all up dancing and having a great time.

My favourite song 'Grace' came on and we all swayed arm in arm and sang along. But two minutes later, one of the guys broke the chain and went over to the front door to greet what must have been the rest of his friends.

Caitlin and I were singing at the top of our lungs with the inflatable groom stuck between us.

When the song came to an end, we applauded the band and headed back to the table when I stopped in my tracks.

What the?

I honestly couldn't believe it…

Standing in front of me, in the middle of a small Irish bar in Santa Ponsa...

Chris.

I squinted my eyes to see if I was dreaming, or if it was someone who just looked like him but no it was him. Chris, in Santa Ponsa!

Is this real life?

My jaw was on the floor.

I walked up to him in total shock.

'What are you doing here?'

'I'm on a stag do.' He laughed, equally as shocked to see me.

It all made sense, they two guys we had met were his friends.

You couldn't make this up.

'It's nice to see you' I lied, it wasn't really, every time I thought I was over him he just seemed to pop right back up.

'You too. Do you want a drink?' he asked.

'No thanks, I'm all good,' I said, pointing to the jug of cocktail in my hand.

And that was it, we both just kinda smiled awkwardly at one another and I turned on my heel and headed straight back over to the girls to tell them that the guy from the story I'd told earlier that day at the pool just walked into the same bar.

'What? No way! That's unbelievable!,' Julie said, gobsmacked.

I honestly couldn't believe it.

It was so weird how I'd just spoken about him today for the first time in ages and here he was, in the Dubliner in Santa Ponsa of all places.

After the band finished for the night, we all moved back outside and the friend of his that we had met earlier asked if we knew each other.

'Em, yes, you could say that.' I laughed taking a draw of my cigarette.

'Yeah, we go back a while.'

We spoke for a bit, and I just asked him how he was getting on, if he was still working for the same company and small chat like that, nothing interesting, but one thing I did know for sure, was that the spark that was once there between us was well and truly gone.

I didn't even really find him attractive now, it was strange because he just looked the same.

Just as I was about to get up and say goodbye to him, Jodie and Rachael came over with two trays of overflowing shots in their hands.

'Oh my God. Are you the water jug guy? Oh my God! Do you know that me and Rachael crashed your date that night?' Jodie howled.

'What?' Chris said, confused.

'Yeah! We were there that night when you two first met, look here's the picture.'

Jodie whipped out her phone from her pearly 'Bride' clutch bag and showed Chris the photograph that they'd snapped of the two of them with me and him in the background with the caption 'When you crash your pals Tinder date'.

He didn't really look too impressed; he just did a really fake laugh sort of thing.

I was mortified to start, but then I remembered all that had happened between us and just didn't give a fuck.

We chatted a bit more, he asked if I still went to the football and if I was still working at the paper.

The conversation was dry, and it wasn't like it used to be at all. I remember asking myself, 'how did I ever think he was The One?'

And that was the last time I ever saw him.

I checked his Facebook after our Santa Ponsa reunion and it turns out that Laura was his girlfriend now – lucky her!

I still sometimes catch myself thinking about him from time to time, and wonder if in the future we'll randomly bump into each other maybe in another fucking country like we did in Santa Ponsa.

But I had Jack now, sort of, so I shouldn't have been dwelling on the past.

IT THEN REACHED September; Wine Thursday had happened consecutively for the last six weeks.

Again, I knew it only was what it was, I didn't want to be seen out in public with him and the only time that ever happened was on the work's Christmas night out, and even that was bad enough.

Jack brought over two bottles of wine, as usual, and pizza, as usual.

It was just so predictable and same-y. I didn't complain though, wine, pizza, and yer hole? That really was all he was good for.

I took a picture of my wine in my hand and put it on my Instagram story.

I wrote under it, *Wine Thursday* as an inside joke for Caitlin.

I didn't even have him on Instagram anymore since he blocked me back in March and I didn't care less.

In the corner of the picture, the very tiny corner, you could see the sleeve of his T-shirt, no one would notice though, it didn't identify him in the slightest, thankfully.

I didn't want anyone to know I was shagging a total loser.

The next morning, it was the same as every other Friday morning… morning sex, coffee, and toast in bed with the news, before saying goodbye.

I was going to Liverpool after work with Heather, Shanice, Hayley, and Samantha for a night out and I was the designated driver. I was so looking forward to a change of scenery and for some quality time with my girls.

I'd been running around like a headless chicken all day, getting organised for my trip and packing my bag that I hadn't even text Jack at all, and I didn't plan on it.

As we drove down the motorway, five girls and five suitcases bundled into my little Audi A1, I filled them in on my secret Wine Thursday dates and they, like everyone else I told, warned me to be careful.

After my lecture was over, we all sang along to my Apple Music playlist, which was a total mix from Kasabian to Destiny's Child to Abba. The girls were all drinking, and I couldn't wait to park up and pour myself a well-deserved vodka.

We soon arrived in the town of Cilla Black, The Beatles, and Scouse Brows.

We dragged our overnight bags through the cobbled streets until we finally reached our hotel. Making our way up to our room, we discovered that our friend Lucy had sent us up a bottle of prosecco as she couldn't make it and let me tell you the first sip tasted like heaven.

We cheers'ed to the weekend and I had the proper Friday feeling, I was ready to go out dancing, maybe winch some Scousers and get absolutely shit-faced drunk.

I checked my phone for the first time in about four hours, and noticed I had a message request…

Kayleigh wants to send you a message
Kayleigh? Who the fuck is Kayleigh?

15. Hey, Hunni...

I quickly realised that this girl had just started following my Instagram account last night, but I'd not seen nor heard of her before, so I took one look at the message, and I nearly choked on my drink.

Hey, Hunni... I really hope you don't mind me messaging you. But I've been seeing Jack Devon for the best part of a year now and I'm now finding out he's been seeing you. Just in case he's been feeding you lies as well x

What. The. Fuck!

I stared at the message blankly and cogs in my head started turning, things started adding up.

'Are you OK, Kirst? You've went all quiet.' Shanice asked taking my glass to top up my prosecco.

'You're never going to believe the message I've just been sent.'

I passed my phone over to them and took a large sip of my prosecco.

'Oh my God! What a dick!' Hayley said, handing back the phone.

'What do I say to that?' I laughed.

A few different things ran through my mind of what I should say but I just got back to her saying I didn't know anything about her, which was the truth.

Hey. No, not at all. Really? This is news to me. Yeah, he has been feeding me lies too then as I met him in November. Have you been in a relationship with him then? How did you find out? Sorry for all the questions, obviously just a shock x

But then it wasn't really a shock. I always knew there was something weird about him, he was always so secretive about his phone and I only saw him once a week but fuck's sake I didn't expect that total loser to be living a double life.

Kayleigh responded to me almost immediately.

Thanks for being understanding. I also met him in November on Tinder and we've been together since. I noticed you on his Facebook commenting and stuff when he was in Mexico, and I naively asked who you were out of interest, and he has you on his profile. So straight off I thought that was strange. Yeah so, we've been together, so I've been thinking. Met up with his mum the other week. Have you met any of his family or anything? Have you been like regularly seeing each other? x

Fucking hell.

She had met his mum! The same mum with the lump in her stomach, I presumed. Well, if that was even true.

I told Kayleigh about Wine Thursdays, how it was mostly just sex and that it had been on and off for about nine months and that

295

I was sorry this had happened to her, and within seconds she got back to me.

Oh my God he's been leading a double life. Like spends his weekends at mine, comes over during the week too, mostly at mine because his house is being 'done up', is that what he says to you?

It sounds crazy but I added you tonight randomly totally out the blue and noticed his T-shirt in the corner of your story, the blue one.

Honestly don't be sorry one bit. He's told me in the past that he's cheated on girlfriends and stuff so I've never really fully trusted him but anytime I questioned him he always got annoyed at me.

I'm totally in shock, he was texting me last night like most of the night (obviously when he was with you). Shows you how sneaky he's been. Have you been like going out and about and stuff? I'm sorry for the questions too. I asked him about you there and he admitted it straight away. Think he's in total shock. Has he been in touch with you?

This is too much.

What a wee rat bag bastard! He's been sleeping with us both? Obviously without protection, which is fucking disgusting, what an absolute vile wee worm!

I could feel my blood boil beneath my skin, not because I liked him in the slightest but that he thinks he can get away with this or that it's OK.

I replied telling her no, thankfully I'd never been seen out in public with him except the time he came to my Christmas night out, and that he fed the whole 'doing up the house' bullshit to me too.

Since this revelation, Jack hadn't messaged me or gotten in contact at all, but I knew he knew, that I knew, so I didn't message going absolutely tits at him, instead I just sent a screenshot of Kayleigh's message and wrote a few words.

You going to explain to me what the FUCK is going on? With loads of laughing emojis after it.

He replied within minutes.

I dunno… I'm sorry, I fucked up. Like I dunno what to say, I'm sorry.

I didn't even bother to reply to him because I didn't give a fuck, Kayleigh was probably making him sweat more than ever with her grilling and for me, she'd answered any questions that I had, plus I wasn't letting that wee fucking weasel ruin my night out.

I also told Kayleigh that I was just about to go out with my pals in Liverpool and that I would catch-up with her tomorrow.

I found it quite easy to totally put the whole scenario to the back of my mind and had a brilliant night with the girls.

We drank shots and danced, got a McDonald's on the way home, and I'm pretty sure at one point I was swinging from the Cilla Black statue absolutely steaming – God rest her soul.

As much as the five of us are respectable professionals by day, we're a bunch of fucking irresponsible idiots with a drink, and I wouldn't have it any other way.

We got back to the hotel and into the jacuzzi bath and tanned more prosecco, at one point there were bubbles fucking everywhere – just an FYI, shower gel and power jets are never a good combo, it was like being back in Ibiza 2012 at one of the foam parties – absolutely fucking chaos.

The five of us were running about in our bras and pants too as no one had enough sense to pack a bikini or bathing suit, so in the drunken states we were in, we headed straight in the jacuzzi with the underwear on.

As we climbed into bed that night, soggy from our late-night dip, my damp head hit the pillow and sleeping was the last thing on my mind.

I finally had time to properly digest what the fuck had actually happened to me today.

I was alone with only my thoughts as I began to dissect every single situation I'd been in with Jack and started to pinpoint the several red flags over the last nine months.

I mean, I already knew they were there in all honestly but I didn't think they would be so fucking obviously waving me in the face.

It was 3.30 a.m., I picked up my phone and messaged Kayleigh.

Hey, I can't sleep for thinking about all this. It's actually fucking disgusting what he's done and now that I'm thinking about everything and it's all making sense.

Within minutes I had a message back from Kayleigh saying she was the same and was also still up at this ridiculous hour of the morning.

We began chatting big, huge, lengthy messages about different times that obviously we 'crossed over' and she began to ask me more and more questions and things got a bit weird.

This may seem weird right, but did he ever use Viagra with you?

Sorry, what?!

Viagra?

Obviously, I knew what it was but I generally thought it was from men in their 60s who had erectile disfunction.

No? Why do you ask that? I typed, confused.

She explained.

One time, I looked through his wash bag to find that he had like empty packets of it in there, so I asked him about it and he got all embarrassed and I always caught him going down to his car to take it and he would always wake me up at ridiculous times to have sex.

Oh my God!

I googled 'side effects of Viagra' and it was like the missing piece of the puzzle for the late-night shagging and the serious sweating.

'Difficulty sleeping, restless sleep, excessive sweating, flushing, prolonged erection of the penis.'

I literally was speechless.

How did I not realise this was what he had been doing this whole time?

This information was madness, it was like something from a film, seriously, it was so fucked up.

That explained the drenched bedsheets, the constantly wanting to have sex, and also the fact that the bastard never slept, ever.

He was clearly addicted to Viagra and had been popping them like sweeties.

Kayleigh also said that the two of them had gone on an overnight to Edinburgh one time and he was proper sweating and saying he had to go to a pharmacy to get 'cold tablets' despite not having the cold.

He left her shopping in Zara to go to Boots and later that night in the bathroom she discovered again in his 'wash bag' over the counter pills he'd bought that day to obviously boost his sexual performance.

I laughed at this, not because he was clearly relying on pills to get hard but the fact that he took her on an overnight in the capital and all I got was a bottle of red wine and a Marks and Spencer's pizza.

My conversation with Kayleigh that night was so interesting because I found out more and more about how much of a twisted wee fucker Jack really was.

The time he went to Newcastle with his pal from the army?

He was actually there with Kayleigh to meet her sister, who lives down there.

And he had the fucking audacity to send me a picture of their dinner receipt? And text me the whole time he was there?

Kayleigh said that when he was there, he was constantly on his phone and when she questioned it, he said it was his 'football group chat' he was talking to.

Also, the Gucci belt for his sister?

For his sister fuck all, it was for Kayleigh! The same Kayleigh who he spent Christmas morning with and gave him that Louis Vuitton wallet he carries around.

He literally sent me a picture of it saying 'best brother' like that's so fucking fucked in the head.

Honestly, I was lost for words, it was like he literally got a kick out of playing with fire.

My head was buzzing with alcohol and also all this new and absolutely mental information I was receiving from Kayleigh, so I told her I needed to head to bed and I would chat to her tomorrow when I was home from Liverpool.

Good night x

Opening my eyes, our room looked like a fucking bomb had gone off.

There were chips from our steaming scran, smooshed into the floor.

I had one strip eyelash stuck to my elbow, there were empty bottles covering every single table and unit and piles of soggy clothes and towels at every corner.

The room stank of drink, dampness and stale McDonald's and it was absolutely bloody grim.

I looked over at Shanice who was lying next to me with her head buried under the pillow, clearly suffering from the inside out.

Hayley and Sam were in the bed across from us, dead to the world, and still very much in a Tequila Rose coma.

Heather got papped on the sofa bed because for the twenty years I've known her she's always a nightmare to share a bed with and looking at her now in her hung-over state, she was still the same, arms and legs everywhere.

As we all started to spring back into life, although hung-over, we laughed as we looked around at the state of us and our surroundings.

I told the girls about my late-night chat with Kayleigh, and they couldn't believe when I told them about the belt and the dinner receipt.

'He's a scumbag!' Hayley scolded.

'Yeah, imagine doing that!' Heather chimed in.

I still couldn't believe the audacity of this prick, seriously?

How bold do you need to be to see two girls at the one time and send risky pictures and messages when you're with one of them?

It honestly blew my mind.

As the check-out time loomed, we attempted to tidy up our drunken antics from the night before and I balked as I scooped up the soggy chips from the carpet and tossed them in the bin.

We were absolute mingers.

After handing back the keys at reception, we rolled our cases and ourselves on to the street and were on the hunt for somewhere decent to get some good food to banish our hang-overs for good.

I was absolutely fucking starving and needed to be fed and watered asap before I drove us all home in just a few hours.

WE ARRIVED AT the cutest wee place that according to Trip Advisor, did the best breakfast in Liverpool.

I ordered some sort of halloumi and chorizo dish and a coffee, I would need the energy to keep my eyes open for our road trip back, which was never as fun as the one on the way down.

I passed the waitress the menu and glanced at my phone and noticed that I had a Facebook message from another name that I didn't know.

Someone called Nadia.

What's this?

I opened it and my heart just about fell out my arse hole.

Hi doll, have you been sleeping with Jack Devon? xxx

No fucking way. This can't be another one, surely?

I looked at my other messages and I had one from Kayleigh saying she'd found another girl who had also been seeing our charming Jack.

I burst out laughing. Was this really happening?

Our brunch arrived and I was sat at the end of the table with my head stuck in my phone.

'Come on, Mrs Anti-social. Eat up!' Shanice frowned, looking at my untouched plate.

I didn't even feel hungry, I felt sick.

Again, it wasn't in a hurt way, it was more about the fact he had been sleeping with three girls, what if I had the fucking clap?

Can you imagine?

Obviously, I am a responsible adult and go to get checked after every 'partner' kind of thing, but then between times of Jack, I'd also slept with Dave and Chris so what if I did have it and then passed it on to them?

I pictured the conversation in my fuzzy head.

'Hi, Dave, Hi, Chris, now I know you both have girlfriends now, good for you, but mind that time we banged? Yeah, well I may or may not have given you the clap because the guy I was seeing (at the same time as our encounter) seems to be dipping his dick in two others, so maybe best get checked out? Let your girlfriends know too. Thanks.'

Thoughts burled around my hazy hung-over head.

Fucking hell.

Kayleigh had text me again and asked me if I was ever suspicious of any other girls. I racked my brains and got back to her, saying that at the time, I noticed a girl called Laura comment on his stuff a lot, but Jack had openly spoken about Laura as she had cancer and said she was his friend from years ago.

He said he kept in touch with her to see how she was doing but that was really the only person I could think of, and as he spoke about her openly, I didn't really suspect it.

Back in my inbox, I stared at the message from this Nadia girl and replied to her.

Hey, Nadia, yeah, he was at my house on Thursday. Kayleigh messaged me last night. I can't believe this, he's had a girlfriend this whole time!

She got back to me instantly.

I've been going with him as well LOLOL

I rolled my eyes. He was unbelievable!

How has he pulled this off? He's so full of shit!

Nadia and I chatted back and forth for ages, making a joke of the whole situation. It appeared we were the side chicks and Kayleigh was like the actual girlfriend.

Nadia told me that she and Jack had went on one actual date and then he just came over to her house after that, he sometimes brought her flowers but not like florist flowers, like the wee shitty ones you get outside the petrol station.

She said her situation was basically the same as mine in that she didn't really like him that much but saw him for the convenience of it being once a week.

Nadia was a few years older than me, a sports therapist, and had a four-year-old daughter called Darci.

She said that Jack was always asking when he could meet Darci but she never let him because she doesn't let just anyone meet her wee girl.

That's so fucking wrong, why would you want to meet someone's daughter knowing you were shagging two other people?

Sicko.

Nadia and I went back and forth for ages and it turns out, she knew my sister-in-law Paula, she seemed hilarious, and had the same sort of sense of humour as me.

We tore Jack a new arse hole in our chat, nitpicking everything about him, comparing notes and joining up the dots.

That bastard!

We were similar in the sense that we both had long dark hair and were quite short, whereas Kayleigh had blonde hair and looked nothing like us, a pretty girl but doesn't wear a lot of make-up unlike me who has Daisy the coo lashes on every day of the week.

I continued to message both Nadia and Kayleigh separately. Kayleigh seemed to be extremely heartbroken which was understandable whereas me and Nadia's conversations were full of banter, we slagged him and his pinky ring, and had a real laugh about how we were the bits on the side and had ended up being in some sort of shagging square, while Kayleigh was treated to a Gucci belt.

I told her about the 'Wine Thursdays' and she said he always came over to hers on a Wednesday to chill and watch TV.

Again… the bastard!

Just as we were chatting, I got another message from Kayleigh, she'd found yet another girl, it was Laura, the girl who had cancer.

What a sick fuck!

I felt an awful feeling in the pit of my stomach this time, how could he do that to a girl who's battling fucking cancer? This has gone way too far. He can do that to me, no bother at all, but not to a vulnerable cancer patient.

My phone exploded like never before, between finding out the details from Kayleigh, conferring with Nadia, and consulting my group chat on the latest Jack scandal.

My head was absolutely fried with it all between that and my terrible hang-over from last night, I was in a tizzy.

I pushed my breakfast round my plate, I didn't feel hungry at all, I just wanted to get home, jump into my bed, and never see the light of day again.

The drive home was horrendous, the three in the back napped almost the whole journey, and as I drove up the motorway the whole scenario just buzzed about my head, thinking of all the times I should have called it quits, all the times I saw him again after he was a pig to me. But then I reminded myself that I didn't see him romantically the last wee while, the only thing he was good for was sex.

The sex was decent, but was that because he knew where the G spot was as he found four of them per week? Or the fact that some over the counter pills gave him a raging hard on?

Ugh, what a grim thought.

After what felt like forever, I finally arrived home and got the proper chance to look at my phone.

Kayleigh suggested that since we were both sending huge paragraphs to each other that might be nice to meet in person, maybe for a coffee…

I scratched my head.

Is that a good idea?

I'd told her everything she needed to know basically, but why not? I supposed if I met her for a coffee maybe that would be it? Case closed.

So it was arranged, me and her, Starbucks on Sunday at 2 p.m.

But after accepting her offer, it wasn't long before my phone bleeped, it was Nadia.

Are you going for a coffee with Kayleigh on Sunday?

My phone buzzed again; it was Kayleigh.

I've asked Nadia to join us on Sunday.

Aw great, it's going to be us three girls sitting around a table like a fucking AA meeting for the one guy, I pictured it in my head.

'*Hi, I'm Kirsten and I was shagging Jack Devon between November 2018 until September 2019, I've been clean from him for about three days now.*'

I laughed at the thought.

Kayleigh also told me that she'd messaged Laura to ask if she wanted to join too but she was ill in hospital so she wouldn't make it.

I still couldn't believe he had done this to a girl with cancer. Kayleigh had told me she'd spoken to her quite a bit about us all and she was just as shocked.

And just at that, I got an Instagram message… It was Laura.

I gather you're one of Jack's other women too? Haha, absolute madness!

She must have searched for me on social media after Kayleigh told her all about it. So, I replied.

Hey, Laura! Yes, unfortunately I have also been tarred with that brush too – the bastard! Just a wee message to say though I hope you're OK and you deserve the world! He's a wee loser who isn't worth your time, girl!

I still couldn't believe he could do that to someone who was so ill. That another human being could do that to someone who was going through the worst time of their life, fucking scumbag.

Laura replied.

He's not well in the head. He visited me in hospital, bought me the new Celtic trainers, etc. I can't believe he targeted a girl with cancer. He didn't start to see me until my second diagnosis, promising me to be there through it all, weirdo! I actually don't care anymore, I don't have feelings for him. I didn't have actual feelings for him, anyway, just liked him as in fancied him. Thanks so much, sweetie. You deserve the world too! You are far too good for him. Well done on raising so much money for cancer, you angel.

Laura must have seen that I was raising money for the Beatson on my Instagram and also running the Pretty Muddy Race for Cancer Research.

I messaged her again.

Did you call him out on it? I know that's what I said to Kayleigh, he actually told me about you, he said my pal's cancer is back or something like that and I found that odd that he was telling me a wee bit then nothing! Yeah, I was the same he just passed the time for me tbh, he was Mr Right Now, not Mr Right!

I also told Laura all about my fundraising and how what Jack had done to her turned my stomach and she told me more about it.

He disappeared from my Facebook and Insta, so I asked him about it and he said he deleted both due to it effecting his work productivity. Then we were lying in bed, and I could see past his wee flip phone cover that he was on Insta... He said he just got it back and I must be on his as he only paused it. No, no, he had to add me again. I said that shouldn't happen if he only paused his account. He flapped and his only answer was he didn't know. That's when he knew I was on to him, and he went weird after that. The next day he was so quiet when he usually texts me all day. I thought, naah! I'm so glad I stopped talking to him. I can't believe he told you all about me, though, like I needed people feeling sorry for me. He really did use the fact that I was ill to his advantage. Thanks for being so sweet, honestly, I believe girls should always stick together. I'm doing as well as I can, trying to always keep my positive pants on.

It was Sunday now, and I was preparing for my big date, or the JJ meeting as I'd named it, what were we really going to talk about?

I cringed a bit at the thought of us three meeting for a coffee to talk about some guy we'd all been shagging.

Kayleigh was still texting me back and forth, she actually sent me a picture of myself that I'd posted on my Instagram back in the summer.

Is that Jack's green toothbrush in the back of your picture?
What?!

This chick surely must have a secret degree in journalism or was an undercover detective because the background of my picture was all blurred out but indeed, it was his toothbrush. I couldn't believe how much she was looking into things.

Fucking hell.

At this point, I was texting Kayleigh, Nadia, and Laura, how did Jack really keep up with this for a whole year? It was exhausting.

16. The 'JJ' Meeting

My friends thought I'd absolutely lost the plot going to meet this girl in person, Caitlin especially, she called me as I got ready.

'Hen, what the fuck are you thinking meeting her? You've told her what she wants to know, what more is there to say?'

I wasn't sure, closure maybe? Did I even want closure? I didn't even like this prick, but I was going to go along for the sheer hilarity of the whole situation.

I made a bit of effort with my hair and make-up that day, I didn't really want to seem like I'd got overly done up for this 'date' so I shoved a hoody and gym leggings on to tone my face down a bit.

And about twenty minutes before I was due to meet them, I jumped in the car and headed there.

My heart raced as I pelted across the motorway, my palms sweated underneath the steering wheel and I had this horrendous feeling in the pit of my stomach much like the feeling of a first date but this time it was with a girl – two for that matter.

What was going to happen?

Was she going to asked me forty-five million questions?

Would she cry?

Oh fuck, I don't know what I'll do if she cries.

Would I cry? Would I fuck! He wasn't worth my tears.

I pulled into the Starbucks car park, and I squeezed my car into a space before noticing that Nadia was parked directly in front of my car, I just knew it was her from her pictures and she immediately started waving and laughing.

This is going to be a hoot, I thought.

I laughed too, while feeling a bit nervous, what the fuck was I doing here?!

I glanced at myself once more in the rear mirror, I didn't look like a slob so that was something. I tweaked my strip lash into place and fluffed my hair once more.

I hopped out the car and went right over to Nadia, who was already giggling before me.

'This is like a first date!' I blurted out.

'A first Tinder date!' She laughed.

'I can't believe we're here and we're doing this. What the fuck!'

'Oh my God I know. I just can't believe he did this to us! That bloody loser.'

I honestly couldn't believe it either and my blood boiled to think he got away with it for so long.

We went inside to order some drinks, I got a bit of chocolate cake too, to ease the blow possibly, but looking back I should have probably just brought popcorn for the absolute scandal I was about to hear.

I picked up a latte and a frozen tea at the end of the bar we headed outside.

It was a mild September afternoon and the decision to sit outside was made because I might want a stress cigarette to cope with the incoming details.

I fiddled with the tassels on my hood, I was nervous, and it showed.

Nadia seemed very much like me personality wise. I'd only been in her company for a few minutes, but I could already tell she was bubbly and fun.

It was just the two of us for a while, so we exchanged brief stories and laughed at how similar they were.

The funny thing was we both looked quite similar. We were short, dark-haired, curvy gals…the total opposite of Kayleigh.

We waited on her arriving in anticipation. She was the actual girlfriend after all, she'd met his mum, been on an overnight, and been gifted a Gucci belt for Christ's sake.

That feeling in my stomach intensified as I really didn't know what to expect from this whole meeting, but it wasn't long before Nadia whispered, 'Here she comes.'

I gazed up and there she was, a natural looking, petite blonde pottering over to our table.

Kayleigh had a blousey-like top on, with black trousers and a pair of pristine dolly shoes, she looked very smart and made me look like a total tink.

'Hello! I would say nice to meet you, but I mean it's not really the best circumstance, is it?'

I didn't really know if she meant that comment in a light-hearted or serious way, but I just laughed and introduced myself as girl number three, I thought it might break the ice a bit.

Despite not knowing her at all, I could already tell Kayleigh was stressed, she looked tired and worn out.

I noticed the bags under her eyes, disguised by thick foundation, she was broken and it was obvious.

Poor girl.

My heart went out to her a bit but then in my head I changed my tune because we were all victims here, Gucci belt or not.

I'd been shagging a guy who was shagging other people (three to be precise) behind my back and every time I thought about it, I felt sick, and now two of them were sitting here in front of me.

My mind started to wander and in my head, I imagined Jack being with both of them, pottering about their houses like he did in mine.

Did he wake them up at ridiculous hours for sex too?

I wasn't sure if it was too much of a touchy subject to ask so I kept quiet and decided to let Kayleigh take the lead on this whole fiasco.

As I zoned back into conversation, I stared at Kayleigh as she mentioned that someone else would be joining us and that it wasn't Laura.

What?! Don't tell me there's another one, surely to God? If this boy was shagging any more girls in one week, surely his dick would have fallen off by now?!

Kayleigh went on to say that she'd contacted Jack's long-term ex-girlfriend and asked if she'd come and chat to us, to (in her words) give us 'background'.

FUCKING HELL.

As if this whole situation isn't bad e-fucking-nough without the ex-girlfriend here to laugh at us all!

I was mortified at the thought.

I closed my eyes for a moment to gather the thoughts rushing around my head, then just burst out laughing.

Surely there couldn't be anything else more to this absolute fucking idiot than I already knew about.

This whole thing was an absolute shit-show and at one point I was just expecting Ashton Kutcher to jump out and tell us we'd been *Punk'd* but it didn't happen, sadly.

Kayleigh said Emma would be joining us for our coffee date just shortly.

So, before her unwanted arrival, Kayleigh began telling her story.

There were parts of it I already knew from messaging her, but it was interesting to hear the similarities.

She also matched him on Tinder in the November time, but the difference between us and her was that they went out for dinner and overnights together.

Kayleigh had met his mum, and he met her family.

I felt a rush of only what I can describe as shame wash over me.

Did he only really see me good for one thing? Sex?

Was I not good enough to be taken for dinners and overnights?

To be honest, as I've said before, I wouldn't have been seen dead with him out in public, but it just made me question my worth – and that feeling itself, as many girls know, is horrendous.

I looked down at my short-bitten nails, I'd always been a nail biter but the past few days with what had been going on, I'd bitten them right down to the skin.

They looked raw and painful, but I just couldn't stop myself. The pain felt weirdly nice, almost like a stress reliever.

We established that he told us all about his 'building site' house and it turns out that none of us had actually been to it. Did he even have a house, or did he take the pictures from Google?

Kayleigh went on to reveal that she actually knew that he did own it as she had one of her lawyer friends look into it.

My God, is that girl totally invested or what? She would definitely give Miss Marple a run for her money.

Jeez.

Kayleigh went on to ask if we had ever received gifts or anything like that from Jack.

I told her about the gin I bought him for his birthday, and I saw a smile creep across her pale face.

'Did it come in a box with a teacup?'

'Em, yeah?' I mumbled, wondering what she was about to say next.

'Oh my God, he told me he got that as a birthday present from his mum and brought it over to mine and we drank it together.'

I shouldn't have even been surprised by this but something about Kayleigh's smile struck me like a knife in the gut.

It wasn't about him, it was about the absolute audacity of his actions.

Did he get a buzz from seeing his 'girlfriend' drink from a bottle he knew his bit on the side bought him? Kayleigh also mentioned that he'd brought over the Clinique face wash that I'd bought him to keep at her house.

The fucking cheek of it!

I really couldn't help but feel embarrassed that this had happened to me, my cheeks burnt red. I took a sip of my coffee and wanted the ground to swallow me up.

It wasn't long before the ex-girlfriend Emma swanned over with a denim jacket draped over her shoulders like a WAG, I could tell she was loving every moment of this.

Emma also had dark hair and was a curvy girl. But I don't know, there was something about her that I just didn't like right away.

She introduced herself and told us a bit about her relationship with Jack. Sitting looking smug, Emma revealed that they'd been together for six years and even lived together but his crazy gambling problem drove a wedge between then.

Of course he had a gambling problem. Was there anything else that could come to light that would shock me?

As we continued to talk and fill in the gaps, the whole story was just like something from a film – unbelievable.

I studied each person as they spoke and then searched for everyone else's reactions to it. My initial thoughts about Emma were right. I noticed that she didn't once bad mouth Jack, and I could tell that each time one of us spoke she was drinking it all in and loving every taste.

Emma didn't hang about very long at all and soon left but we all agreed there was something about her that seemed a bit off.

Nadia had to leave as well to pick up her wee girl so at the end it was only me and Kayleigh left.

ME AND HER chatted about all the weird things that he had said and done that was similar in both our situations or they crossed.

Here's a handy list:

1. The night I was followed home, Jack told Kayleigh about it and said he seen a post about it on Facebook.

2. Kayleigh actually called out Jack when I commented on his photo from Mexico, and he told her that he only knew me because I was 'shagging his pal' but he deleted me so I wouldn't comment on anything else.

3. Jack had taken Kayleigh to the football on Valentine's night, the same night he was texting me throughout the game.

4. The final night he was in my house for the last Wine Thursday he was texting Kayleigh, trying to smooth out a previous argument they'd had.

5. It was actually Kayleigh who told Jack about the 'Devil's wine' and he didn't read an article about it.

6. He had a green toothbrush at her house too.

7. Also refer back to the belt, dinner receipt, and gin story above.

THERE WERE SO many things that he did that were absolutely appalling, so much so that Kayleigh said she wanted to get his tyres slashed.

It was a bit extreme. We all wanted revenge on this prick, so we settled on something more mild and Nadia put his number on Gumtree, saying he was selling his car and a litter of puppies.

And not surprisingly, it transpires that Emma ran back to Jack and told him everything about the 'JJ meeting', and he called Kayleigh and begged her not to get his tyres slashed.

Emma was probably still shagging him too – so that makes five of us.

We decided to make a group chat, aptly named 'Jack Devon Renovations Ltd' and had a giggle in there.

Jack actually text me, apologising and blamed his behaviour on being in the army.

What the hell?

The text came through from a number I didn't have saved, so I assume he changed it, as he was probably getting harassed by people wanting to buy his car and non-existent dogs.

Hi, hope you're well. This is not a message for anything other than to say I'm really sorry about the full mess as you deserve better than that. Every part of my life was fucked, and I was absolutely fried and in no a good place at all. I've put stuff in place to sort it out, again I can't apologise enough as the way I was acting was not really me. I don't expect a message back just wanted to say sorry. J.

Of course I text him back and said how embarrassing it was and that he was a total nobody.

He got back to me right away.

I can't explain it through a text it's too much. I know and no one is more embarrassed than myself. I just was not coping with the full being at home and stuff like I have been away since I was 15.

Jack then said he could explain it all to my face, but I didn't care enough about him to want to hear it – I just told him there was absolutely no excuse for what he had done and that he was disgusting and that was that.

He also text Nadia and Laura to apologise, but not Kayleigh. She was so upset about it she went to his mum's door and told her everything.

She also spoke to him face to face and if I remember rightly, she said he cried like a big baby.

As the situation unfolded, the main thing that I was worried about was the possibility of having a STI.

Jack had been sleeping with four different girls at the one time (potentially five) that we knew about, and that was so dangerous.

So I took it upon myself to get booked in at a clinic to get checked out.

As I sat in the waiting room, I felt sick to my stomach.

That horrible clinical smell wafted in my nostrils. If this guy has given me chlamydia or any other disease, it would probably tip me over the edge.

Practicing safe sex is so important – please take note.

Of course, I should be to blame too because I should have been taking precautions, but it's definitely a lesson learnt.

As the nurse put my swab in a test tube and took a blood sample, she asked all about my sexual past.

'When did you last have sex?'

'Was it unprotected?'

'How many people have you slept with in the last six months?'

'Was it consensual?'

I'm not really sure how it happened, but I think I wanted the nurse to know that I was here because I'd been betrayed, so I ended up telling her all about the escapade and explained that was the main reason I was there.

She couldn't believe it as much as I still couldn't and laughed with me as I told her a very brief description of my encounter with the snake. She asked what his name was and said that she'd look out for him in the clinic.

What a gal.

I KEPT IN touch with the 'JJ' girls in the group chat and when I got my negative test results back, I sent a message to them all to congratulate us all on not having the clap, Laura and Nadia saw the funny side but I don't think Kayleigh really quite appreciated my humour.

Well, if you don't laugh, you would cry, right?

We chatted to each other often for a few weeks and a night out was even arranged later in the month for me, Nadia, Laura, and Kayleigh under the agreement that the J word was not mentioned.

A few days before we were due to go, Kayleigh announced that the whole situation had badly affected her, and she had to remove herself from the chat, even though it was her who brought us all together in the first place.

You're all lovely girls, ladies. So so nice but all the going back and forward with him and his mess really isn't helping me move on. It's making me feel worse about it all. I need to, for me, remove myself from it all to forget about it.

'Kayleigh left'

Fair enough.

But she then blocked us all on Instagram, Facebook, and WhatsApp.

Laura, Nadia, and I went on that night out and had a great day.

Nadia and I become very close and honestly, now I class her as one of my closest friends.

I kept in touch with Laura too and we liked each other's Instagram posts and stuff as she continued to update everyone on her cancer journey.

Last year, Laura tragically lost her battle to breast cancer and to this day I feel sick to my stomach to think about what Jack did to her.

That absolute bastard.

I wish I could tell you what happened to Jack but the honest answer is that I don't know.

I've tried to search him on Facebook multiple times but to no avail.

Not to get in contact with him by any means, no, but just to see if he ever ended up with someone – dumb bitch if he did!

Actually, I did see him again, I came across him on Bumble last year and out of spite, I reported his profile immediately so who knows what happened with that.

But he has quite literally dropped off the face of the earth and I'm glad.

One thing that Jack taught me was that I should always trust my gut.

He was good for one thing but I shouldn't have let him stay in my life any longer than the first meeting.

I feel sorry for him in some ways because he could have really had something special with Kayleigh.

She told him she loved him and he shit all over her, and will probably leave her scarred for life when it comes to men.

Trust is one of the most important things in a relationship. If there's no trust then what's the point, really?

I'll admit as much as I knew Jack wasn't 'The One' from early on, he is the reason I find it really hard to trust men.

The lies, the betrayal, the unsafe sex – he was so convincing and that's the scary part.

If someone can barefacedly lie to you, and not only you but to three others too, that's a real problem.

I just feel silly for allowing it to happen and getting myself caught up in a such a mess where so many feelings were hurt.

I wish nothing but the best for Kayleigh, I really mean that.

I hope she finds or has found someone who treats her the way she deserves to be treated. I don't know if she has because I'm still blocked but I know she'll be reading this.

To Nadia, you're the one good thing that's come out of this absolute shit-show. Keep being you and being the amazing person you truly are.

To Laura…

I think about you often. I'm sorry that your precious time on Earth was wasted by him. You deserved the world and so much more. You were a beautiful girl, with a beautiful soul. A fun-loving, larger-than-life party animal and I hope you're up there drinking all sorts of pints. I know you will be x

And to any girl out there reading this and thinking that maybe they're the 'other girl' – trust your gut. If something doesn't feel right that's because it probably isn't.

When red flags are waving you straight in the face, don't ignore them and assume things will get better. Act immediately... shove the red flag right up his arse and be done with it.

And to Jack... I don't really have much to say to you, but what I will say is, I hope you're miserable. I'm all about forgive and forget, usually, but not for you. I hope your 'house' is still a fucking pigstye like you and that you never find happiness because you don't fucking deserve it.

17. Waving Goodbye to the Penthouse

So there I was once again, totally and utterly, fucking over this 'single life'.

I'd got more grief being single this last year than I had in any relationship I'd ever been in before.

After Jack, I began to question everything about myself.

Why was I letting these guys like Dave, Chris, and that worm Jack walk all over me, all the fucking time?

I will admit, that after Jack dropped off the face of the earth, I felt a bit off with myself.

I was in the same cycle with these disposable men, they didn't want me as a girlfriend, but they wanted me for sex and I just let it happen.

I nit-picked things and put them to the question.

Is this why I'm not 'girlfriend material'?

Was I not skinny enough?

Was I not pretty enough?

Was I not funny enough?

Was I just not enough, full stop?

I just couldn't put my finger on what was wrong with me, but it was just a horrendous feeling that I just couldn't shift.

As I sat on my sofa, not heartbroken by any means, but just numb to the world.

I felt used in so many ways.

I looked around my pokey flat and imagined all the guys that had come and gone through the door over the last three years and sighed.

I wanted a change, and I wanted it now.

After much deliberation with myself, I decided that it was time to move out of the top-floor penthouse.

The last wee while I'd been here, I'd been in quite a shitty place.

I was drinking a lot, partying a lot and sleeping with all the wrong guys a lot – and I just wanted out of this space for a new start.

Because of my chaotic social life, I didn't have quite enough savings to actually buy somewhere at that moment in time so I asked my auntie Elaine if I could move in with her.

My auntie Elaine is absolutely wild, that must be where I get it from.

She's a single, self-employed hairdresser in her 40s and lives with her Frenchie, Grace – I love them both to bits.

After speaking to her, she said I could stay in her spare room until I'd saved up enough to eventually buy somewhere and I was so grateful.

I didn't really want to move back home with my parents just because that felt like a step backwards.

Whereas moving in with Elaine was like moving in with my cool big sister, she was so laid back she was horizontal and a brilliant laugh, it wasn't a bad idea at all.

Within a month of my conversation with Auntie Elaine, I packed up my belongings and handed back the keys to my first ever home of my own.

Shutting the door for the final time, I remembered the pre-night out selfie spot in the hall that me and all my friends posed at in our best outfits for the 'gram.

I laughed as I thought about the several times I'd hung my head out the Juliet balcony and puffed on a menthol when I was drunk.

I also smiled for the abundance of laughs I had in this place.

Walking down the first flight of stairs with the remainder of my belongings, I remembered every single guy who scaled them in order to get in between my sheets and I smiled and cringed at the same time.

Regardless of there being no happy ending in the romantic side of things, the real happy ending was actually a new beginning.

I was about to embark on a new chapter of my life.

The end goal was to get on the property ladder and saying goodbye to this place was my first steppingstone to that dream.

The Gorely Place Party Penthouse 2016 – 2019.

Gone but never forgotten.

18. The Absolute Wanker

When I first arrived at my new home, my brother Jonny, Auntie Elaine, Auntie Pauline, and wee cousin Ellie set up a human conveyor belt to get all my belongs from Jonny's van and my tiny A1 into my new bedroom.

Flitting is a bloody shift by the way, but we got there in the end and when I eventually flopped down on my bed, I felt a pang of sadness.

The contents of my two-bedroom flat surrounded me in the second bedroom in Elaine's house.

I started to question if I'd made a mistake or not as I couldn't believe I'd left my own place behind, I felt like I'd given up freedom and independence.

Anyone who knows me knows that I have more clothes than every shop in Argyle Street put together, so I had to put most of my things in a storage unit owned by my other cousin, Hayley.

Following my penthouse departure, I had to scatter my possessions all over Lanarkshire. My mum had some of my clothes stored in her garage, my other auntie kept my TV and cocktail glasses (priorities) and the rest of my things were staring at me in the face in my new bedroom.

The only thing in Elaine's spare room prior to my arrival was a random freezer so I had to stack a chest of drawers on top of it and make the most of the space.

From my old flat I also brought a double bed, a clothes rail, a bedside table, a washing basket, a small TV, another chest of drawers and boxes and boxes of shoes.

One thing was for sure, I certainly wouldn't be bringing any man back here, it was like Aladdin's Cave!

Despite giving up my freedom, I absolutely loved staying with Elaine.

She really is the kindest soul I know, who would do anything for anyone.

Elaine's hairdressing salon was at the back of her house directly below my room, so the only downside of staying there was getting woken up by the sound of hot hairdryers and hairdresser chit-chat on a Saturday morning, but I didn't mind so much.

Grace also chewed my favourite slippers on my first night, but she's extremely cute, so all was forgiven pretty quickly.

On my first Friday night in the house, we toasted to the weekend and to being housemates for the foreseeable and sat down to a bottle of wine and an Indian takeaway. I tried to convince Elaine to download Tinder as she'd been single for a few years but she was having none of it so I let her play on mine with the hopes that she'd help me find the man of my dreams.

We would sit on her sofa in our pyjamas each night after work, occasionally, more so than not, with a glass of wine, watching EastEnders, having a giggle and savagely swiping left and right.

Elaine encouraged me to go on dates, but I hadn't come across anyone I wanted to date on there… yet.

The good thing about not having my own place anymore was that I couldn't exactly bring anyone back on a whim because it wasn't my house. I thought this might actually be good for me to actually 'date' and not just shag and dispose like history would suggest.

One night when we were fuelled with wine, I ended up matching with a guy called Jake.

Jake was stereotypically my type, but the name Jake even gave me PTSD as it was so similar to Jack.

Dark hair, dark eyes… the usual.

From his pictures he looked like a good laugh although his fashion choices were a bit off the wall.

In every picture on his profile, he had a different funky patterned short sleeved shirt on from leopard print to zebra to Hawaiian to polka dots.

His bio described him as having a 'dad bod' but in these times that doesn't always mean you have a child.

Jake opened the conversation by commenting on how nice my eyes were and we went from there.

He was cheeky, funny and was certainly handsome… a route I'd been down oh so many times before.

But this time, we're dating and not shagging, remember?

This was my new motto. I don't have crazy house bills to pay anymore so I could go out for as many dinners and drinks as a I wanted, although I should really have been saving every single penny, I made towards buying my first proper home, but forget that for now.

Jake told me he was actually English but was living in Scotland because he was in the Navy.

Hmmm.

Red flag?

Jack was in the army and we all knew how that ended so I was sceptical because the Navy was basically the same thing, wasn't it? Probably not but you know, it's similar.

In true Kirsten fashion, I chose to ignore said red flag waving me in the face and continued talking to Jake. I'm sure not every guy in the Navy is bad but I was just going from my previous experience.

As our conversation got deeper, it transpires that Jake is newly separated from his soon-to-be ex-wife who lives down in England with their three children.

Now, this isn't a red flag by any means, but it already seems like a tricky situation.

Jake was thirty-three years old, but even going by his chat, he was a man child who loved to party.

Now this is where it gets slightly odd.

I can't remember exactly how he worded it but he said that there would be days at a time where we wouldn't be able to speak because he would be working for two days and wouldn't have his phone because… he was on a submarine.

A submarine?

What the fuck?

I've never even met anyone in the Navy before in my puff except that random I winched at the Fringe but we hardly spoke so I wouldn't know if this is true or not but, I wouldn't hear from him for a few days at a time.

Again, another red flag perhaps? If it was… I ignored that too.

I already knew this would never go anywhere but he seemed like a nice guy to chat to, plus it must be quite lonely living up here and having next to no one but your work mates.

Did I not say earlier that I should never waste time on something I know isn't going anywhere?

Yes, I did.

The chat between Jake and I was just OK. He often pestered me to meet up with him and took the huff when I made excuses.

I knew the whole ex-wife and kids in England thing was a problem in itself and I just knew he wasn't 'The One' either – even without even meeting him.

It was hassle I didn't need to be involved in.

I made several excuses not to meet up with him, but one Friday night around 6 p.m., he cornered me over text.

What are you up to tonight, then?

Not much, just chilling probably. What about you?

Fancy going for dinner, since you're free

FUCK.

I couldn't really say no, but I didn't really want to go.

A bit short notice, is it not? I replied, hoping he would agree.

It's now or never really. I go back to Bradford to see the kids on Sunday for two weeks.

Jesus.

Right, OK then, what's the plan? I panicked.

Why don't we meet halfway in Braehead about 8? He suggested.

Yeah OK, I'm away to get ready then.

See you soon x

I ran into Elaine's room in a total flap.

'OH MY GOD! I NEED YOUR HELP! I HAVE A DATE IN AN HOUR!' I wailed.

She looked up from her magazine.

'What?! With who?' She laughed.

'One of the guys you matched me with last week! The guy with the weird shirts.'

She beamed, proud of her work.

'What are you going to wear then?'

'God knows! What have you got!?'

Elaine tossed her magazine on the bed and dashed over to her wardrobe and together we rummaged through the packed rails to come up with something quick.

I was going to Braehead shopping centre for fuck's sake! I didn't need to be glammed up at all.

We settled for a pair of black skinny jeans, Elaine's Dr Marten boots, and a black blazer with a bright scarf – also Elaine's, she really was a saviour.

I blew the dust off my Chanel perfume and scooshed it all over myself as my fabulous hairdresser auntie straightened the back of my barnet.

To be honest, I think Elaine was more excited about my date than I was. She cuddled me as I shot out the door, shouting, 'Good luck!'

Jake had told me to meet him at the front door of Braehead.

How romantic.

After a twenty-five-minute drive and the usual pre-date pep talk with Caitlin on the phone, I parked my car, checked my lip gloss in the mirror quickly and I still couldn't believe that I'd agreed to a first date at a shopping centre, it was like the coffee in Next all over again!

It was a cold November night, and the icy air stung my cheeks as I made my way to meet yet another Tinder date.

Would he be wearing a crazy patterned shirt? I hoped not, especially that Kat Slater-esqe leopard print one from his pictures. I couldn't be seen dead with him in that.

Hot air blew on my freshly GHD'd hair as I walked through the automatic doors to the shopping centre and there he was, leaning casually on the wall looking at his phone.

AND JUST LIKE his pictures, he was handsome.

He had a lovely, dazzling smile and his brown eyes gazed right over to me when he eventually looked up. There was no horrid shirt in sight as he opened his arms to give me a cuddle.

The thing that struck me though was his accent, a broad English accent.

'All right, love, how ah ya? You look luvely!'

In my head, I cringed. Love?

'Where do you wanna go for dinner?' He asked, cocking his head to the side.

'I don't mind really. Anywhere!' I smiled back.

As we looked around at the busy food court, everywhere was packed except one place, that sat in the corner looking sad and empty.

Chiquitos.

'Do you like Mexican food?' he asked, peering over at it.

'Yeah, I do actually,' I lied.

Well, it wasn't really a lie because I did like Mexican food, but I hated Chiquitos. I'd been a few times before and every time I had been it was rotten and by rotten, I mean afterwards — spending the rest of my night in the toilet.

We walked up to the entrance and some cheery waiter with a sombrero on showed us straight to a booth at the window — for the whole world to see.

I didn't know if this was an attempt to make the restaurant look busy, but I winced a bit at the thought of anyone I knew walking by and being able to see me on this first date.

I don't know what it was, but I just didn't have a good feeling about it at all.

We ordered colas and browsed the menu. The safe option would have been quesadillas, but the thought of mispronouncing it and making a tit of myself in front of this guy I've only met about six minutes ago made me opt for fajitas.

After giving our order to the cheery waiter, I then panicked for a minute about how I would construct the spicy wrap, eat it, and have a 'get to know me conversation' all at the same time.

Multi-tasking wasn't really my strong point, but I couldn't change it now.

After the menus were whipped from our hands, there was a small awkward silence between us.

The buzz of the cheesy Mexican music rang in my ears, and I began to wonder if going for a meal with this guy was a good idea.

'So how far do you live from here?' he piped up, looking at me dead in the eyes.

His brown eyes, my god they were magical. I was so drawn to them that I hardly took in what he said.

Then I snapped back to life.

'Oh, em, about twenty minutes in the car?'

I sipped on my Coke through a paper straw. God, I hated those things.

My sticky lip gloss practically sealed it together, so every time I tried to take a sip, my cheeks drew in.

I spotted him looking at me intensely every time I sucked the straw. It was all very odd.

By the time our dinner came, we'd gotten into the conversation about his ex-wife and children.

He said he saw them every three weeks as he would travel down to England during his time off.

This may sound harsh, but he didn't strike me as the doting dad at all, if I'm honest.

He didn't gloat about them or even really smile when he spoke about them, which I found a little strange.

I could be completely wrong. Maybe he just didn't give strangers details about his kids, but then there was something about his dismissive manner that I found a little weird.

I picked at my food with a fork. I really didn't feel like eating.

But Jake, on the other hand, gorged his way through an extra spicy burrito.

With bits of rice falling out of his mouth, he went on to ask me about my work and what it was I 'actually did' and all the rest of the predictable questions that are asked on first dates.

I would say something about myself and he would always refer back to his life in the Navy, and it was pretty annoying. I just felt like if I'd been to Tenerife, he'd have been to Eleven-erife.

He proceeded to tell me he lived in a Navy house with his friend and that I should come over one time and he'll cook me dinner.

I looked up at him after pushing a bit of chicken around my plate.

What?

In the back of my mind, I'd already written off seeing him again after our Mexican feast, for being a bit arrogant and someone I didn't have a lot in common with, but strangely, he seemed keen on a second date.

Jake cleared his plate and I indicated that I'd had enough by placing a napkin over my barely touched food, and the cheery waiter came over to take them away. I took one last sip at the dregs of my cola.

'You have the most beautiful eyes,' Jake whispered, leaning his chin on the palm of his hand.

I raised my eyebrows.

'Eh, thanks!'

I hated compliments. They made me feel awkward.

Know that way, you think, are they saying that for you to say, 'Aww, so do you'? It made me cringe.

When the bill arrived, I pulled out my purse and offered to pay half, but he insisted that he was getting it, which was nice.

I thanked him.

'Should we head?' He grinned.

I grabbed my coat, and he ushered me from the booth and I thanked him again for dinner.

'I had a great time, you're so gorgeous you know,' he told me.

I blushed again. Why does he keep saying it? What do I say back? Thanks?

As we walked through the shopping centre, I could feel his hand brush the base of my back.

I didn't know how to feel about it. He was a nice guy, attractive, but I just knew he wasn't for me.

I didn't even think he was Mr Right Now, never mind Mr Right.

'Shall we take a walk?' he said, tilting his head to the side in thought.

Part of me just wanted to go home as I was slightly concerned the fajitas would bag me a spot on the toilet for the rest of the night, but I agreed, feeling OK in that moment.

We strolled around the outside of the shopping centre – how romantic – and just as we went to turn a corner he grabbed me and pulled me in for a kiss.

Jake was a great kisser don't get me wrong, but he literally caged me in his arms to the point I had cramp in my neck, it just didn't feel natural, but I kissed him back anyway and finally broke free from his arms for air.

'I think I'll head soon, I need to get back,' I told him not being able to think of any sort of excuse to back up my exit.

'I'll walk you back to your car, make sure you get there safe,' he replied, taking my hand.

We had parked at opposite ends of the car park so as we began to head for mine, the grip of his hand on mine got tighter.

Again, I wasn't a huge fan of this but given the temperature of the cold November evening, I welcomed it, plus it really wasn't that far to walk, and no one could see us, he was slightly warming to me… he seemed like quite a gentleman.

As we approached my white A1, I geared up to say my goodbyes when he suggested that I drive him over to his car because it was cold.

I looked at him thinking it was a bit of a silly suggestion, but he was right, it was freezing beyond belief.

He hopped in the passenger side and moved the junk that I'd gathered on the seat into the back. The minute he shut the door over, he leant over and kissed me again, this time pushing me right over so my head was pressed against my window with my wrists in his hands.

It took me by surprise, if anyone could see us, we looked like a pair of teenagers getting off in a fucking shopping centre car park.

His hands began to wander down my jumper and that's when I knew I needed to get rid of him.

'No, enough!' I whispered, not wanting anymore.

'But why? You're so hot!' he purred, grabbing my back of my head with his two hands and sticking his tongue further down my throat.

I pushed him off again.

'No! We're in the middle of Braehead fucking car park!' I snapped.

As he fell back into the seat from me pushing him away, he was panting, clearly aroused and wanting more.

'OK, I'm sorry, I just couldn't help myself, you're so gorgeous.'

It was like a completely different person to the guy who sat across from me and wolfed down a burrito about twenty minutes before.

I was so confused.

I didn't say anything, I just strapped my seat belt in and asked him where his car was. He pointed over to an isolated Audi A3 a little in the distance and I put my foot down on the accelerator.

Pulling up next to it, I thanked him again for dinner and once more he went in for the kill.

I kissed him back for about two seconds and then pulled away.

'Text me when you get home safe, thanks for a great night!' he winked.

'Thanks, bye!'

As soon as he shut the door over, I sped off.

On the drive home, I tried to process everything that had just happened.

Was it a good date? I didn't even know.

He was nice, a good kisser but very full-on from when we got in the car, but at dinner I didn't think we gelled that well?

I was very confused.

The only thing I think that sizzled on the date were the hot fajitas and not the chemistry.

I called Pam on the way home, obviously leaving out the detail about the weird car kiss, but I told her that he was not 'The One' but would maybe see him again just to be sure.

'You can only see how it goes,' she chimed back, feeling happy that I was back on the dating scene once again.

Such a typical maw thing to say, wasn't it?

But I still knew deep down this wouldn't be anything serious.

After about half an hour, I arrived back home to Elaine's and got ready to give her a full debrief about the date.

I opened the front door and was greeted by Grace, jumping up, clearly happy to see me.

'Well... I want to know everything!' Elaine beamed, as I flopped on to the sofa feeling deflated.

So I told her about what happened and that I just knew it wasn't going to work out.

'Oh well! Thank you, next!' she giggled.

'You're right, I might see him again just for something to do, anyway, I'm away to get my pyjamas on, get me a wine poured – pronto!'

As I glanced at my phone for the first time since getting home, I had quite a lot of messages.

A few from the group chat asking how it went, one from my mum too.

Let me know when you're home!

And three from Jake.

What the...

I opened it and gasped.

I really can't stop thinking about you since I got home, so here's what you've made me do...

Hope you like it, babe.

And there, attached to the messages was a video of Jake stroking his manhood for about two minutes, then finishing off with a happy ending – all over his bed covers.

Instantly repulsed by its contents (or lack of) I screwed my face up and died inside a little.

The last thing I expected on the back of this date was to receive a wanking video upon my arrival home.

I replied.

Really didn't need to see that tbh. Not for me.

But you made me so horny, I wanted to rip your clothes off in the car.

As much as I would love to tell you I never seen him again after this, I did, as we know, I have a tendency of being a two-date wonder.

Stupidly, I took him up on that offer at dinner at his one night after work.

His house was the oddest wee house I'd ever seen. It had no character whatsoever.

Two navy-blue dinky sofas and a matching navy carpet with a TV which looked like it was from the 90s graced the living room and that was it.

I'm not judging him on that, obviously, it's his home for work but after he 'cooked' me an M&S pizza, he was extremely pushy in wanting me to go all the way with him, which I declined.

He used the tactic to 'show me around' and up to his room, which I only can describe as a uni halls room.

A basic double bed, a dark wood standing wardrobe, and one bedside table.

He kissed me and manoeuvred us over to the bed but when he tried to go further that's when I really knew this wasn't for me.

I felt uncomfortable and I just really didn't want to be here anymore.

When I said no, he respected it and we went back downstairs.

It was so awkward. We'd exhausted every bit of conversation we had so he turned on the TV as a distraction.

We watched a bit of *I'm a Celebrity Get Me Out of Here* and I knew that I had to 'Get Out of Here' so I made an excuse that I was tired and left shortly after.

And I never heard from him again.

WHAT DID I learn from my experience with Jake?

1. After they send you wanking videos on the first date, run for the hills.

2. Jake and Jack are my new red flag names.

3. It's OK to say no. Don't EVER feel pressured to do anything you don't want to do, and don't just do it because the other person really wants to.

19. Sunday Stew

The girls in work hardly entertained my dating stories anymore, nothing I could possibly say would shock them now.

After the Mexican wanking story and the fact I went back for a second serving, Stef said she didn't even have sympathy for me now – touché.

Where are the normal guys? The guys that just want to go on normal dates and do normal things?

It was now a whole month since my stint at the Navy house and my God I was ready to meet someone.

I was absolutely over Tinder and was focusing on just Bumble because I wanted to test Claire's theory that it's 'more up market' again, so I gave it another go.

I matched with a guy called Scott. He fell into the 'mountain scaler' category but despite previously swearing that these guys were not for me, I had to try out different options because let's face it, workies, football fans and guys in the army had not been successful thus far.

Scott seemed nice, his chat was fairly bland but there is only so much you can get a feel for someone over texts.

He worked for a technology company and seemed like a bit of a geeky gamer type, I really was clutching at straws here.

Scott had mousey brown hair, blue eyes and was quite skinny… not my usual brown-eyed guy but again, they hardly had a track record for sweeping me off my feet, did they?

Scott asked if I wanted to go out for a drink that weekend but I was working a double shift at Starbucks, so we agreed to meet on Monday night at a bar in Glasgow.

Monday night dates? I was really changing up my technique here, and at this point I really was willing to give anything a go.

Was it desperate? Maybe. I was absolutely looking too hard.

I'd now been properly single for almost three years, and after being at Jodie's wedding in the October and being the only single bridesmaid there, part of me just ached to be loved and to be wanted.

I wanted a plus one at a wedding. I wanted the weekends away. I wanted to be adored by someone like so many of my friends were.

Did I feel like I was left out? Absolutely.

Scott had arranged to meet me in O'Neill's bar in Merchant City. Not the most amazing place but I didn't really care.

It was absolutely dead on a Monday. There were a few old men sitting at the bar stools but that was it.

I shamelessly wore the same outfit I had on when I met Jake because let's face it, black is super flattering.

As I looked around the empty bar for Scott, there tucked in the corner I could see a guy sitting with his back to me.

That must be him, unless he was the balding man in his 70s in the other corner.

I got closer to the table and glanced at him up and down and the first thing I noticed were his boots.

Scott was wearing totally battered, brown, suede Chelsea boots and they were really awful – they'd definitely seen better days.

This guy hadn't even clocked me yet and I'd already written him off.

I tapped him on the shoulder to grab his attention.

'Hi! Sorry I'm a bit late.' I smiled, examining the front of him.

'Heeeey, Kirsten! So lovely to meet you!' His high-pitched voice let out.

Oh dear, I already didn't fancy him.

Scott wore a tight-fitting T-shirt, and his glasses were thick rimmed ones, like those 'geek' specks you used to wear at Halloween when you had last-minute plans and had to scramble for an outfit.

'What do you want to drink?' He gestured towards the bar as he already had a pint of Guinness sitting in front of him.

'A pink gin and lemonade please.' I smiled.

I studied him as he leant on the bar on his elbows. He made me cringe and I didn't know why. He seemed... I don't know the right word... camp? I just got camp vibes from him, but I had to remind myself that I was trying new things and not going for the norm, so I had to give him a chance. It was only a date anyway; I didn't really need to see him after this.

I couldn't help but stare at the Chelsea boots though, they really were awful. I never really judged a guy by his shoes before but now I was – they bothered me, they really bothered me.

Scott returned from the bar clutching the goblet of gin and was smiling like a maniac and we began to get to know each other.

As he spoke about his life, telling me that he had just bought his first flat and all about his decor ideas.

I couldn't help but notice that he was really animated, he used so many hand gestures when he spoke. He would also touch my forearm sometimes after he told me a story and say, 'you know?'.

It was just bizarre.

We got on fine, but I definitely got more friendly vibes from him, but the gins kept flowing and I wasn't having a terrible time.

Scott didn't blow my socks off but let's be honest what else would I be doing on a Monday night?

I think I'd had about four gins when he suggested that we go to the little Irish bar across the road called Connelly's.

I agreed, again thinking that the only other thing I would be doing otherwise would be watching *EastEnders* on the couch with Elaine plus I loved a good Irish bar.

I grabbed my blazer and we headed for the door.

We stepped outside and as I fixed the strap on my bag to my shoulder, Scott tugged me in towards him and started to kiss me.

His glasses banged off my face a few times, it was pretty awkward, but I kissed him back anyway and when he pulled away I had to wipe his saliva off my chin, there weren't fireworks by any means but the gins made it a bit more tolerable.

Inside Connolly's, I swear we were the only two people there apart from the guy behind the bar and a man sitting near the door with a fiddle.

The man with the fiddle looked delighted that he finally had someone to play to so he struck up a tune and I couldn't help but once again feel awkward, we were being serenaded.

I decided to get the drinks in this time, so I ordered a Guinness for him and another gin for me.

After swiping my card on the contactless machine, I shuffled over Scott, who was sitting at the table in the far corner, out of eye shot of the fiddle man.

As I sat down, he planted another kiss on me and at this point, I was thankful for his choice of seat, I was dying at the thought of anyone witnessing this sloppy scene.

We began talking about something and as I was telling Scott more about myself, he gazed at me very lovingly as I spoke and tucked a bit of my hair behind my ear and began stroking it, which gave me the absolute ICK.

Why would he do that?

I wasn't a dog?

I don't know why I didn't have the balls to say 'Right, mate, enough's enough, can you stop that please?'

Once again, he stuck his big lips on me and I quickly kissed him back, before insisting that we must head for the train soon.

The ICK was peaking, get me the fuck home!

The way it worked out Scott and I got on the same train, and he would get off about five stops before me.

Five stops wasn't soon enough.

We sat at one of those seats with a table and across from us at the other table were about four teenagers blaring out songs from their phones.

Scott kept trying to kiss me on the train too, does this guy ever stop?

And all I could think about was one of those teenagers recording us for their Snapchat, saying 'look at these weirdos'.

I brushed him off me numerous times and soon he was getting off.

As we were approaching his stop, he tried to ram his rampant tongue down my throat once more, but I opted for a peck instead.

'See you soon!' He smiled skipping out of the automatic doors and waving through the window.

I let out a sigh of relief and just kind of nodded back to him.

Pam had said she'd come and collect me from the station, and take me back to Elaine's, obviously just wanting all the date gossip.

'Well!? How did it go?' she beamed as I hopped into her car.

'Naa, too much, he had the most awful pair of boots on ever.'

I then received a lecture from her for not giving anyone a chance, it's true though, the boots didn't do it for me, neither did the hair stroking or train winching, I just knew he wasn't for me.

IT WAS THE weekend. Nadia and I were going to the football together and we planned a whole day shot.

It was a 3 p.m. kick off and I actually arrived at her house at 10 a.m. with a bag full of drink ready to make the most of it.

I'd still been texting Scott briefly, but I was playing it very cool and trying to subtly drop the hint that we wouldn't be seeing each other again.

I told Nadia every last detail of our date and she burst out laughing each time.

'Where do you find these guys?' She giggled, knowing fine well the answer.

We toasted to the single life and downed our first vodkas just shortly after 10.

I already could taste the hang-over in my mouth, but I didn't care one bit.

Nadia and I had a great day at the football, we were absolutely blitzed by the time we even got to the game, but afterwards, we decided to head to the pub, to most likely continue with our shenanigans.

Jumping into an Uber, we told the driver to take us to Grace's bar, you know the one, to drink more venoms.

I absolutely did have PTSD after walking into the bar that basically helped me ruin my life the night I took Chris home, but at this point I was so drunk that it was soon a distant memory once the first sip of venom crossed my lips.

We danced to Irish music, took shots of tequila, ordered more drinks, and chatted up some very unattractive men at the bar, my God those beer goggles are so deceiving.

I pulled my phone out of my bag.

Scott text me asking what I was up to and if I wanted to go meet up with him after the pub.

I laughed and showed it to Nadia.

'Are you going?' She laughed, drunkenly.

'I mean, he gives me the ICK, but I've not got anyone else on the go at the mo' I said chugging back my fourth pint of venom.

Before I knew it, I was in a taxi, on my way to Scott's flat.

Bad decision? Absolutely! I didn't even like him in the slightest for fuck's sake.

In all absolute honesty, I don't even remember getting into a taxi at all.

I vaguely remember climbing stairs with my football scarf dragging on the floor and Scott greeting me at the door.

The rest is a blur.

THE SOUND OF busy traffic outside woke me up.

I was alone in a bedroom, bundled among beige and brown bedcovers.

I looked at my surroundings and spotted a free-standing mirror in the corner.

Crawling out of the bed and on to a manky brown carpet, I padded over to look at the sight of myself.

I actually let out a gasp.

I had one of my high-top Converse still on and the other one was lying at the other end of the room. My clothes were still on, and my hair was like a bird's fucking nest.

Oh my God. What the fuck happened last night?

Where was Scott? Obviously, I didn't sleep with him because my one lace was still triple knotted on my foot, meaning my trousers definitely didn't come off unless I shagged him with one shoe on.

Na, I definitely didn't. I knew it.

I picked up my other shoe and put it back on and decided to venture outside this brown room to see if he was still here.

I creeped along the long and dark hallway, light belted out at the end of the corridor, and I could hear a few noises.

I walked past those godawful Chelsea boots sitting at the door and winced a little; they were still as awful as I remembered.

I peeked my head around the door; it was the kitchen and there was Scott standing chopping carrots and throwing them into a slow cooker.

He peered up over his glasses.

'Good morning, how's the head?'

'Not great. I'm so sorry, was I a riot, what happened last night?'.

'You were very drunk weren't you – don't worry you were fine. I'm just making stew for my family coming over later, I'm going to pop to Lidl and get some bits do you need anything?'

Oh my God, get me fucking out of here right now!

Chopping carrots?

Stew?

Lidl?

Absolutely not. I need a taxi and I need one like yesterday.

'No, I'm just going to get a taxi home'.

I booked an Uber as soon as possible and text Nadia saying I was coming to hers asap for a debrief.

It was about 9 a.m., and I had another bout of The Fear.

Scott gave me yet another kiss as I walked down the stairs of his flat and into my Uber, I was surprised he even came near me again after my drunken antics last night, oh God, what did I do?

I tried to so many times figure out what exactly happened and how I ended up being in the pub with Nadia, to being in the most horrendous beige and brown room I'd ever seen.

As I sat in the back of the cab trying to avoid that terrible small talk with the driver, I began getting flashbacks of being in Scott's flat.

I *think*, I'm trying to convince myself for my sanity that we didn't, but I think some 'bits' were done, I possibly maybe even tried to pull my trainers off, but to no avail?

I didn't even want to try to remember because what an absolute RED NECK!

Before the taxi stopped at Nadia's, I jumped into Tesco to get some rolls and square sausage and two cans of Irn-Bru for us to try to curb the hang-over, what a fright those Tesco customers must have gotten that day.

When I arrived outside Nadia's house, I handed the driver a crumpled up £20 note and went on my way.

I chapped her door, and when she pulled it back to welcome me, I'm not sure who looked worse if I'm honest.

But as we glanced up and down at one another, we both burst out laughing at the same time.

I did the walk of shame up Nadia's steps swinging the bag of hang-over goodies in my hand.

'What the fuck happened last night?' she giggled, cracking open one of the cans of juice.

'I don't even know, and I don't even want to know,' I replied, shutting my eyes in pain at my actions.

The both of us crawled into Nadia's bed and spent the day eating hang-over food and cry laughing as the flash backs continued from the night before.

Scott had been given the new nickname Puss in Boots, also due to the fact that I couldn't get mine off to actually sleep with him.

We laughed, and we laughed, and we laughed.

There really is nothing better than lying in bed, hung-over with one of your pals. I may be single, but I definitely wasn't alone.

That day I did nothing but smile. I may not have heard from Puss in Boots again, but I didn't care one bit.

WHAT I DID take away from the situation was:

1. See when you're not feeling a winch? Don't just do it anyway.

2. I never want to see stew in a slow cooker ever-a-fucking-gain.

3. If you're trying to pull, don't wear triple knotted high tops.

20. Mr Golden Shower

It was now January 2020, and I was moving out of Elaine's house and into a place all my own.

I'd planned to stay there much longer but I just really missed having a space of my own and living in a tiny second room crammed with all my belongings was really grating on me.

My friend Samantha had sent me this two-bedroom flat in Motherwell on her daily snoop of Rightmove and I went to view it right away.

I knew more or less instantly that I had to have it and that was that.

Not really having a fucking clue what I was doing, I put an offer in and it was accepted straight away… I was going to be a HOMEOWNER!

It was all systems go to move into my new pad and while I was picking out paint samples and deciding on what new dinner sets to buy, online dating took a back seat.

At this moment in time, trying to entertain a man was the least of my worries and I had all the apps deleted from my phone – plus I was sleeping on a mattress on the floor for seven weeks until my bed was delivered so I didn't want to bring anyone back for a shag and for them to think I was living in a crack den, you know?

I threw myself into making this house a home for a few weeks before jetting off to Copenhagen with Caitlin for our annual football jaunt.

As always, pints were consumed, boys were winched and we had a fucking ball, if I told you some of the stories from that holiday, I would have to kill you.

What happens on tour, stays on tour, right?

At the time, it was the end of February, there were whispers of something called 'coronavirus' but apparently it was only in China, and no one really thought much of it.

After the Copenhagen saga, I got home and decided to once again to reinstall those dreaded apps back on my phone to curb the boredom.

I was ready to play the swiping game once again for what I promised myself would be the last time.

I was bloody skint, nobody really tells you exactly how expensive it is to buy a house or about all the hidden costs you need to pay, so I had no money to do anything except sit in my new gaff and hopefully meet the man of my dreams online. Where the fuck is he?

By this point, I'd been properly single for three years, three whole years since Dean and I split. I felt so ready to meet someone, but I was also ready to not have my fingers burnt again or get way ahead of myself and imagine my wedding with the next guy I matched with online.

I decided this time with Tinder and Bumble that I had to be ruthless, and I shouldn't just give sympathy swipes for people who I thought seemed 'just OK'.

'Just OK' wasn't good enough anymore.

'Take it seriously this time Kirsten,' I told myself as I uploaded the same Dubai tit picture on to my profile for what seemed like the 40-millionth time.

It was honestly as bad as I remembered it to be, and I even spotted some of the guys who had profiles when I first joined.

It really was quite depressing.

I matched with a few people, surprise, surprise, another gas engineer, a banker, and a mortgage advisor.

I left it a few days without appearing to be too keen. I sent a few messages and left some others to message me first but once one week went by and if their chat was shit or they hadn't spoken, I swiftly unmatched them – I was taking it seriously this time plus I couldn't be arsed with time wasters or silent duds taking up my inbox.

I was busy painting my bedroom one Thursday night, when my phone flashed – I had a message 'request' on Instagram... I immediately had PTSD from when Kayleigh dropped a message request in my inbox for the Jack drama, but I hadn't been chatting to anyone for a while so the possibility of me being involved in another love triangle was relatively slim.

It was a message from someone called Robert, that I wasn't following and didn't follow me... weird.

I opened it.

Hey. Sorry for the random message. We matched on Tinder and with the whole Covid-19 thing last week, I never replied as was so busy dealing with angry customers. I went to message you today and realised you had unmatched. Disappointed as I think you're a really good-looking girl and have a super cute smile. So was hoping you'd still want to message me but understand if you don't or have met someone else x

I won't lie 'super cute smile' really made my toes curl but the fact he went out his way to track me down meant he must be keen but I was torn, 'super cute' wasn't in my vocabulary... was I being a bitch?

I had a quick look at his profile. He seemed pretty attractive and met the usual physical criteria for me – 'dark hair/brown eyes' so I thought why the hell not.

This coronavirus thing seemed to be much closer to home now too – we really didn't know what was happening with it at all, but again, I thought nothing of it.

I replied to his message saying I didn't mind chatting to him and we went from there.

Robert was thirty-eight, so more than ten years older than me, but he didn't look it really, or did he just take a good picture? He was a mortgage advisor, had a wee white dog called Russell, and had his own place in Edinburgh – a bit away from me but it didn't really matter.

He seemed really, really, REALLY keen. Like the keenest bean I'd ever spoken to in such a short time.

Despite being much older than me he seemed to have decent chat, appeared to have his head screwed on, and also appeared to really want to get to know me and evidently – date me.

He also subtly reminded me of Dave in so many ways and not just because he was much older… because the chat quickly turned into sex talk.

Aside from that, though, he seemed like a pretty decent guy, and I was willing to see where it went, so we continued to text all day and night.

Robert was so interested in my job, my life and, most of all, my house.

He quizzed me on the decor of my newly bought flat, which was kind of odd – none of my Tinder suitors had done this before.

I'd recently made an Instagram account (@gaffatthegrange) to document the DIY/decorating progress I was making, and Robert wanted to know where everything was from, how I was going to do things, and was always telling me ways I should do certain DIY projects. Early on I got the vibe he was a bit of a control freak – first red flag noted, maybe? Or was he just being nice?

I thought he was maybe just being nice and trying to form some helpful chat which seemed sweet, I supposed.

At the start of the month, I left my job with my local paper and moved to a different role within the company. I'd landed my dream job as a showbiz writer, and I was absolutely over the moon about it.

However, my showbiz bubble soon burst only three weeks after starting as I was sent home to work due to this coronavirus palaver.

It wasn't ideal but I was told it would be for a month max so it shouldn't be too bad, really.

After slogging away in my spare room, 4 p.m. soon rolled around and I text Robert saying I'd just finished.

Within seconds my phone started ringing, but not with a phone call, it was FaceTime!

Oh no, he's not a FaceTimer is he?

I screwed up my face, is there anything more awkward or embarrassing than FaceTiming someone who you've never met before?

I hesitated before shyly answering. I'd never even spoken to this guy on the phone before never mind a FaceTime.

I was cringing but I decided to be polite and answer.

Robert was giving it the 'hello you' chat and quizzed me on how my day went, our conversation seemed pretty normal and didn't have to be forced so that was something, but I didn't know, there was something about him that I just felt was a little off, but I gave him the benefit of the doubt.

'So, when can I take you out on a date?' He smiled as he walked his dog in the street.

Robert had a bit of an Edinburgh accent and even though he wasn't that far away, sometimes he didn't really know what I was saying.

I was from Lanarkshire, so not quite a Glaswegian, if you're from here you'll understand what I mean.

Who knew you could have a language barrier from forty minutes down the road?

We chatted for a bit more and eventually had arranged to go out on Friday, March 20th.

But then it transpired that this coronavirus thing really was actually quite serious and Scotland's First Minister, Nicola Sturgeon, made the decision to shut the pubs, restaurants, bars, and all social venues.

Fuck. This is absolutely mental!

Robert and I decided that he would come over to mine and just stay the night, he was from Edinburgh, and he couldn't leave his dog so he would bring him too.

I mean I didn't mind; it really couldn't be helped, we didn't have the option to go out on a real date, plus we had spoken on FaceTime.

Did I like him?

Probably not.

Did I get the vibe he was 'The One'?

Definitely not.

After our official 'date' was re-organised, Robert's texts began to get a little strange.

First, he asked me what 'I would call him' when we were 'together'.

Em, Robert, because that's your name, no?

And when he said he meant pet name, my cringe scale skyrocketed.

I wasn't a pet name kinda gal whatsoever and I was very up front about that.

He asked if he could call me 'babe' to which I said absolutely not, I didn't want to be called anything – and that was the end of that.

Robert would then say things to me like 'when you're my girlfriend', 'when we live together', and 'you'll see that when you meet my family' when we hadn't even met.

Again, this gave me the ICK, he was so keen, and it really put me off, 'when we live together'? UGH!

As our 'first date' got closer, Robert tried on the extra dirty chat with me and even dropped a few dick pics in our WhatsApp.

ICK.

I mean, the guy was clearly gifted in that department but fuck's sake, I couldn't cope with them, I didn't even know what to say back?

Em, Nice?

Dicks are ugly.

Much like the pet names, I told Robert that I was not a 'send nudes' type of girl either – I was really sounding like a frigid wee bitch but sending pictures and messages with the aubergine and water emoji?

No, ta!

I enjoyed sex, like most people because it's normal but he was just taking it to a whole other level.

His sex chat sometimes was too much, that I had to draft in Claire once again to help me out.

I would again message her, 'What do I say to this?' or 'Help me reply!'

Sexting absolutely is not my forte.

After his dick pic debut, they just kept coming, and then they even upgraded to a video, and I just couldn't cope but I couldn't back out our 'date' now... he was coming tomorrow!

Every time I tried to chat to him normally, he always managed to revert it back to sex.

I was talking about one time I went out and was hung-over the next day and he then asked if I ever got the 'hang-over horn'.

Doesn't everyone?

But it didn't stop there. Robert asked me if I liked to be spanked, if I liked anal, if I liked being told what to do in the bedroom...

If there ever was another red flag waving me in the face, this was it, but what did I do? Like all the other red flags I'd seen before in my life, I chose to ignore.

Was I colour blind?

Perhaps that would be the only logical reason or I just really liked the colour red.

The man was an utter sex-fiend, and it was on his mind twenty-four hours a day.

Me on the other hand, I hadn't had sex in months (apart from a one-night stand in Manchester in January but that doesn't count) so maybe this was just what I was after. God, it was definitely what I was after – minus the anal.

But I'll give him his due, he still spoke about 'serious' things like me being his girlfriend which to be honest, made me feel more uncomfortable than being asked if I liked anal… (the answer to that is no, by the way, in case you're wondering).

Robert also told me, after FIVE whole days of chatting (yes, he really was talking about moving in together after five days) and having not met yet, that he was deleting Tinder.

I couldn't help but think that he was moving way too fast.

During those five days, I realised that he did a lot of things that put me off, including the sex chat, the unsolicited dick pics and videos, and him basically marrying us off. I should have run for the hills, or just ghosted him immediately (I should have probably done that when he sent me a video of himself wanking) but I'll admit I just wanted to see him for the sex, he seemed to really like me, like I didn't need to try very hard, that may seem harsh but it was true.

Another thing that put me off him was the fact that he was like the female version of Mrs Hinch. Not for the being a crazy cleaning fanatic because there is nothing wrong with having a clean and tidy house by all means, but it was the decor.

He had sent me pictures of his mirrored furniture, crushed velvet sofa, his white fluffy rugs, silver candlesticks and the rest, it just didn't do anything for me – his house was girly-er than mine with his 'live, laugh, love' sign and all. When he wasn't turning our conversations sexual, he was asking me my opinion on new vases for his hall, an animal print dog beds for his beloved Russell, and which fragrance of Jo Malone candle he should get for on top of his shoe cabinet.

I honestly had such mixed opinions on this guy. He seemed like two different people.

DATE DAY FINALLY arrived.

It was the Friday and as soon as I finished work I was hanging over the bathroom sink removing all traces of the grains… one leg up on the toilet with shaving foam slapped on up to my belly button. You get the gist…

I pottered about for ages tidying up the house before he arrived.

It wasn't long before I heard loud music out my front and I peered out the window to discover a white Mercedes convertible was sitting in my drive.

I caught a glimpse of Robert grabbing a bag from his boot.

He wore a tight black V-neck T-shirt, ripped black jeans, and a pair of mirrored sunglasses, he reminded me of some Premier League footballer from the early noughties – think Kyle Pascoe in *Footballer's Wives* but he also gave me Dave vibes, older guy who dresses like he's younger.

On closer inspection, it wasn't a bag he was grabbing from the boot, it was… a dog bed.

Oh, my fucking God, this is too much!

I walked over to the front door to welcome the first ever male into the new gaff, no stairs of doom either which was a bonus, and as I pulled the door back, Russell ran straight into my hall.

'Hello, you,' he said whipping off his ridiculously uncool sunglasses and grabbing me in for a kiss.

His cringe catchphrase sent a shudder up my spine, I'd barely even shut the door and he was ramming his tongue down my throat and grabbing my arse with one hand while clutching Russell's bed under the other.

The thought pained me, so I quickly pulled away and ushered him into the living room.

By this point it was about 7 p.m. and we were both absolutely starving so we decided to phone a Domino's and the minute I put the phone down from ordering a large pepperoni pizza, Robert pounced over the sofa and began to kiss me passionately.

Now it had been a while, so I wasn't really complaining but Jesus Christ, the guy didn't even have his jacket off.

371

Before I knew it, we were in the bedroom. Clothes were flying everywhere… it was all happening so fast. What the hell?

From the corner of my eye, all I could see was poor Russell standing in the doorway not knowing what was going on.

Oh my God, this is just such a bizarre scenario – there was a dug watching me get off with its human!

I honestly couldn't believe how quickly this had happened from him getting here to ripping my clothes off.

Obviously, I must say he was an attractive-looking guy, and was probably more attractive when he took the boy band clothes off, but I was not expecting to sleep with him as soon as I did, but there we were.

And just as there was passion in the air and I was fully in the scud, the door went – it was the pizza… SHIT!

Startled by the loud knock, I pushed Robert off from on top of me and scrambled to get my clothes back on to answer the door. I shoved on a Nike vest quickly and a pair of shorts and bolted to the door.

When the poor guy handed me over my pizza, he looked a little startled, embarrassed almost, and when I turned around and shut the door, I realised it was because Robert was standing in my room in full view with not a stitch on, with his dick in his hand.

Lord above.

To make matters even worse, when I looked down at the box in my hands, I realised that my tit was hanging out my vest, the poor guy, it's no wonder he looked flustered!

It's safe to say I never ordered a Domino's again!

After exposing myself to the pizza delivery driver and him definitely getting more than he bargained for, Robert finally got dressed and joined me in the living room. It was literally like nothing had happened at all.

He was pleasant enough and I still kept asking myself quietly 'did that just happen?'

The one thing I hated about Robert was the way he spoke to his dog, not that it was bad or anything but just the way he shouted 'Russell' in his Edinburgh accent kind of made me die a bit, he was very abrupt, and I didn't like it.

I didn't even know it was possible for someone to be rude to a dog, but apparently it was.

But aside from that, we got on fine, although I'll admit, apart from being in the bedroom, there weren't massive sparks flying.

As my heart rate began to come down slowly, we sat on my couch, ate pizza and chatted about things we had already chatted to over FaceTime and texts.

It was weird just chilling out with a total stranger that I'd just met but already had sex with.

I almost instantly regretted it because I felt like a bit of a slut but like I said, it had been a while, so who cared really?

He wasn't from here either so it's not like it would be the talk of the toon.

We watched a few films, he spoke about himself having a big dick a lot and how some girls didn't like it.

I really couldn't take listening to him much more, and I decided that we should go to bed and watch TV there.

I gave him a spare toothbrush from the multipack I'd bought previously for going to Manchester and the thought of him even standing in my bathroom brushing his teeth gave me the ICK.

It was a bizarre feeling having a man in my house, particularly a man over ten years older than me that had a dog in tow.

After brushing his nashers, Robert came out the bathroom and placed Russell's bed in the corner of my room. Russell just looked at it and looked back at him, as if 'Am I fuck going in there' but after a few minutes, he did.

As we came together in bed, it was inevitable that Robert insinuated round two, but I just didn't think I could do it.

Robert had such a massive dick that it actually scared me a bit, and some of the time, having sex with him really wasn't that enjoyable.

When you chat with your pals, everyone always jokes that the ideal man would have a huge penis, but see when it's the size of Robert's, I was worried I wouldn't walk again, and I won't lie, it really hurt.

Another thing about him that totally turned me off was that he loved to talk dirty in bed, again much like Dave, he loved to call me 'baby' and tell me what he was going to do next... was it an older guy thing? Perhaps!

So when he whispered in my ear that he was going to 'spank me' I didn't expect for one minute to be thrown over his lap with his forearm over the base of my back pinning me down.

He forced the palm of his hand down on my jiggly bum not once, not twice but about six times.

I jumped and winced every. single. time, it's like that scene in *Fifty Shades of Grey*, I knew he had definitely seen it before and taken inspiration.

After the sixth time, my arse cheek literally burnt, so my automatic reaction was to try to break from his hold.

And I just told him that I'd had enough.

'OK, baby,' he purred, attempting to rub it better as he kissed my neck.

I just wanted him to fall asleep so that he would leave me alone. I didn't want or need him to rub my arse.

Feeling the heat come from my sore behind, I knew right away that I was red-raw and not one single bit turned on by what had just happened.

I'm always here for trying new things, but I knew that this extreme spanking wasn't for me.

But Robert wasn't quite finished there, he continued this raunchy escapade by kissing me and demanding I go into another position.

Don't tell me, how about you just throw me into it? I thought.

And although the rest was reasonably enjoyable, at the back of my mind all I could think about was, not the fact that I'd just been slapped to fuck, but that it was weird that we were having sex and there was a dog in close proximity.

It freaked me out, knowing that he was lurking about, although he wasn't in the room, I felt like I was being watched.

After the grand finale, let's just call it, I turned off the light and began dosing off although it took a while as my arse cheek pulsated for a while afterwards.

But when I eventually did nod off, it wasn't long before I was woken up with Russell perched on my head. I tried to wriggle down so he would move over a bit, but he was literally sitting on my hair like a bird on a nest, it was the worse sleep of my life.

If he wasn't actually sitting on my head, his fluffy white tail wagged in my face.

At one point I woke up as I got such a fright as he howled in his sleep. Robert woke up too, after hearing me pant from being disturbed.

But he just rolled over, kissed my head, and whispered to me, 'Don't worry, he's just having a bad dream.'

I was starting to think this whole situation was 'just a bad dream', why did I ever agree to him staying over?

His words gave me the ICK. Why? It was just so weird, one minute he was this horny shagger who could be starring in a porno and the next he was this weird dog dad that made me cringe beyond belief… how could he be both?

I liked him, but I liked him when he didn't talk.

After the 'bad dream' I thought this might be it and Russell would eventually settle, but I was wrong. If Russell wasn't sleeping on my head, he was down by my feet or moving about, and that was on top of Robert's loud snoring.

I mean, I'm blaming the dog. He was in a strange place, so I suppose it's understandable.

The next day my sex-fiend guest was working so had to leave around 9 a.m., which I was extremely glad about, although he briefly mentioned coming back on the Sunday to stay, which I wasn't overly bothered if he did or didn't.

The sound of his alarm echoed in my bedroom and Robert scrambled at the bedside to turn it off. I woke up infuriated due to the lack of sleep I had; I was so grumpy.

Despite not having to, I got up and seen him out; he kissed me and placed his sunglasses on his face as if the paparazzi were going to get a glimpse of him outside my house.

Again, I ICKED.

I was conflicted. The sex was decent (when I wasn't being spanked) but him as a person? Not so good.

It was only the first time we had properly met though, so I should really just give him a chance, although I already knew this 'wasn't it'.

After he left, it was all I thought about the rest of the day.

Since everything was more or less shut because of this bloody coronavirus, my day out with the girls had been cancelled so I decided to fill them in on the details about my latest house guest in the group chat.

Sex – good

Him – not so good

The dog – doesn't sleep!

The group chat was laughing emojis galore as I told them about Russell sleeping on my head and also the fact that Robert had basically spanked me into next week.

I text Claire too to tell her all about the first meeting with Robert and how I'm probably barred from Domino's…

But do you want to see him again? she asked.

I sent her a photo of my black and blue arse cheek.

I'm not too sure I could deal with doing this again!

OMG! What the hell!

I told Claire all the details, that's what I loved about her, she didn't judge at all, was always just there to listen and often gave good advice.

But do you like HIM? she quizzed.

Not particularly, I think I just like the company.

I just couldn't get over how sometimes I would just look at him and wouldn't be able to think of anything worse than being in his company.

I thought back to when we were lying on the couch and just how much I hated every minute of it, the way he got up to let Russell out of the door, his attitude, the fact that he couldn't understand certain things I said, and he just didn't get my humour really.

Robert seemed to get quite up tight when I would talk about myself and my work – like he was such an adult that didn't have fun. At one point, he actually lectured me about spending too much money on 'pointless things' like holidays and nights out.

I frowned – but I enjoyed those things?

Robert actually let out a sigh of relief when I told him that I did actually have a pension and one thing that stuck with me was that he said something like 'when we're together I'll look after you financially anyway'.

What?!

I didn't want to be 'looked after financially' or any way for that matter, I was perfectly capable of looking after myself thank you very much.

And anyway, see if I wanted to take a lighter and burn my cash to a crisp, then I would because it was mine and I'd earned it.

He was old-fashioned and I didn't like it.

I remember at that point just thinking that we were from completely different worlds and the only thing we had in common was enjoying sex.

That was it.

But I promised I would give it another go, just to be sure, you know me by now, two dates is my thing!

We chatted most of the day on Saturday over text and we agreed that he would come over on Sunday as he said he would cook me dinner.

I'd never really had anyone cook dinner for me apart from the M&S pizza Jake made for me, so when Robert said he would be cooking me venison, potatoes with a red wine jus, it was like one extreme to another.

ON THE SATURDAY, I spent the day in the house just pottering about, my arse was still stinging like how can someone who gives me the ICK so bad do something like this to me?

I was minding my own business, when I noticed that I had the red notification of doom when I opened my Facebook app.

There in the top hand corner, I had a friend request from Robert. I just hate when guys you're 'dating' add you on Facebook because it's different from Instagram.

On Facebook, I have my mum, people I work with and my family all on there, I didn't want him to have access to my 'real' life.

I was in a dilemma though, it looked really rude of me if I didn't accept him, plus he was coming over tomorrow so maybe he would bring it up if I didn't?

Feeling confused on what to do, I consulted with Claire, and she said I could always delete him after if it went tits up, and she was right, so I reluctantly accepted.

Of course, I couldn't resist browsing his profile. I snooped around to see what hidden information I could find about him that was a red flag and although he didn't have much on it at all, I went far enough back that I also stumbled on pictures of him and his ex.

Looking at pictures of them both looking ridiculously happy swimming with dolphins in Mexico, I noticed that she was completely the opposite of me.

She was pretty, blonde, and petite. I literally couldn't find one similarity between us, and it really made me wonder what his actual type was, did he prefer blondes or brunettes? Petite girls or girls with a bit of chub like myself?

Why was he talking about being with me if this is what he had previously?

Apart from the ex, I couldn't really suss anything else out about him except that his awful fashion choices weren't just a recent thing.

It was late Sunday afternoon and once more, Robert's flashy white car pulled up outside my house, with some really loud old school R&B blaring from it.

I had only moved into my house less than two months ago, I didn't really want to attract attention to my new neighbours or give them much to talk about, so when I opened the door to him calling 'Hello, beautiful!' I ushered him in as quickly as possible, hoping and praying that no one noticed.

The only thing about having your own front door was that everyone could see who was coming and going, not like my last party palace where the close door made visiting guests a bit more discreet. They could be going to anyone's house after all!

Robert grinned like the cat who got the cream as he walked into mine with Russell down by his feet.

As I closed the door behind him, I noticed he was wearing a very boyband-esq, light grey Boohoo man tracksuit and also that he was clutching a Waitrose bag in his hand with our dinner. I'd never shopped there before in my life.

1. Is it not like Marks and Spencer on steroids?
2. I didn't even know they existed in Scotland.
3. I was more of a Lidl girl...

Robert also had a rucksack draped over his shoulder, with what I assumed were his overnight belongings and Russell's 'things'.

The proud doggo-dad that he was.

He kissed me, but in return I gave him a peck, there's no way he was ripping my clothes off straight away. I still felt uneasy from the last time that happened.

Popping his shopping bag up on my kitchen worktop, Robert unpacked his dinner ingredients and got started on the cooking. I asked him if he wanted help, but he just told me to show him where things were and he would be fine.

After giving him a run-down of the cutlery drawer and the pan cupboard, I headed into the living room with a glass of wine.

Russell followed and sat up next to me on the couch.

I laughed to myself when he just stared and stared and stared at me; it was awkward. Weirdly, I was being made uncomfortable by a dog in my own house, and despite clapping him and putting his toy down next to him, I could tell he still wasn't best pleased.

I began to wonder if Russell had this a lot, strange girls around his human, or maybe he was mad that I tried to move him off my head the other night and disturbed his sleep? I wasn't sure, but he seemed unsure about me, but I would keep trying.

After Robert had got his Jamie Oliver on, he brought through our dinner of venison with a red wine jus, mashed potatoes and veg and another glass of wine.

I sat at the dining table feeling slightly awkward and uncomfortable, like I said, this was the first time I'd ever been cooked for properly and it just didn't feel normal.

But as I made my way through my plate, I looked up at Robert, who was sitting in the chair across from me and I watched his mouth move round and round like a washing machine as he chewed on his food, and I screwed my face up a bit.

Was I just really looking for things to be put off by?

I internally rolled my eyes. I was trying to like him I really was but every little thing that he did really just put me off, so I brought my eyes back to my own plate and tried to get the 'quick spin' image out my head.

When we finished, I cleared up the plates and did the dishes and we sat down to watch another film.

He pulled me in for a cuddle and scooped Russell up in his other arm.

It was like an outer body experience because I was looking down at this image of myself sitting there and absolutely howling, who the fuck did I think I was, playing happy families with this thirty-eight-year-old man and his dog?

Halfway through the film, Robert mumbled something about the back door, but I didn't really hear him properly, so I got up to open the door thinking it was to let the dog out.

When I sat back down, he looked at me and smirked.

'No, you know what I really meant.'

I stared at him blankly.

'What?'

He started to laugh.

'When we go to bed tonight'.

Oh. My. God.

He was referring to doing anal – my back door.

He just asked me to do anal and I got up and opened the back door, oh my God.

'Absolutely not.' I scolded, squeezing my bum cheeks together at the thought.

'You don't ask you don't get!' He winked.

I was dying inside at this point, not only at the fact that he outright asked me but the fact I misheard what he said and opened the back door. I gave myself the ICK.

That night, no back doors were entered, thankfully, much to Robert's disappointment, but I'm telling you, he was absolutely obsessed with it and continued to mention it at almost any point he could.

I mean, I know many people who do enjoy it, but it's just not for me and even more so with the size of Robert's manhood, I'd end up with piles!

The thought made me shudder, and I tried to think of a happy place.

The following morning, Robert had to get up for work pretty sharp and so did I. I jumped in the shower quickly and made my way through to my new working from home set-up as Robert had a shower after me.

When I was sitting at my desk, logging into my emails, I felt a claw at my feet.

It was Russell, staring up at me as if he wanted up and on to my lap.

With my hair dripping wet, I picked him up and cuddled up to him, realising that he didn't think I was so bad after all.

Quickly, I snapped a selfie with him and fired it in my group chat as his 'dad' showered before leaving.

The girls were pissing themselves after they saw it, when I captioned it 'That's me a dog stepmum now!'

I'd already started working by the time Robert was fully ready, so I only managed to briefly see him off, on his journey back to Edinburgh.

My day at work was really bloody busy, this coronavirus thing was actually getting really real now, people were dying all over the world and it was getting closer and closer to home by the day.

I went into my room to get my charger for my work phone, and at the corner of my eye, I noticed that Robert had left the dog's bed behind.

This soft black and beige bed with 'Russell' embroidered on it still graced the corner of my room.

When he text me later on in the day to see how I was getting on with work, I mentioned that he left the bed behind.

You've left Russell's bed here.

I think I was tipped over the edge by his reply.

I know. Hope you don't mind. Didn't see the point of bringing it back if I'll be coming back. It can just stay at your house!

Oh my God. I wasn't so sure about this.

I think my time with Robert and Russell had run its course and I really didn't see it going anywhere if I'm completely honest. He was too cringe, a freak in the sheets yes, but not the type of person I could see myself with at all. I could take him in small doses, but I definitely couldn't take being his girlfriend or his beloved dog's new mum.

We continued to chat, but I kept it at a minimum, I figured if the chat dried up I could just ghost him and that would be that.

Can I tell you something? he text me that evening.

Yes?

Are you sure? I don't want to freak you out?

386

Oh God. What could it possibly be now?

What do you think about Cuckolding? Do you know what that is?

Absolutely not knowing what it was, I quickly took to Google to investigate before messaging him back.

"Cuckhold: A man whose wife is sexually unfaithful, often regarded as an object of derision."

What the actual fuck!?

Was he into swinging? Did he want me to be a swinger with him? This went from 0-100 really quick.

I replied.

Like going with other people?

Kind of, swinging haha.

No, thank you.

Although only the woman does anything. The guy is faithful.

Would you want that? I typed in total disbelief that we were even having this conversation; I didn't think I could be anymore shocked than the back door comment.

He replied.

I have done it before.

Wow, I definitely wasn't expecting this... I needed to know more.

Tell me about it.

I was totally intrigued but at the same time, slightly repulsed.

After a few minutes, I opened the huge message from him.

It was with a previous ex years ago, about five years ago. Was with my girlfriend for around a year and we were in bed talking about what we could do to spice up our sex lives. She had a child so it wasn't like we could just go away all the time.

So I said I would let her fuck someone else if she was honest about it and told me what happened. Like it was only sex, nothing romantic of or dating. She wasn't sure if I was kidding or if it was me asking for an open relationship, but I said I wouldn't want to do anything, I'd be faithful.

So a few weeks went past and we were watching TV and she told me she'd fucked someone else and she would sometimes stay at his house if she was out drinking with friends and I wasn't there... it wasn't every week or that. Just random times.

Holy shit!

I was in utter shock. I couldn't imagine ever doing anything like that, particularly in a solid relationship, but each to their own I suppose.

But I had so many questions about it, so I quizzed him some more.

And you were OK with that?

Yeah, it turned me on.

Whaaaattttttt!?

Haha not impressed?

I mean, not really.

Yeah, I like my girlfriend being so dirty.

This is a bit much! I typed, just being honest.

Too weird? She would tell me how much he fucked her and how much she enjoyed it and how naughty she felt.

Each to their own. I typed back, trying to put this conversation to be*d.*

I know you wouldn't do that though, even if I said you could, he replied.

Na, I'm a one-man kinda gal. Would you actually really like me to do that?

Yeah.

Sorry, it just doesn't sit with me.

How do you know unless you've tried it?

But the sex chat didn't stop right there. Things certainly took another turn.

Robert then asked me if I'd ever been pissed on or if I ever fancied being pissed on.

Ew! Absolutely not. The thought of a 'golden shower' absolutely repulses me, if I'm honest.

Absolutely fucking not. Why? Are you into that?

I have done it once, with my ex in the bath. I stood up and did it over her tits

I was so over this conversation, and I was so over Robert. He was just absolutely everything I didn't want. This was the red flag I could see so very clearly, and it absolutely stank of piss.

I didn't reply to him and went to bed.

21. Lockdown 2020

On Monday, March 23, 2020, one week before my twenty-sixth birthday, the UK went into lockdown.

The coronavirus was spreading and fast, people across Scotland and the rest of the world were dying from this unknown virus and it was honestly terrifying.

The government had ordered everyone to 'stay at home' and only leave for essential purposes.

It was a total shock. How was I going to cope living on my own?

Robert had been texting me back and forth about it, he lived in his flat with a flat mate and obviously had Russell to keep him company, but it was nice that he wanted to check in with me – despite me now being completely off him and his swinging and 'pissing on tits' ways.

The next few weeks were extremely tough, being single and living yourself during a global pandemic was hard going and I struggled every single day.

For me particularly, I found it really hard not physically seeing anyone as I was literally down at my mum's house almost every day. The other thing was that I'd just moved into my new house, I didn't even really know my neighbours yet. I felt totally isolated.

I would speak to Robert every few days, our chat certainly dried up after he realised that I wasn't into going to let him shag my arse, become a swinger or let him piss on me.

There wasn't really much more sex chat although he would occasionally, out the blue, send me links to items from Love Honey or Ann Summers and just say, *'thoughts on this?'*

One day he just dropped a PVC pair of hog ties in our WhatsApp chat with no context. He literally thought about sex 24/7.

I always killed the mood when I replied, *NO.*

Never for one moment in my life did I think that a lockdown would ever happen and oh my God was it tough, as everyone knows.

I'd never experienced anxiety until 2020. Being stuck inside with your thoughts and no one to off load them to in person was so fucking difficult and I'm sure so many people can relate.

Things went downhill for me quickly and I began drinking most nights and binge eating. I put on a shit tonne of weight – 1 and a half stones to be precise – and I was absolutely miserable.

I think the thing I struggled with most is that 2020 was meant to be the best year of my life.

I'd just bought a home of my own, started my dream job, I had planned to see more of the world, go on more adventures and make the best memories of my life. I was going to go on dates and hopefully find 'The One' that I'd been searching for for the last four years.

I was twenty-five when we went into lockdown and twenty-seven and a half when it ended although it's still kind of ongoing.

I truly felt like I was missing out on what was supposed to be the year of 'finding myself'.

I was mourning the loss of something that hadn't even happened and I spiralled into a state of depression.

I tried to plod along as best I could and see the best of a bad situation.

One thing I decided to do which would better my life, was to get rid of Robert.

Partly because I couldn't deal with being sent another link to a pair of Love Honey restraints or handcuffs, I made the decision to completely remove him from all my social media platforms.

I couldn't be bothered entertaining him anymore, I knew I had no one else to fall back on this time but I just couldn't afford to waste energy on him, God, I hardly had any left for myself.

A few weeks later, after we hadn't chatted at all, I got a message from him on Instagram, after he noticed that I deleted him.

Guessing I should take the hint since you unfollowed me, etc. but thought be a shame as we got on well, didn't we?

I just got back to him saying we were different people, who didn't have very much in common and evidently wanted different things.

Robert had taken it quite badly and blocked me on WhatsApp and that was the end of that.

I kept my Bumble and Tinder account open during the first lockdown and spoke to a few people to pass the time but there was literally nothing to talk about.

I'd started chatting to one guy who was from Dunoon, who FaceTimed me and stuff but again, we had nothing to talk about plus he just wasn't for me and I knew that almost right away so I didn't see much point in even entertaining that either.

The chat on dating apps at this point was abysmal it had totally dried up. No one was up to anything or going anywhere so there were no hot topics of conversation at all, and no one could go on actual dates.

How's lockdown treating you?

You need an isolation buddy?

If corona doesn't take you out, can I?

It was absolutely mind-numbing and I couldn't take it anymore.

The apps were once again removed from my phone, and I tried so desperately to focus on myself.

I planned to get things done around the house and even went as far as to tile my own bathroom – I would literally do anything at this point to save my sanity.

For the next five months I, along with the rest of the nation, stayed at home.

We Zoom quizzed.

We clapped for carers.

We wore masks.

We sanitised.

We cried.

We drank wine almost every night.

We did home work-outs or home baking.

We then were allowed out for walks.

We tuned into daily briefings.

We waited for normality to return.

It really was the most bizarre time of my life. I learnt a lot about myself, I learnt that I wasn't as strong as I initially thought I was and that I heavily relied on other people for happiness. I'd never been truly alone, and it took a lot of getting used to.

I cried most times on FaceTime to my mum because I just missed her so much and I also missed my old life.

I hoped and prayed every day that we'd get back to normal or this 'new normal' that they always spoke about on the news.

It really was a dark time in my life, but I muddled through and started to make the best out of a bad situation, like most of us.

22. Finding Love During a Global Pandemic?

After working on myself for a few months, I was starting to feel like a better person.

It was now July and I'd ditched the weeknight wines and takeaways, I was working out from home, reading more, writing more, looking after myself more and starting to accept that I either made the most of this time that would probably never happen again or I sat feeling sorry for myself and did nothing about it.

After being stuck in the house alone for what felt like an eternity, Nicola Sturgeon announced that you could now have visitors in your garden and that soon beer gardens would be open for business again.

It was the news that I so desperately hoped for, and I couldn't wait to see all my friends and family again and hug them as tight as I possibly could – if restrictions allowed that was.

With the world looking like it was opening back up again, was it may be time to download my dreaded apps once more?

I'd been off them for four months and was never tempted to re-download until now, when dates could potentially happen again.

The new rules meant that all bars and restaurants were doing table service only, so the chances of me being chatted up at the bar ever again looked highly unlikely.

On one of our daily walks, my pal Natalie had mentioned another app that I should try called Hinge. I'd never heard of it before but according to Natalie, the guys on that were a bit more 'normal'. I took what she said with a pinch of salt because Claire had said the exact same thing about Bumble and look how some of those dates ended.

But I mean, what had I got to lose now?

I really had changed during lockdown and had a totally different outlook on things, plus I hadn't spoken to anyone since that terrible 'FaceTime date' back in April and obviously hadn't actually met up with anyone since Robert.

I was more than ready to get myself back out there but at the same time, I wasn't desperate to meet anyone, I was more desperate to get back into the pubs if anything.

'If it happens it happens' was my new approach to life, and I felt like if I chased something so much it wouldn't be real, or it would be forced so going with the flow would be my new motto.

And now that it seemed like the summer was a goer again, the girls and I planned to make the most of what was on our doorstep and booked a weekend away glamping, a road trip to the Highlands and instead of the usual Tenerife holiday with my mum, we decided that we'd go to St. Andrews for the weekend and stay in the caravan.

We might as well make the most of beautiful Scotland while it was the only place we could go.

When it came to dating apps, I decided to leave behind Tinder and Bumble and take up Natalie's advice and get Hinge to see what all the fuss was about and if I could in fact, find someone 'normal'.

I told myself if it didn't work out on there then I was deleting them all and joining a convent because I didn't think I could put myself through anymore dates with strangers. Particularly ones who were sex fiends, had more than four girls on the go, that were personality catfishes or that had secret children.

Was there literally anything else worse that I could uncover?

Let's find out!

After downloading it, I quickly realised that Hinge is more of a profile situation than a swiping scenario. You get to know a bit more about a person as you need to answer three different questions that appear on your profile, and you can react to things people post.

Your answers to the questions appear on your profile along with your pictures and your info such as age, height, smoker, drinker etc.

So I decided to have fun with it because I didn't think I could take online dating seriously anymore.

The first question was, *'What was your latest shower thought?'*

When the fuck will this all be over.

The next question, *'My most irrational fear is…'*

That the pubs never open again.

And finally question three was, *'We'll get along if...'*

You love Celtic and the sesh.

I wasn't taking myself seriously and hopefully they would get my sense of humour, because if they didn't then I wasn't interested anyway.

As I began flicking through profile after profile, I was starting to wonder if having more info on the Hinge profiles was a good thing or not because I didn't really seem to swipe anyone because the things they said made my toes curl.

I only had the app for two days when I matched with a guy called Nicky.

When I studied his pictures, I realised that I knew his face.

We had a few mutual friends, but I didn't think I'd ever actually met him before. All I really knew about him was that he was a triplet, lived about five minutes up the road and was a Celtic fan.

It took me by surprise when I saw that he had messaged me first about one of the questions I answered, and we went from there.

He was a few years older than me and worked for the council.

I hadn't come across that profession during my dating diaries, so that was a new one to add to the list.

Nicky had dark hair and of course he had brown eyes didn't he, it's rare that I opt for anything else.

398

He just seemed like a genuinely nice person, and I was up for getting to know him.

We went back and forth for ages, and he was really quite funny.

Going by the chats we had on the app and after speaking for about a week, I just cut to the chase and asked for his number.

I was going to do things differently this time, I was going to be forward because I couldn't be bothered messing about or playing games or anything like that. I wanted to speak to him over text and that was that.

So when I sent him the first message on WhatsApp, we just seemed to have loads to talk about.

It transpired that he was not long out of a long-term relationship and had just got back on the dreaded dating scene. I remembered it well, although it was much more advanced now than four years ago when I first came across it.

But regardless of him being a newbie, I felt like we could talk about anything. The more we chatted, the more we realised how much we really did have in common – freakishly too…

It turns out, he went to uni with my best friend Shanice, had also been on a stag do that my brother had been on, our mums were pregnant at the same time and went to the same maternity classes and our grans both knew each other, how bloody weird!

Was this fate? I wasn't sure I believed in the whole fate thing after my situtionship with Dave, but it was really bizarre, what a small world!

The longer our conversations went on it was evident that we got on really well, even if it was just over text for now.

Soon enough, Nicky finally asked me when I was free to go out.

Since things were starting to open back up, I had so many plans with my friends which meant that I just really didn't know when I could meet up with him for a date.

Plus, that weekend was my first big proper night out after a hellish start to 2020 and the 'Gals Gals Gals' and I were going out for lunch and cocktails.

We managed to book a table outside at the Cranside Kitchen in Glasgow and ordered every single cocktail on the menu – twice.

I was drinking everything. Cocktails, pints, shots – literally anything I could get my hands on. This taste of freedom was exhilarating, and I wanted to soak up in every single bit of it. I cannot explain how amazing it was to be reunited with my besties, it's a feeling I'll never forget it was like having first date butterflies times ten, but it was more a feeling of content, a little slither of the life we used to live and took for granted.

After our allocated time slot was up at the Cranside, we decided to continue the much-anticipated session back at our local Jack Daniels.

Since the bar service was scrapped, we started up a tab for table service and the pints of venom just kept coming and coming.

I'd text Nicky a few times throughout the day, he was also out at the pub with his mates. I think everyone in Motherwell was out that day, making the most of it, of course they were, everyone had been locked up for five months!

I didn't really tell my pals much about my latest dating conquest like I usually did, I just told them that I was chatting to someone Shanice went to uni with and that we'd see what happened.

But as we sipped on our drinks, the girls tried to prise more and more information about Nicky out of me, but we had only been chatting for about a week or so, I didn't have anything to tell! For now...

After a few hours of knocking back copious amounts of booze, our Jack Daniel's bar tab came and £217.10 later, it was home time.

Nicky had text me asking how my night was and said that he was sitting out in his mate's garden having a drink which was literally in the street behind mine.

Fancy going a walk?

I was pretty drunk and had only just gotten home. It crossed my mind that I could easily just ask him to come around to mine but we all know the outcome of that.

I ummed and aahed over it but after a few minutes of deliberation with myself, I decided against it. I wasn't about that anymore so I would go the walk instead.

I couldn't think of anything worse than having sex with yet another dating app stranger and then waking up with them awkwardly the next morning, I just wasn't willing to put myself through it again because I remember vividly what it's like.

I caught myself smiling my decision because last year drunk Kirsten would have invited him round in a heartbeat, but I wasn't her anymore, I'd changed, for the better.

I pulled my shoes on again after just taking them off and walked to the end of my street. And there he was, standing underneath the lamp post, wearing a khaki green jacket.

'Hi!' He smiled.

'Hi!' I giggled, finding myself out again just past midnight after a full day of drinking. Would I soon turn into a pumpkin? Time would tell.

I studied Nicky as he stood in front of me and right away, I got a good vibe from him; he ticked most of my usual boxes. He had longish dark brown hair, due to the barbers being shut for about five months, brown chocolate button eyes and was just a bit taller than me. He was handsome and a good beard going on – we can all appreciate a good beard, can't we?

But the one thing that struck me the most about him was that he really did seem like a nice guy, you know, the type you wouldn't mind your mum meeting.

God, here I was again, getting way too ahead of myself.

Stop that right now, I thought.

It was obvious we were both very drunk, but before meeting him I'd psyched myself to not expect much from this except a drunken blether and perhaps a kiss.

I think that mindset was clever of me because then I wouldn't be disappointed.

We began walking and chatting, asking about each other's nights and where we had been. I don't even think we reached the end of the road when I decided to pull him in for a kiss.

The drink made me confident and bold, plus I wanted to see how I felt about it. This was my situation, remember? We're doing things differently now.

As I ran my fingers through his lockdown locks, I weirdly got butterflies. I was pleasantly surprised, as it turned out to be a really good kiss.

We pulled apart and laughed together; I don't think he saw that one coming at all.

Nicky and I walked and talked a little bit more and ended up sitting on one of the benches further into the scheme. There wasn't much else to do at this time on a Saturday.

Although, I could have just asked him around to mine, but again, we all know what happens when a guy comes to your house after midnight at the weekend and that wasn't happening, not on my watch, not this time.

We chatted and chatted and chatted; it was now about 1 a.m. I was sitting cross-legged on this bench, and he was facing into me, we seemed to just have loads to talk about and it was so nice.

In the middle of a conversation about our mutual friends, an old man who had evidently sunk loads of beer earlier in the pub, approached us and decided that he was going to join us on the bench.

It was really random if I'm honest, but you know what it's like when a drunk person stops to talk to you – there's no getting rid!

I shuffled up and so did Nicky and 'Frank' joined us.

'She's got dead nice eyes by the way – you should keep a hold of her!' Frank slurred to Nicky, who nodded in agreement.

He started telling us all about his night, when all of a sudden, we heard a voice shout from one of the towers.

It was a woman's voice, and she didn't sound happy one bit.

Nicky, our new pal Frank, and I all turned in the direction of the shouting to see a woman in her 30s race towards us with the most twisted look on her face. She was furious.

'HOW DARE YOU!' she screamed as she began to hammer her fists down on Frank's head.

What the hell!?

She was going crazy shouting about things that didn't make sense. Was this really happening?

'Stop it, leave him alone!' I shouted to her as she kicked off on a total rampage.

Turning to me she went to pounce in my direction but Nicky stood out in front of her and told her to calm down.

She was basically squaring up to him when Frank butted in, and she turned to him began screeching at the top of her lungs. It became evident that they knew each other.

'Come on, hen, it's no that bad.' Frank laughed, holding her shoulders as she bawled in his face.

That was our cue to make a swift exit before she actually did give one of us a black eye.

'Come on, let's walk.' I turned to Nicky, grabbing his hand to leave.

We walked down the hill, leaving those two to sort out whatever differences they had.

As we walked, I looked down and realised I was still clutching Nicky's hand. I must admit, it didn't feel weird in the slightest. I didn't really even realise I'd grabbed it in the first place until five minutes later when our fingers were still entwined.

I hated to admit it, but I liked it, it felt... nice?

I wasn't shaken at all by what had just happened to us really. I was more mortified that I found myself in a situation like this with a guy I'd only met an hour before. Just my luck!

After the initial adrenaline wore off, we both giggled.

'Some first date that! Nearly getting battered by a drunk!'

We laughed and had another kiss and again, those butterflies I'd been searching for forever were suddenly present. It was such a nice feeling.

By now it was edging towards 2 a.m. and Nicky said he would walk me home.

And true to his word, he walked me to my door, and we had another kiss and said our goodbyes.

I was unsure if this was just a drunken one-off thing, but I hoped not because I had a good time regardless of nearly getting a bloody nose or not.

Locking my front door behind me, I felt giddy for the first time in a long time, and I couldn't sleep that night for the massive smile slapped across my face.

Although it did cross my mind that Nicky might not want to see me again after nearly getting into a fight on the street, but it wasn't my fault at all.

I was working the next day but still managed to find the time to voice note Claire to tell her all about my late-night outing.

She laughed and said that only me would end up nearly boxing with someone on the street while also on the pull. She was right things like this only ever happened to me, maybe that's why I'd been single for four years.

I filled her in and told her all about Nicky and even sent her a picture of him for context.

Awwww he looks like he's dead thoughtful. I don't really know how you can tell that, but he just does. He's very your type, isn't he?

I think he is too. When I went home after it, I had a wee skip in my step. I felt happy and he properly made me laugh, but we'll see what happens.

She replied.

Yeah, that's true. If he makes you happy, then that's the main thing, but I mean what's the worst that could happen? Worst-case scenario, you'll get a pump out of it!

I told Claire that I was going to try to see if I could make it to the third date because with practically everyone else before, I saw them twice and then never again.

I also added a bonus experiment into the mix and said that if it did get beyond two 'dates' then I was going to wait until at least date five before inviting him to 'stay the night'.

Claire laughed and told me that she knew my history and that I would never last that long, but I was determined to prove her wrong.

And I did... even after date number five he was still hanging about.

Dating during a global pandemic really is bloody difficult.

It was hard to really do anything with not everything being open, no alcohol inside and also the two-hour booking slots.

So, after having no option but to have a few 'house dates', we finally got to go out for dinner and some drinks about three or four weeks after meeting.

I can honestly say it was the best first date I've ever had. The food was good; the cocktails were exceptional, and the company was even better.

We were doing things backwards, and it appeared to be working.

Five dates turned into ten dates and ten dates turned into me somehow ending up with a boyfriend!

Yes, you heard right a bloody boyfriend!

Nicky and I just totally clicked, it's the most natural thing I've ever experienced in my life. He just gets me and I get him without giving myself the ICK, it's like we were made for each other.

Who would have thought it would have taken a global pandemic for me to finally meet someone who ticked all my boxes.

It just feels… right.

I still can't believe that the guy I met absolutely steaming after drinking several pints of venoms on a random walk one night, where we nearly got leathered, is now my boyfriend.

Who would have thought? Twelve months later…

We've just celebrated our one-year anniversary and I can honestly say that I haven't been this happy ever in my entire life.

Nicky makes me laugh every single day and I can't see my life without him. I'll stop going on about how great he is before I give myself the ICK.

When I began to pen this book back in 2019, this wasn't the ending I'd envisioned. I planned to still be very much single by the end and to still be on the hunt for 'The One' which would have probably given me a head start for book number two.

But I truly believe that every single thing happens for a reason, we meet people in places when the time is right, and everything just falls in to place.

C'est la vie.

There's a theory that I read a while back that you have 'Three Loves' in your lifetime and that we need all three of them for a different reason or lesson.

1. *The First Love* – The young love that we enter into thinking it will be forever. It doesn't really feel right because it's all we know.

Dean was my first love. We basically grew up together and I shared many special memories with him and a lot of 'firsts' but it was evident that we just weren't each other's 'person'. He'll always be the first person I ever properly 'loved'. We just grew up and apart, and that's absolutely OK.

2. *The Hard Love* – The one that teaches us lessons and also shows us who we are, what we want and what we don't. This love hurts at the time but makes sense in the long run.

The 'situationship' with Chris may have been short, but the feelings I had for him were extremely intense.

Although the L bomb was never dropped, I did fall for him hard. And if anything, it taught me that I had so, so much love to give.

3. *The Love That Lasts* – The one that you don't see coming. It comes up to you when you least expect it and smacks you right in the face. The surprising and pleasant one that just fits in your life like never before.

Nicky came into my life unexpectedly and much to my surprise we just immediately clicked.

He makes me happy beyond belief and of course he is the brown-eyed guy that I'd been so eager to find all this time.

I really believe that it could be the 'Love that Lasts'.

But the 'love' that this theory doesn't talk about is the one with yourself.

I was in a very dark place for a while and I really, really did forget my worth.

I didn't love myself and I didn't believe that I deserved the best so I put up with being treated like shit by so many people – mostly all the men you've just read about.

It was only when I actually started to value myself and realise that I do deserve the world and more that I started to feel genuinely happy.

I stopped wasting my time on mediocre men and drove that energy into bettering myself and when I started doing that, that's when my life truly changed for the better.

It's easy for me to sit here and say looking after yourself will solve all your problems, it won't but it's a great start.

Happiness attracts happiness, good vibes attract good vibes, and the grass is definitely greener where you water it…

It's important to remember that the being in a relationship isn't the be all and end all. You should never depend on someone else for happiness that should come from you.

Don't get me wrong, yeah, it's great to have someone there to share things with, but they should only add value to your life.

The last few years of my twenties have taught me a great deal, of course, I look back and wince at some of the things (or men) that I have done, but every single decision I've made in the past has made me the woman I am today.

The heartache, the questionable drunken one-night stands and of course, all the swiping.

Life is a journey, it's never going to be plain sailing, and it really has a funny way of working things out to lead us on the right path.

But right now, after a few bumps in the road, and from what I can see so far, I'm right where I need to be.

THE END

23. Your Tales

Since I started writing this book, many people have reached out on social media to share their short dating app disasters with me, so I thought it was only fair to include some of them here too.

Enjoy!

"I was chatting to this guy from Tinder, and we got on really well it seemed. When I was looking through his pictures on his profile, I noticed that he was posing with like plastic cutlery and stuff. I thought he might be into camping or something, so I quizzed him about and he was like yeah I'm in jail for murder. As casual as you like, he was in a prison cell – ON TINDER!

"He'd phone and text me all the time, then one time he said he was with his 'pals' and they were all chatting, and a buzzer went off and he was like I've got to go – it all makes sense now. He told me he wanted me to come and visit as he wanted to get 'sticky fingers'. I blocked him but he kept phoning me from different numbers, so I changed it."

"I went to a guy's house once, and he had an orange lilo instead of a bed. There was no way I was going to have sex with him on that!"

"I'd been chatting to this guy on Tinder and things had been going well. We went out for dinner and at the end of the date after he paid, he asked me to tap him ten pounds for gas and electric. I left and never saw him again."

"Went on a first date with a guy and he was asking about my sexual past and said, 'If you're not a slut you may as well walk home'."

"Girl from Tinder came up to the house. Things were going well, then I got a phone call from an unknown number, and it was this English guy shouting and swearing, asking why I was with his girlfriend and was saying he was in the army and was mental.

"He said he was off duty up here and knew where I was so was going to come down and batter me! I panicked and started pure questioning her, saying why didn't you say you had a boyfriend and what was she thinking!? We got into an argument and eventually I told her to leave and never contact me again. So she left the house after about forty mins in, it was pure awkward. Then suddenly I get a phone call again... this time it was my pals. They knew she was coming over, pranked me on that call and I'd just went and chased her out the door panicking."

413

"I was meeting a guy in a bar for our first date. We had only just sat down to our drink when he was insisting that we move to a different bar, like a specific one. I thought it was strange, but I thought 'OK', so we downed our drinks and headed there.

"En route, the guy said he had a text from his ex saying she was in trouble and that she was in that very bar we were headed to – also on a Tinder date. How odd. So when we got there all seemed to be well and they chatted to each other. I was left sitting with her date and it turns out it was some sort of weird role play fantasy thing! I swiftly left and he later text me saying he was sorry! Safe to say that I deleted his number."

"Guy told me his name was Paul Davis*.

We went on a date and he left his card on the table to pay the bill and went to the toilet. When I looked at his bank card, his name was Ryan Evans*. Boosted after that."

"I'd been seeing this guy for a few weeks.

Things were going pretty well until he suddenly ended things. When I asked him why, he said that he basically started talking to me because I had the same name as his ex-girlfriend and he got excited when I text him because my name came up and he imagined it was her."

"I met up with a girl I used to see when I was at uni after she came back home from living abroad.

She seemed different to when I knew her previously, but it didn't matter and I invited her back to mine. We were kissing and about to do the deed when she stopped and put crystals on my bedside table and said she wanted to 'cleanse' my bed before we got down to business – let's just say, the cleanse killed the vibe."

"I got so drunk on a first date and when I went to the toilet to fix myself, a brawl started just as I was applying my lippy.

I tried to stop the two girls from punching each other when the bouncer walked in and dragged me out thinking I was the one who initiated the fight. I had to text my date and tell him I was outside because I got thrown out. Good job he believed me because he's now my husband!"

24. Your Chat Up Lines

"I'd hide every chair in the world just so you'd have to sit on my face."

"I'm not a dentist but I could give you a filling."

"I wish you were my wee toe, so I could bang you off every single bit of furniture in my gaff."

"Here, you African?"
"No, why?"
"Cause you're African stunner, hen."

"Do you work at Subway? Cause you just gave me a footlong."

"Do you want to play sunbeds? You lie down and I'll tan you."
"If coronavirus doesn't take you out, can I?"

"Are you a haunted house? Because I'm going to scream when I'm in you."

"Hey do you like dragons?"

"No?"

"That's unlucky because I will be dragon my balls across your face shortly."

"B5"

"Sorry?"

"Oh sorry, thought this was a vending machine and you were a tasty snack."

25. Acknowledgements

Throughout my life I've always had the most amazing people around me to pick up the pieces when things haven't always worked out the way I wanted them to.

They've laughed with me, cried with me and have always been there for me through the good times and the bad.

Without sounding like I'm about to pick up an Oscar, I want to thank those special people for being truly amazing.

First, I need to thank my wonderful mum, Pamela.

Even though she's probably read majority of this book and cringed at my stories, she is hands down the most special and important woman in my life.

My biggest cheerleader and my best friend. My true inspiration in life. I love you more than words, Pam.

I couldn't do this life without you. Thank you for everything you do for me.

To my stepdad Graham,

I know you'll only be reading this end part (thankfully) but thank you for being the father figure I needed in life, you're truly one of a kind.

To the rest of my crazy family,

My brother Jonny, sister-in-law Paula, Auntie Ellen, Elaine, Pauline, Anne, Ellie – you're all amazing and thank you for all the advice you've given me over the years. Particularly to my auntie Elaine, the best flat mate I've ever had! Love you lots.

To my 'Gals, Gals, Gals',

Caitlin, Hayley, Heather, Lucy, Samantha, and Shanice, I would be lost without you girls. Thank you for always being there for me and sticking by me even though my life decisions weren't always the best ones. My bestest friends in the world. I love you all to death.

To my crazy pals,

My cousin Jodie and the Spoon sisters. The sisters I never had. The most amazing bunch of gals I could ever meet, who really are all like family rather than friends. Thanks for the slaggings, the wild nights out and for always being there for me too when I've felt at my lowest. Some of the best nights of my life have been with you girls, and I'll take those memories to the grave. You mean the world to me.

Caitlin – I'll not say much as we both might get in trouble. The YHYH and grain life might be behind us, but the memories will live on forever!

To my wee mate Claire,

The evil genius behind the sexting when I didn't know my arse from my elbow… thanks for the constant words of wisdom, the laughs and the late-night voice notes and for keeping me going through lockdown. You're one in a million!

To Nadia,

One of the best things to come out of all my dating app dramas was definitely you. And although the way in which we met wasn't the most ideal scenario, I'm so glad it happened and that you and Darci are part of my life. Fate was meant to bring us together.

To David, Darren, and Molly,

My unofficial, dysfunctional family. My husbands and wife who always save me in my time of need, who are brutally honest when they need to be. These three have collected me in drunken states more times than I care to count, and I thank my lucky stars to have friends like them.

To Bryony,

Thank you for always being there for me and being the most amazing friend. For being my shoulder to cry on during every break-up. I love you so much.

To Anne-Marie and Barry,

Thank you for unofficially adopting me during lockdown and never giving me back. Truly the best neighbours I've ever had.

To Rachael Proctor (RRRETRO.INK),

Thank you for listening to all my dramas during our time in Starbucks and checking out my star sign compatibility with potential suitors on our lunch breaks. Thank you for making me an absolutely banging front cover for this book too. You're the best!

To Paula Johnston,

Thank you for everything you've done for me in helping get this book out there. I genuinely could not have done it without your knowledge and endless talents.

Thank you for also being the best podcast co-host a gal could ask for and for being a top-notch pal in general. The only decent person who has ever slid into my DMs.

To Nicky,

Thank you for being you. For making me laugh, and for making me see why it never worked out with anyone else. Without sounding cringe… you're everything and more.

And to you!

To every single person who has supported me on this journey, to every person who has shared their dating app dramas with me and has cheered me on along the way. Thank you, thank you, thank you!

26. Keep in Touch

If you pick up a copy of *The Swipes of My Life*, make sure you follow the official Instagram page @theswipesofmylife and tag me. Don't forget to use the hashtag #theswipesofmylife

You can follow me on my social media accounts too!

Personal: @kirstenmcstay

Home: @gaffatthegrange

Podcast: @twoburdsandapodcast

Twitter: @KirstenMcStay

Printed in Great Britain
by Amazon

17003274R00244